M000274248

# A VERSION OF REASON

Also by Rob Jovanovic

*Beck! On a Backwards River*
*Adventures in Hi-Fi: The Complete R.E.M.* (with Tim Abbott)
*Perfect Sound Forever - The Story of Pavement*
*Big Star: The Story of Rock's Forgotten Band*
*Nirvana: The Complete Recording Sessions*
*Kate Bush: The Biography*
*George Michael: The Biography*

# A VERSION OF REASON

## In Search of Richey Edwards

### ROB JOVANOVIC

Copyright © Rob Jovanovic 2009

The right of Rob Jovanovic to be identified as the author of this work
has been asserted by him in accordance with the Copyright, Designs and Patents Act 1988.

This edition first published in Great Britain in 2009 by
Orion Books
an imprint of the Orion Publishing Group Ltd
Orion House, 5 Upper St Martin's Lane,
London WC2H 9EA
An Hachette Livre UK Company

1 3 5 7 9 10 8 6 4 2

All rights reserved. Apart from any use permitted under UK copyright law, this publication
may only be reproduced, stored or transmitted, in any form, or by any means, with prior
permission in writing of the publishers or, in the case of reprographic production, in
accordance with the terms of licences issued by the Copyright Licensing Agency.

AGATHA CHRISTIE® POIROT® Copyright © 2009 Agatha Christie Limited
(a Chorion company). All rights reserved.
'The Disappearance of Mr Davenheim' Copyright © 1924 Agatha Christie Limited.
All rights reserved.

A CIP catalogue record for this book is available from the British Library.

ISBN: 978 0 752 89835 3 (hardback)

Printed and bound in the UK by CPI Mackays, Chatham ME5 8TD


The Orion Publishing Group's policy is to use papers that are natural, renewable and
recyclable and made from wood grown in sustainable forests. The logging and manufacturing
processes are expected to conform to the environmental regulations of the country of origin.

Every effort has been made to fulfil requirements with regard to reproducing copyright material.
The author and publisher will be glad to rectify any omissions at the earliest opportunity.

www.orionbooks.co.uk

For Carolyn

*'What no wife of a writer can ever understand is that he's working when he's staring out of the window.'*

– Burton Roscoe

*One tap of your finger on the drum releases every timbre*
*and founds the new harmony.*
*You take a step and new men materialise; they march out.*
*You turn your head away: the new love!*
*You turn back: the new love!*
*'Alter our destiny,' you hear these children sing.*
*'Stamp out plagues! Stamp out time, for a start!'*
*Everyone begs you: 'Raise the substance of our fortunes,*
*our desires, whatever you can.'*
*You – fresh out of forever. Making for everywhere.*

– 'To a Reason', from *Illuminations*, 1886, by Arthur Rimbaud

# PREFACE

*'If the whole of his poetry can be read as a denial of the values of the present civilization, as I believe it can, then [his] disappearance . . . becomes as symbolic an act as Rimbaud's flight or Crane's suicide.'*

– Donald Justice

The day that he left was shrouded in mist and gloom. The conditions weren't unusual for this place at the time of year. This weather seemed to fit the ambience of events quite well. He was interested in T. S. Eliot and often spoke of Malcolm Lowry's *Under the Volcano*, but there was a dark beauty to his own writing, too. Some of the texts he'd written meant that his life would be analysed, but after that day this interest was amplified. If his car hadn't been found abandoned near the bridge, then the theories about what happened to him might all be very different. He was unusual for a man in his position. He was interested in writing, reading, art, and was even a bit of a musician.

When he couldn't be found in the morning his friend spent the day thinking what might have happened the night before, because when he'd last seen him all seemed well. His friend knew that he had an interest in both suicide and in attempting the perfect disappearance, but had he actually taken these interests a step too far? If it was suicide, then it wouldn't have been his first attempt. If it was a disappearance, then he certainly had the knowledge to pull it off. Leaving the country with or without a passport to head south wasn't out of the question. He knew about suicide, he knew about famous suicide notes. He'd written about them before and would probably have done so again had he stayed around. It was fair to say that he collected suicide notes in his mind. Remembering this near-obsession and knowing that no suicide note had been found gave heart to those hoping that he was alive and that the railings of the bridge weren't an ending.

He hadn't been eating well recently, but better than previously. He was also taking prescribed drugs. James Reidel, in *Vanished Act*, noted that he looked 'so gaunt that sometimes, from certain angles, he seemed to be almost bodiless inside his clothes'.

Some overseas work was lined up but perhaps he wasn't as keen about it as he'd seemed. The next morning, his door was locked. The police were called and his apartment was searched for clues but they could find nothing conclusive. The books he left behind were scanned for subtle hints but this only complicated matters. Later, when his car was found by the end of the bridge, there was still no note. His bank account was never used again. Years later, there is still no sign of this man – a man regarded more as a writer than a musician.

This was the mystery surrounding the poet Weldon Kees, not Richey Edwards. The bridge in question was the Golden Gate Bridge in San Francisco, not the Severn Bridge in South Wales. Kees was last seen on Monday, 18 July 1955. The following day, a highway patrolman spotted his car parked at the Golden Gate Bridge. The keys were still in the ignition. Nobody has seen or heard from Weldon Kees since. Before vanishing, he'd told some friends of his desire to commit suicide but he'd spoken to others of his plans to disappear and start a new life in Mexico. Which did he choose? History repeats itself. Forty years later, on the other side of the world, the similarities were chilling.

*'He was a loveable person and I think it's sad that some of our fans don't even know he existed. Maybe it's time we re-educated all those Mondeo drivers in Northern Europe . . . '*

– Nicky Wire

# CONTENTS

# BOOK 2

# AUTHOR'S NOTE

## When you were young

I first really heard about Richey Edwards after my girlfriend and I split up. I'd had glandular fever – no, really – but I won't go into that. There was something about him that I couldn't put my finger on, and yet for a while I kept away from immersing myself in the band. Now it's too late: Richey's long gone and I've spent the best part of two years thinking about almost nothing else. Just like now. There's been this photo staring down at me whenever I sit at my desk. I stare back, but inevitably I'm the one that blinks first. Then the spell is broken and I glance around. I wonder if my environment would tell a voyeur anything about me or my writing. I often spend a few minutes looking at the *Writer's Room* picture in the Saturday *Guardian*, wondering why each particular writer sets out their writing space in the way that they do. Maybe I'm looking for inspiration or an insight into the brains of the authors that I admire. I reckon, after months of these pictures have passed by, that my writing room is a mish-mash of all the cluttered ones that I've viewed. Full of books, magazines, music, notes, and – as my wife insists – a fair amount of junk. I don't have as many Post-it notes stuck up as Will Self does, but I have a lot. There are lots of pictures on the walls, but this particular one is looking down its nose at me, presenting me with an almost palpable challenge. Daring me to go on. Of course, this is a picture of Richey Edwards. Taken by the elusive Japanese lens-man Mitch Ikeda, this picture shows Richey crouching at the side of the waterfront outside his Cardiff apartment in the months before he disappeared. His arms casually cross at the wrists, his sleeveless T-shirt exposes four tattoos – two on each upper arm – his head is slightly tilted back, his expression borderline contemptuous as he stares into the camera. The image captivated me from the first moment I saw it in Ikeda's book *Forever Delayed*. I always planned to find the exact spot and take a picture of the exact same view, but of course without Richey in it. In the summer of 2008, I did just that. Now there are two pictures looking down at me: a kind of 'before and after'. One monochrome, one colourfully lit by a sunny day. Not much has changed between the images, apart from the obvious. Do ghosts cast shadows? Didn't someone else say that you don't have to die to become a ghost? Well, the shadow and the man are both gone. And I'm tired of being asked by well-meaning friends who are trying to be funny, 'Have you found him yet?'

## He doesn't look a thing like Jesus

Press 'Rewind': now I'm sitting here in the middle of France, and I can really appreciate how easy it would be to disappear. And I thought that *before* my copies of *How to Disappear Completely and Never be Found* and *Cover Your Tracks Without Changing Your Identity* arrived through the post. Robert Louis Stevenson disappeared here for twelve days over 130 years ago, the same year in which he published *The Suicide Club*. With just a donkey to carry his luggage, he crossed the Cévennes before dropping into the valley and arriving at Saint-Jean-du-Gard. Today, the roads are beautiful to drive along, with swooping, majestic bends that dip into lush valleys and run alongside rushing rivers. We've been listening a lot to The Killers, especially *Sam's Town*, which is the perfect, if slightly clichéd, driving accompaniment.

Each late-summer morning I've been driving from our rented house, perched up on the steep hillside, into the small town for fresh bread, newspapers and sundry supplies. The pale-blue-eyed sky is spectacular, and the only wispy clouds are far away on the mountain-framed horizon. Each and every day I've spied a chap walking in the opposite direction out of town. There are no pavements so he's always on the roadside gravel or grass verge. He's always wearing shades and a hat, always has a small backpack. He has a bit of grey in his stubbly beard and is quite slim. For all I know, he could be Richey Edwards. He doesn't look 'French' to me. One day I almost stopped the car to ask for some fake directions. Just in case. Richey Edwards has been gone for years and could be absolutely anywhere. The longer I spend here the more I appreciate that I could just melt into the landscape if I really wanted to. If I hadn't told anyone back home where I was going, would I be found? The rental house isn't in my name so that wouldn't show up on any searches. I've been using only cash. The Channel Tunnel ticket was the last time any trace of my name would be noticed. I could be anywhere by now. And today I am. Brandon Flowers is telling me that the hurricane started spinning when I was young. Back in 1995 I was young.

Rob Jovanovic
Saint-Jean-du-Gard, France

# BOOK 1

*'I would have thought that it would be almost impossible for anyone to "disappear" nowadays.'*

– from *Poirot Investigates* – 'The Disappearance of Mr. Davenheim' [1924]

**H**old steady now boys! Revolt, Revolt. Revolution is in the air!' We're marching. Marching through Wales. And there I stand, Owain Glyndwr. Village by village I'm taking back the country. Ever since Richard II's death in February 1400 when the country's future seemed so bleak that revolution was the only way out. By September I was proclaimed Owain Prince of Wales, the last *Welsh* Prince of Wales.

In 1401, it spread – but it had to. If you were Welsh you were outcast. If you were Welsh you couldn't buy land in England. If you were Welsh your children were barred from education. By 1403, village by village had become castle by castle. A year later 'Owain Prince of Wales' became 'Owain IV, King of Wales'. The Cynulliad called for a Welsh state and a Welsh church. In six hundred years a 'rock band' will write a song about me.[1] In six hundred years there still will not have been another Welsh Prince of Wales.

The French withdrew their support in 1406 and I was hunted. Suicide was an option, or rather a suicide raid, but still I did not die. I was captured, ransomed and that was the end. Wasn't it?

Owain Glyndwr then vanished in 1415. Some said he was dead, others that he was alive and that he had withdrawn into himself. By the time English rule had been restored, much of the Welsh farming land had become neglected and was now a wasteland. There were many rumours of sightings of Glyndwr under assumed names or in disguise, but he had effectively disappeared. After that, no one knows what happened to him or where he went. No one turned him in. No one captured him. He was offered pardons but never surfaced.

Now he is seen as a myth, a caricature, his humanity stripped away. But he knew his history, he knew what the prophecies said and when they gave him the best chance to succeed. His followers would cling to his side with an almost religious fervour, it was almost the cult of Glyndwr. He bridged the gap from reality to literature when Shakespeare penned him as Owen Glendower in *Henry IV, Part One*.[2] He wasn't the only Welshman to follow this path and only they could decide when they wanted to be found, when they wanted to return.

# I

# A PROLOGUE TO HISTORY
*Pre-1967*

Blackwood? Where the fuck is Blackwood? Sounds too like 'back woods' for comfort. Blackwood. Coed Duon. Blackwood. Backwoods. These names spin through my head while I wait for Google Earth™ to load. I want a bird's eye view of where I'll be going. The town has almost as many bastardised names as the reason for my crusade. Richard James Edwards. Richie. Richey. Ritchie Vee. Richey James. Richey Manic. Richard. Titch. Android. The last Generation Terrorist.

I used to be a scientist, maybe I still am and always will be, so I know a little about space and time even if I used to hate physics. I know that a scene in a book is dependent on the writer giving the space and time to the reader; in non-fiction it's best for the writer to be able to inhabit one or both to be successful. One should also know their history. It affects the people you write about in ways that you might not otherwise understand. Time is sometimes hard to handle. The zenith of this book involves a man walking out through a door. The man and door are in the past. While I think about the man and the door I see the man's life pass before me, approaching like the proverbial express train. Me standing on the platform as it hurtles ever closer. Then in a blink it has passed and is miles away in seconds. I'm left standing with clothes flapping in the slipstream. Now I have to recreate the journey, walking back along the tracks, noting that some small elements of the journey expand to fill a whole chapter. Other chapters cover many years in just a few pages. The whole effect is a concertina of time:

contracting and expanding as moments accelerate away out of reach. The day of Richey's disappearance glows brightly in people's memories because of the intense emotion attached to the events, while the months afterwards blur into forgetfulness. And so I start back in history.

•

Despite his high intellect, Richard James Edwards of Blackwood never did study at Oxford, but Geoffrey did. Like Richard, or Richey as we shall call him throughout this volume, Geoffrey was from South Wales; in fact he was said to have been born in Gwent. Geoffrey wrote several famous texts, in a language that many would struggle to understand, and in later life he inhabited a priory. Although Richey knew of Geoffrey, the two never met, mainly because Geoffrey died in 1151 after writing one of the earliest known histories of Wales in his *Historia Regum Britanniae*. If Richey – who had a keen interest in history – had been born eight hundred years earlier, he could have been Geoffrey. Geoffrey wrote that Wales was first inhabited in 1170 BC when Brutus, a descendent of the Trojans, arrived by boat. Geoffrey decided that apart from the few giants that already made Britain their home, Brutus was the first human to live there. Of course Geoffrey was using a large portion of his own imagination to stir this truth, but it was *his* own truth, his own *version* of Wales and how it had all began.

This book is my version, but like any non-fiction it becomes a kind of fiction as soon as I begin deciding what to include and what to leave out, what should be highlighted and what should be downplayed. As soon as I start making those choices it becomes mine alone. Someone else would make different choices. That fact can't be escaped. Time is a large factor in this. I know exactly what happened to Richey Edwards on certain days and during certain weeks, but there are months and, in his early life, even years where virtually nothing is known. Inevitably the dreadful parts are swollen by import as they slow right down under my magnifying glass, hour by hour, and then the story flies off at an ever faster pace.

We know that the first real recorded version of Wales comes from an account of a Roman battle with local tribes in AD 48. As far as I can tell, there weren't any giants involved. Wales, with about 70 per cent of its border being coastline, has changed considerably over the years because the sea level around its shores has varied up and down by over 150 metres across the millennia. The area we now know as Wales came into existence with the building of Offa's Dyke around AD 790, the name 'Cymru' had been in use for around two hundred years by then. Richey knew history. He knew what it meant and how to use it. He knew that you had to understand the past in order to decipher the present.

•

The world of rock music has its own private universe of myth and legend. The stories of the deaths of Jimi, Janis, Jim, Ian, Kurt and the rest are well told. The fact that a guitar player can become an icon for a generation – a soothsayer for the masses – when he dies, but not before, is quite confusing to those with no interest in the genre. Wales, with its Celtic heritage, is also a land of myth and legend. King Arthur and Owain Glyndwr will rise again to save the country in its darkest hour. Another of these ancient stories involves the Welsh prince Madog, who disappeared from Wales and supposedly turned up in America several hundred years before Christopher Columbus. Though there is no hard evidence that this actually happened, there were later reports of Native Americans being able to speak Welsh. In 1669 a Revd. Morgan Jones was captured by a tribe, which was going to kill him, until the chief heard him speaking Welsh and understood what he was saying. This saved his life. Another story had an explorer finding a tribe that owned a copy of the Bible written in Welsh. This last point might not be quite as astounding as it seems. After rejecting the church of Rome in the sixteenth century, Wales, on the whole, turned to Episcopalian values for the next 250 years. John Wesley first spoke in Wales in 1739. Methodism then spread in part due to the large numbers attending its Sunday schools, which were an integral part of religious teaching. Both adults and children would attend to read the Bible, and this was the major function of the schools. Because so many attended, by the late 1700s Wales was one of the few countries that had more people who could read than couldn't. Early in the nineteenth century, twenty thousand Bibles were printed in Welsh – a massive print run for the time – and these slowly disseminated around the world. These chapels and meeting rooms gave people a sense of community and the preachers provided leadership – things that had been missing since the English lost interest. In an entry in his journal dated 27 August 1763, Wesley wrote a description of a sermon given by fellow preacher William Williams: 'It is common...After the preaching is over, for anyone that has a mind to give out a verse of a hymn. This they sing over and over with all their might, perhaps above thirty, yea, forty times. Meanwhile the bodies of two or three, sometimes ten or twelve, are violently agitated and they leap up and down, in all manner of postures, frequently for hours together.'

Religion wasn't the only thing to transform Wales. Soon, industry was growing at a pace never before seen anywhere in the world. Coal mines were dug into the ground, copper and tin plate industries expanded, and ironworks grew to meet the demand for tram and rail lines. The tramways spread across South Wales to move the people into work and the goods that they were producing to market. By 1840, South Wales was mining 4.5 million tonnes of coal a year. About three million tonnes were used locally: the majority of this went into the local iron works, while the rest was exported – leading to the building of a massive dock in Cardiff.[3] Between 1850 and the start of World War I, the population of Wales more than doubled from approximately 1.1 million to approximately 2.5 million, with workers flocking in from other parts of Wales and all over the British Isles. Wales' agricultural workers shrank in number as heavy industry called. By the start of the war, Wales was exporting thirty-six million tonnes of coal annually. During this period, Wales was turned from an almost forgotten backwater on the world stage to an important financial power. This new wealth helped to fund museums, a national university and a string of new libraries.

'Libraries gave us power.' Nicky Wire wrote the words. James Dean Bradfield sang the words. I sat in Blackwood Library thinking about the words. On a Tuesday afternoon the library was pretty quiet. A couple of pensioners browsed the new novels, and another was slumped asleep on one of the chairs. I looked for some in-depth local history but could find little. To make matters worse, the photocopier was out of toner and I had to write out everything by hand. The ordering of new supplies seemed to be the highlight of the afternoon for the staff. The building was smaller than I'd imagined, nestled at the end of the shops on the High Street. I thought about all the trips Richey Edwards made here while he was growing up and I realised that I was still closer to the beginning than the end. Prior to the building of the Sirhowy Tramroad, which opened in 1805, there was not a single building in what is now known as Blackwood. A chap called John Moggridge from Wiltshire settled in the area and eventually owned 450 acres of land, on which he built cottages with one eighth of an acre each of land and rented them out at the equivalent of eight pence a year. This social experiment gave local people some advantages but also made a bundle of cash for Moggridge.

The Beer Act of 1830 saw a massive increase in the number of places that were allowed to sell beer and by 1842 there was one tavern for every five inhabitants of Blackwood. In response, Temperance societies sprung up to cater for those disgusted by the excessive drunkenness, the beaten housewives, the employers with missing workers. One such society allowed members to drink two pints a day, but manual workers would save up during the week and then neck fourteen pints on a Saturday night. At the same time, there were thirty collieries within two and a half miles of Blackwood, and the biggest local deep pits – Oakdale, Wyllie and Markham – were still to come. At its peak in 1908, Oakdale was supplying a million tonnes of coal every year and employing two thousand men. When it closed in 1990, it signalled the end of two hundred years of mining in Gwent.

The Blackwood Miners' Institute was built in 1925, and still stands at the opposite end of the High Street to the library – these two buildings providing the only cultural refuges to the townsfolk and book-ending the strip of shops. The impressive multi-storey

Institute included a stage and dance hall, library, music rooms and areas for the use of local clubs and societies. Its completion coincided with the onset of a crushing depression: by 1932 unemployment was running at 43 per cent and continued to cripple South Wales until World War II, when most other countries had been over the worst, five years earlier. The transfer to oil from coal caused many of the Welsh problems. This was an area, and a town, that had endured its fair share of hardships before the Manics were born.

•

In 2007, the *Independent* printed a picture of the Blackwood Miners' Institute. It was an article about yet another TV Top Ten list. *VH1* had listed Blackwood, which has produced one nationally known act, as number eight in its Top Ten of influential music towns in the UK. Someone must have been having a laugh. Somehow the town got listed ahead of, for example, Sheffield, home to acts as diverse and influential as Arctic Monkeys, ABC, Pulp, Richard Hawley, The Human League, Def Leppard, Joe Cocker, The Long Blondes, The Comsat Angels and Heaven 17. Despite all that the Manics have achieved, there are suprisingly few bands that are overtly influenced by them.

Until the 1990s, the rock and pop music of Wales was decidedly 'old school'. Tom Jones, Shirley Bassey, Bonnie Tyler, Shakin' Stevens, Badfinger, The Alarm. As Britpop took over the mainstream in 1995, a sub-cult of Welshpop gained a wider following too. Catatonia, 60ft Dolls, Stereophonics, Super Furry Animals and Gorky's Zygotic Mynci led the way. When *Melody Maker* changed to a shiny magazine format to try and stave off its demise in 1999, it pulled off a publicity stunt of projecting huge images of Catatonia's Cerys Matthews and the Stereophonics' Kelly Jones onto the facade of Buckingham Palace with the headline 'The New Prince and Princess of Wales'. But the real 'Cool Cmyru' only emerged in 2008. The broadsheets were all over themselves proclaiming 'Wales Swings', 'Dragon Force' and 'A Good Time To Be Welsh', with celebrities draping themselves in the Welsh flag at every opportunity. Why? Because the rugby team won the Five Nations, Cardiff City got to the FA Cup semi-finals and Duffy was at number one. Add in *Gavin and Stacey*, Joe Calzaghe, Catherine Zeta Jones and Rhys Ifans, and you had a veritable cultural phenomenon on your hands. 'In Wales at present,' claimed the *Independent*, 'no matter what your line, you're feeling pretty confident.'

This was all very different to the Wales that Richey Edwards knew and grew up in. 'Where we come from there is a natural melancholy in the air,' he said. 'Everybody, ever since you could comprehend it, felt pretty much defeated.' In the early 1990s, it was reported that Gwent had the highest rate of alcohol poisoning in the UK. When the mines closed and the jobs vanished, there was little else to do. 'It's a museum, everything is closed, it's like a long walk down a graveyard,' said Edwards. '[Wales is] a soul destroying place; we'd rather say we were from Europe.' He had nothing positive to say about his hometown at all: 'If you built a museum to represent Blackwood, all you could put in it would be shit. Rubble and shit.' From these initial interviews, Edwards' world-view became clear: rather than look for a sliver of positivity, he chose to accentuate the negative. It might have been bad, but it wasn't Somalia.

Today, Blackwood is a shopping centre and a site for light industry. Sony, Toshiba and Unilever all have factories in the area. With a population of over twenty thousand (and growing), Blackwood is now merging into surrounding villages. It even has a cinema again after the previous one closed down in the 1980s. Even the Miners' Institute has undergone a rebirth. After being left to rot in the 1980s, it was bought by the local council, and reopened in 1992. Jasper Carrott and the Welsh National Opera have since performed there (not together). It is presently under the umbrella of the Arts Council of Wales and thriving once again. But the damp stigma of melancholy remains. Wales *seems* to have a high rate of suicide, whether it's backed up by statistics or not. Going way back in time, Milly 'Peg' Entwhistle left Wales to act on Broadway and then moved to Hollywood in the 1930s hoping to get work in the movies. She famously committed suicide by jumping from the top of the letter 'H' in the giant Hollywoodland sign up in the hills. Alun Lewis, the poet whose works included 'The Suicide', shot himself while serving in Burma during World War II. Some speculation argues that it might have been accidental. These are just two of the many Welsh suicides from the arts world. While this book was being written, more than twenty young people killed themselves in nearby Bridgend. Why was the South Wales suicide rate so high? Many other areas of the UK have been through depressions when the primary industries died out, but few seemed to take it so badly.

Despite there being no proof, the story of Richey Edwards is often reported as a suicide. Should that be expected? You would be forgiven for thinking that the Richey Edwards book had already been written, the mystery explained and it all nicely wrapped up. Surely this was such a story that it had already been told, and would not be sitting around waiting for its author? But it hadn't. So why not? It hasn't been an easy project to research, as I noted to myself at one point, 'When one door closes, another one is slammed shut.' Some Manics fans have been helpful, others haven't. There is certainly a cult surrounding the memory of Richey Edwards and some take it as their duty to 'protect' his name. They, thankfully, are in the minority. Many Richey fans are too young to have experienced his place in the world of pop first-hand. Maybe it's the generation gap of fourteen years and counting between Edwards' disappearance and now. Looking at the age of people posting on various internet forums tells its own story. Looking down a random page I noted that the comments were being written by people who were three, two, nine, three and two respectively when Richey was last seen alive. Like Kurt Cobain and Jim Morrison, there are conspiracy theories revolving around this story and I had to try and work through them. It was highly unlikely that I would literally find the man himself, but I hoped to find his version of reason.

*I saw with my own eyes the Sibyl at Cumae hanging in a jar,*
*and when the boys said to her, Sibyl, what do you want?*
*she replied I want to die.*

– Petronius, *The Satyricon*

**W**riters **often compose their best work** when they are
suffering times of personal upheaval or difficulty. Or maybe it
isn't their best work but it is the work of these times that the critics
and public at large are drawn to in hindsight when they discover
what the writer was going through. It makes them seem more human
to know that the text has been *felt* by the writer first-hand.

'The Waste Land' was one of Richey Edwards' favourite texts.
When Thomas Stearns Eliot was writing it after the end of World War
I, he was experiencing difficult times. His first marriage was falling
apart and he was struggling. During the many years that he worked
on 'The Waste Land', these things contributed to the despair of the
poem and the perceived disillusionment of his generation. His life
was grim, his writing was grimmer. He wasn't just writing of personal
hopelessness but also of the wretchedness of modern society and
the loss of order and faith. Chaos was king, death was everywhere.
Flowing water replaced by hard rock. A 31-year-old woman with no
teeth. A dead tree. Bad sex and gladness when it's over.

Edwards was drawn to Eliot's obscure, sometimes pedantic, Grail
mythologies that reached into the core of human despair; he could
relate to Eliot's almost prudish outer being, which was at odds with
his writing. Edwards found that someone so calm on the outside
could spew out writing of such horror from within. When Edwards
later studied the abominations of the concentration camps he lost
faith in humankind; to him the whole world had become a waste
land, where the fortunate lived blinkered lives and pretended that

the horror didn't exist while he grappled with a conscience that couldn't bear to live such a life.

Similarities between Eliot and Edwards are many. Eliot was able to use a wide range of different literatures and religions in his writing; Edwards also drew on various religious texts and holy books for his lyrics. Eliot was not averse to pursuing populist culture, just as Edwards did. Eliot was given three months' leave from his job to recover from a 'nervous breakdown'; Edwards was given similar leave in the summer of 1994. Eliot abandoned his childhood religion and turned to the Anglican church when he settled in England; Edwards rejected his Methodist upbringing. Both remained virgins until relatively late (Eliot was 26; Edwards 21), both smoked heavily (Eliot died of emphysema, which was at least exacerbated by his heavy smoking; Edwards was smoking upwards of sixty a day before he vanished), and both were fixated on producing the perfect work.

There were parts in 'The Waste Land' that Richey Edwards could relate to, even reaching back to his teenage years when he first read it. The general mood of decay was around him in everyday life as the industry of Blackwood collapsed in on itself in the wake of the miners' strike; the text hinted at night terrors and problems with sleep and of thinking too hard about things, and these were problems that Edwards would wrestle with his whole adult life.

Many pieces of literature held important places in Richey Edwards' psyche. In later life he became so engrossed in Dante's 'Inferno' that he had his arm tattooed with connected imagery, as his own self-worth dipped and his thoughts turned to an eternity of damnation while musing over the loss of youthful innocence. Edwards' later interest in religion would have a real Old Testament ring to it; he discovered that 'The Waste Land' alluded to Dante in the section starting 'Unreal City'. In the Bible verses referenced by God warning the people that they must remember the days of their youth (for, in their old age, 'fears shall be in the way'), it became almost a self-fulfilling prophecy as Edwards – from his late teens onwards – carried a possibly unhealthy view of his childhood being the best, and only good, part of his life.

# II

---

# THE GREEN, GREEN GRASS
# OF HOME

*1967 to 1979*

On my second day of researching in South Wales, I set out from my Cardiff hotel to drive north under virtually cloudless blue skies. Despite this being a capital city, it didn't take long for me to escape from the grid-locked traffic and I was soon zooming along the green and leafy M4. In the car's CD player was the Manics' best-of, *Forever Delayed*. Now, listening to 'A Design For Life' while driving along hillside roads gives the song more meaning, and perhaps a little more insight, just because this is where the song comes from. You could almost feel the music echoing around the valley. It was the same when I'd previously driven around Memphis listening to Big Star, around northern California listening to Pavement, or rural Georgia with any of R.E.M.'s first three albums playing, although I doubt I'd have felt the same while driving around Liverpool with *Yellow Submarine* on the stereo. On this beautiful day it all seemed so positive and I found it difficult to relate to all I'd absorbed about the place before I arrived.

Down through the years, South Wales has had some unofficial titles bestowed on it that it probably didn't want. 'The divorce capital of the UK', 'the alcohol poisoning capital of the UK', it had some of the country's highest unemployment after mines closed and now – just down the road in Bridgend – the national press was hunting out the reasons why the local youth population all seemed to be killing themselves. All these negative connotations seemed a light year away as I wended through green valley after green valley. This was really pleasant.

Up the valley off the motorway you reach Risca, which seems to have more well-tended cricket pitches than I ever see back in England. I passed the Crosskeys college with its wooden facade. The large wall of high-ceilinged windows was where Richey Edwards would sit looking out at the traffic on the main road while doing his A-Levels here in the 1980s. The next sign said, 'Blackwood 7 Miles'. The thought occurred to me that I was tracing Edwards' life in reverse during this sunny morning. From Cardiff and his flat, which was the end of his documented life in 1995, past his sixth-form college, heading to Blackwood where he spent his teenage years and eventually to the other side of the valley known as Woodfieldside, where his family lived when he was born in the 1960s. In all, I travelled his twenty-seven known years in less than ninety minutes.

Graham Edwards was thirty-one when he married Sherry Davies in 1966 at St Margaret's Parish Church in Blackwood. Sherry, who was eight years Graham's junior, lived with her parents at the time while Graham shared a house on Church View with his mother. The house had been in the family for generations. At the end of 1967, their first child was born – a boy they called Richard, commonly known as Richey. At least one book places Richey Edwards' birth as being in 1966, *The Times* said it was in 1969, while other sources claim it was on 27 December 1967. It's no wonder that his later life seemed almost mythical when simple things such as a date of birth couldn't be accurately pinned down.

In fact, Richard James Edwards made his first live appearance on 22 December 1967. If you believed him in later interviews, life was all downhill from there. 'The only perfect circle on a human body is the eye,' he explained. 'When a baby is born, it's so perfect, but when it opens its eyes, it's just blinded by the corruption and everything else is a downward spiral.' Despite this, Edwards' childhood was a happy one; in fact, it was pretty much the happiest time of his life. He initially lived in a terraced house on Church View, just a short walk from open fields he could play in. Also living there was his paternal grandmother. Shortly before his second birthday he was joined by a sister, Rachel. She was born in the same year that Neil Kinnock became Blackwood's MP. Richey's earliest memory was watching his father Graham put coal on the open fire. Graham's father had been a miner but rather than follow in his footsteps, Graham had served four years in the parachute regiment before setting up a hairdressing business with Sherry on Blackwood High Street. The family unit was close and spent Sunday mornings at the local Methodist church, somewhere that the family had attended for as long as anyone could remember. Richey also started going to Sunday school as soon as he was old enough. Being around his grandmother and organised religion was something that he was presented with from his earliest childhood. The long days that his parents spent at work meant that Richey would spend many hours in the care of his grandmother, which was just fine by him. 'All I remember is green fields,' said Edwards, 'blue skies and Clarks shoes with the compass in the bottom.'

•

In the late 1970s, it wasn't quite jumpers for goal-posts on the Gossard factory playing field. This was a scene replicated on thousands of fields across the country every evening after school. Small groups of boys would gather at different ends and sides of the field to have a kickabout, and they'd gradually meld into one or two matches depending on age and size. Lines would be drawn up with everyone dreading being picked last. The matches would usually last until just before dark on a school night, but this was a Friday – no school and a licence to stay out until dark. On this late spring evening, that meant games running from just after teatime until after eight p.m. At dusk on this night the game was evenly balanced at 12-all, and someone called out that 'Next goal wins!'. Defending wasn't really an issue and young legs chased the ball up and down the pitch with endless enthusiasm. Despite this being South Wales, the players being emulated were the stars of Liverpool and Nottingham Forest, with the occasional Leeds United fan pretending to be Peter Lorimer. Just as with their heroes, there was a trophy up for grabs. This one was a battered old crown green bowling trophy that the father of one of the kids had found tossed into a skip, but it was prized nonetheless and the victors would inevitably parade down the road home with it after the match. With the last rays of the sun disappearing behind the factory, a final burst of energy gripped the players as they knew the end of the game was fast approaching. One of the tallest players, a gangly lad called Jones, skipped past an attempted tackle from a bespectacled kid called Bradfield, and then another from Bradfield's cousin, before slipping a pass to his on-rushing winger. 'There you go Teddy!' called Jones as the winger collected the ball in his stride and slipped it under the on-rushing goalkeeper, before wheeling away in a mock celebration that would have graced the luscious striped turf of Wembley or even the Arms Park. The losing side looked on dejectedly as the winners took turns passing around the knackered old silverware before the winning goal scorer – beaming from ear to ear – hoisted it above his head.

Richey 'Teddy' Edwards was so-named by his friend because of his 'cuddly' nature and the fact that his surname matched that of the Teddy Edwards children's television character. At school, he was also known as 'Titch' because of his small size. The Jones that towered above him was Nicholas Allen Jones; he was just over a year younger than Edwards, having been born on 20 January 1969. The pair had known each other since junior-school age, as both lived on the Woodfieldside estate side of the valley. 'I first met him playing football when we were little,' recalled Jones in 2008. 'I lived on the different side of the street and we'd go on the field and play for this little crappy trophy my dad had found in a skip. He was a decent right-winger. That's my first memory of him.'

Jones' father, Alan, had also served in the army, then worked down the mine before becoming a builder. Nick had a brother, Patrick, who was four years older. In his teenage years Nick Jones would become almost universally known as Nicky Wire due to his tall, gangly, wiry, frame. He had a wide, cheesy grin and a quick mouth if he saw something he didn't like.

Other regular players on the Gossard pitch were the pair of cousins from a mile down the road in Pontllanfraith. James Dean Bradfield was almost christened either Clint Eastwood Bradfield or John Wayne Bradfield by his carpenter father, Monty, but his mother, Sue, intervened and they settled on a third-favourite film star: James Dean. He was just a month younger than Jones (born 21 February 1969) and suffered a number of school-yard nicknames due to an early eye injury which necessitated a pair of thick glasses – 'Radar', 'Crossfire', 'Beaker', and so on, were the usual taunts.

'We played football together and did all the things friends do,' said Nicky Wire. 'I've known James Dean Bradfield since I was five and I think that's why we've stood the test of time. It's very rare that a group of very close friends form a band together.' Bradfield's cousin, Sean Moore, rounded out the quartet.

To this day, Bradfield has the geography of his childhood etched into his mind's eye. 'A long terraced street,' he told Q magazine in 1996. 'Steps down into the valley. Football field. Swimming pool. Then to the left was a big disused slag heap with trees growing on it. We played there, everything happened there – Bonfire Night, Halloween, a lot of people lost their virginity there. If there was a fight between Pontllanfraith and Springfield it happened on that slag heap. It's gone now, levelled. When I go back what strikes me is there's less places for people to hide. Hide and just be innocent. Lose their innocence too.'

The mid-1970s were probably the last generation of kids that could really be kids without the all-permeating fear and suffocating protection of their parents against drugs, knives, abductions and guns. All four of the boys have since recalled how their childhoods were almost too perfect. They spent long, hot summers building dams, playing games, watching films, reading, and playing football. The closest thing they experienced to trouble was when an aunt of James Dean Bradfield had her pony stolen from a local field. Bradfield cried his eyes out when he heard the news and although local suspicion hinted that gypsies had taken it, this couldn't be proved. Even here, the inference was that outsiders must have perpetrated the crime: locals just didn't do that kind of thing.

Richey Edwards started attending Pontllanfraith Junior School not far from the massed allotments at the back of Woodfieldside in the early 1970s. As did Wire, Bradfield and Moore. Just a short walk from home, the junior and infant schools were imposing, Victorian brick monuments that still loom over the main road. Nowadays the school's side gates are all securely padlocked, a simple sign of the difference between Edwards' school days and the present-day precautions that are written in statute. Exactly how Richey enjoyed junior school was relayed by his classmate Maria Gibbs. She recalls that he was a quiet, intelligent boy who kept himself to himself. He enjoyed a third-year project about Concorde and a trip to Bristol Zoo, but otherwise the minutiae of these years might as well have been eaten by locusts. The imposing facade of the school is still impenetrable today, with nary an acknowledgement to repeated phonecalls, emails and letters. Most of the teachers from back then are likely to be retired or dead anyway.

This is all quite different to Oakdale Comprehensive, which they all moved to at the end of the decade. The secondary school is situated just up the leafy Penmaen Road past the funeral directors in Oakdale. It's a modern-looking school, which now has a boundary of high chicken-wire fences all around its perimeter. These wouldn't have been in place when Richey Edwards first walked through the doors in September 1979. 'Endeavour' is displayed proudly on the large school crest above the entrance building. A group of girls were playing hockey when I popped by to take a look and so I didn't think it was a good idea to start taking photos of the buildings. Both schools are on the far side of the valley from the Blackwood High Street so any trip over there would have to be worthwhile, especially for the kids. One such trip in 1978 allowed Richey to buy his first record, 'It's Only Make Believe' by Child. In a funny way, that was an apt choice for young Richey. He was a deep thinker from an early age; it was a problem that would plague him throughout his life – he could be overly sensitive and prone to thinking about things too much. Even before junior school age, this was affecting him. 'Maybe I think about things too much, but everything that happens to me I do feel is deliberate,' he said. 'And that's been the same since I was a child. If something happened in Infants' School I'd be convinced everybody was against me. Which is self-obsession, because the world does not revolve around you. People don't give a fuck.

People don't do things because it's *you*. When I'm driving in my car and traffic lights turn red, I think it's because *I'm* in the car. I feel persecuted. I feel that if anybody else had been in the car they'd have gone through.' Edwards would always have a different view of the world and his place in it. He would struggle with finding any value in himself and would despair at how he perceived the rest of humanity to be acting. He would think about things so intently that the knots his brain tied him up in became more like a noose. He also had off-kilter views of the world around him, which he seemed to get from books, and would refuse to explore new places for himself. In later years, he spoke to one interviewer about the imagery in his lyrics. 'If I tried to write a Springsteen-esque lyric about Wales it'd be, "I went to Pontypool factory / Then drove up Caerphilly mountain / And drank tea from a plastic cup." You can't do it.' In this statement, Edwards revealed his lack of insight both into Springsteen's lyrics and the similarities between the working stock of his home and New Jersey. Both were blue-collar areas with iron works and oil refineries. Springsteen would often invoke the common man and his exit from the factory or road gang on a Friday night. Perhaps Edwards just needed to get out more.

•

Through the 1970s, South Wales had been a Labour stronghold. By the spring of 1979 the United Kingdom as a whole was ripe for change, but the idea that you should 'be careful what you wish for' was never more true than when the area backed the Tory revolution. James Callaghan's dying Labour government was casting around to find something that might allow them to cling onto power, but the Scottish and Welsh referendums of late winter 1979 did little to help. In Scotland a slight majority voted in favour but the Welsh couldn't have made their thoughts more clear as only 12 per cent voted in support of a Welsh Assembly, despite the economic decline that had gathered pace through the decade. The years between 1973 and 1983 would see the number of working Welsh miners drop from 66,000 to fewer than 20,000. Things would get worse still during the 1980s under successive Tory governments.

A couple of months after the Welsh referendum, all of Labour's ideas were swept aside with Margaret Thatcher leading the Conservative march to Downing Street. 'Where there is despair may we bring hope,' she said on her first day in office. The Tories had won eleven seats in Wales – their highest total since 1874. In the north of the country, Anglesey returned its first Tory member since 1784. While the majority were obviously pinning their hopes on the Tories, a minority set about putting their more extreme views into practice. The WAWR (Welsh for 'Dawn'), or 'Workers' Army of the Welsh Republic', went on the offensive against English holiday homes in Wales. The end of 1979 and early 1980 saw thirty houses go up in flames. There was also talk of a bombing campaign. It was a time of political violence in the UK. The IRA troubles were arguably at their height and an aide of Mrs Thatcher, Airey Neave, was murdered in a car bomb as he drove away from the House of Commons. Gwynfor Evans, leader of Plaid Cymru, said he would hunger-strike to death if no Welsh-language TV channel was broadcast. S4C finally debuted in November 1982.

In 1979, Welsh unemployment stood at 8 per cent but by 1982 it had more than doubled to 17 per cent. So much for Mrs Thatcher's speech about bringing hope. Richey Edwards completed his primary school education in the summer of 1979, just as the unrest of a new decade was about to begin. At the time, he was still more interested in playing with his mates than he was in British politics. What would become apparent over the next few years, however, was how his parents and their friends would be affected by the changing political and social environments that the new leadership created in South Wales. Years later, Edwards would say that 'Blackwood is scarred industrially, economically and politically. Everything about Blackwood stands as a reminder of fifteen years of decay. That affects your world-view for the rest of your life wherever you go.' Nicky Wire explained in a Q magazine 'Cash for Questions' feature that 'Our angst springs from coming from South Wales. It's a longing encapsulated in the Welsh word "hireath". The Irish can usually see the better side of things, they have a sense of wonder. The Welsh don't. We think everything is going to turn out shit.' For a while during the 1980s this was something that a lot of people in Blackwood and its surrounds would agree with and relate to.

**T**o say that **Richey Edwards**' teenage mind was like a sponge absorbing everything around it would be an understatement. It was more akin to a machine or super-computer sucking in influences, digesting them and then quickly moving on to the next book, film, album or philosophy. The Parisian uprising of 1968 became one of his touchstones. At its centre had been Guy Debord, who came close to proving that art can change the world – something Edwards acutely admired. Debord's 1967 book *Society of the Spectacle* was at the heart of Situationist International, a group with the view that if art was not revolutionary then it was worthless. Debord, who like Edwards had lived with his grandmother as a child, said that 'The remains of religion and of the family and the moral repression they assure, merge whenever the enjoyment of this world is affirmed – this world being nothing other than repressive pseudo-enjoyment.' Edwards couldn't have said it better himself, especially not in French.

Debord, like Edwards, would polarise views; some thought him a genius and others a motormouth who deliberately made simple theories more complicated than they needed to be with the use of overly complex language. Situationist International's views on art struck a chord with Edwards just as they had with punk in the 1970s. Revolution and sloganeering would be central to his thinking. Edwards would also attempt to use some of Debord's ideas more literally when he strove to have the Manics' debut album sleeved in sandpaper so that it would slowly destroy the albums stored either side of it. Debord's debut book, *Mémoires*, had been bound in sandpaper to do the same with books placed next to it.[4]

Once Situationist International was disbanded, Debord withdrew, Salinger-like, to write in obscure isolation. Salinger's withdrawal was often mentioned by Edwards in interviews. Debord's chosen hideaway was in the tiny Bellevue-la-Montagne, a winding street 110 miles from my own hideaway in Saint-Jean-du-Gard. There, he was free from his past and could drink and write away from the public glare. He rarely left the ancient farmhouse. His alcoholism caused polyneuritis, a painful inflammation of nerve endings, and on 30 November 1994, aged sixty-two, he shot himself through the heart. After Debord's death, Edwards wrote about him for the *NME*: 'True force. No copyright. No rights reserved. No motorcycle emptiness. No modern life is rubbish. No time. No history. The time of life is short and if we live, we tread on kings.'

# III

## SCULPTURE OF A MAN
*1979 to 1986*

Bobby Sands had already served three years for the possession of firearms before he was found guilty for a second time in September 1977. This time he was sentenced for fourteen years and sent to HM Prison Maze, nine miles outside of Belfast. Sands was imprisoned in the infamous H-Block and became the leader of the numerous provisional IRA members incarcerated with him. IRA prisoners had previously been given Special Category Status, which meant they didn't have to wear prison uniforms or do prison work; they were allowed extra visits and food parcels, much like a Prisoner of War. When these privileges were gradually removed, the prisoners rebelled. First, they instigated the Blanket Protests in which they refused to wear prison uniforms and wore only blankets. Next, came the Dirty Protests. After the beating of a fellow prisoner, many others refused to leave their cells even to use the bathroom and began rubbing shit over their cell walls. By late 1980, the first hunger strikes had begun. This seemed to have an effect and they were initially called off, but when it became apparent that the prisoners hadn't won the concessions they had hoped for, these were started again – this time with Bobby Sands as their figurehead.

Sands stopped eating on 1 March 1981, asking for several demands to be met; ultimately these equated to all IRA prisoners being treated as political prisoners. Not long after his fast had started, Sands was given the opportunity of standing for election in the South Tyrone by-election. On 9 April, Sands was elected but of course never had the chance to actually take his seat. On 5 May he died of starvation after sixty-six days of his protest. He was twenty-seven years old.

Richey Edwards, aged fourteen, had watched the unfolding events every evening on the BBC news, sitting with his parents and sister. He viewed the story with a mixture of fascination and admiration. It was a protest that would resonate with him throughout his life, seeing that a person could take such severe action against their own body. He saw it as a method of self-control and to him that was an exquisite thing. 'My idea of purity is completely split down the middle,' he said. 'It's in denial with its own logic. The idea of not eating food, the idea of a political prisoner, say the Maze Block going on hunger strike, when I was young, I thought it was so beautiful, the best thing anyone could do. It's all about injuring yourself to a certain extent. But for a reason, for an absolute reason. That's why I liked Bobby Sands. That's why I thought he was a better statement than anything else that was going on at the time, because it was against himself.' This was the first indication of what would become a growing obsession through his adult life. Weight management equalled control to the extent that he would only allow himself enough food to survive as he became intent on keeping a 'perfect' body shape. But that was later in life – as a child and young teenager he had other things to worry about.

•

When Richey Edwards walked through the gates of Oakdale comprehensive school as one of its eight hundred or so pupils for the first time in September 1979, he probably glanced up at the school crest. He did so alone as Rachel was still at primary school. Edwards was a voracious reader and hard worker. His only misdemeanor occurred when he jumped off a wall and was hit by a car, breaking his leg in three places and putting him in hospital. As Richey Edwards came to the end of his first year of comprehensive school, Joy Division's Ian Curtis hanged himself. It didn't make an immediate impact on Edwards, although Curtis would later become one of his musical heroes. Edwards would buy the odd single here and there, but music wasn't yet a massive part of his life. The other future Manics were also just making their first tentative steps into the world of 7" singles. James Dean Bradfield was famously ridiculed for making the Diana Ross single 'My Old Piano' his first record purchase. 'Everybody was into metal and Whitesnake, but I was into the Nolan Sisters and ELO,' he admitted. 'I just remember buying that single and I remember walking to Blackwood, which is about a mile away, and I saw this bloke walking towards me called Dids, and he was a really cruel bastard. As he got closer he seemed to get bigger and bigger. As soon as I got close to him he just ripped the bag out of my hand and was like, "What have you bought? Ahh, you poof!"'

Around this time, Sean Moore's parents went through a divorce and his mother Jenny decided it was best for Sean to move in with her sister Sue Bradfield. Sean moved into James' room and the two would share a bunk bed until they moved out years later. Moore's father disappeared and only made contact with his son after seeing the Manics on *Top of the Pops*, which prompted Sean to smash up a dressing room with a snooker cue. Bradfield and Moore grew close and remain more like brothers than cousins.

At the end of 1980, Edwards became a teenager and was a typical one in many ways. He suffered from bad skin until his late teens and was shy around girls, although he did have one girlfriend at Oakdale for just a couple of weeks. In fact, apart from a crush on Altered Images singer Clare Grogan he showed little interest in the opposite sex. On one occasion he and a group of friends found a stash of porn magazines under the bed of one of the boys' older brothers. After the gang spent a couple of minutes scanning the pages in stunned silence, Edwards ran from the room and was physically sick outside – an event that resonated through his life. He was always dismissive when asked about public nudity, saying that the human body was an ugly sight, and he mentioned the porn incident in a later song. 'It was one great bloody shock,' he admitted. 'It wasn't the nudity, as such, it was the depravation. They were the saddest pictures I ever saw. It wasn't the girls who were sad . . . I felt sad for the men. The fact that an appetite existed, out there and, I can't deny, I was part of that appetite . . . it was the violence of those pictures that upset me. It affected me profoundly and will always haunt me.'

Well before his O-Levels, Edwards was showing signs of being a conscientious student and insatiable reader. He had little time for many of his timetabled subjects, but English Literature interested him and his favourite early books were *1984* and *Brave New World*. 'When I was thirteen, I did a Shakespeare project that was 859 pages long,' he said. 'Everyone else just did sex. I just had fuck all else to do but sit in and write.'

As he turned thirteen, his life changed in many ways outside of the usual rites of passage. Graham, Sherry, Richey and Rachel moved across town; leaving his grandmother in her own house, he rebelled against going to church and Sunday School and gained the responsibility of a pet dog he called Snoopy. This was a lot for any thirteen-year-old to take in, especially if that thirteen-year-old was becoming more withdrawn and shy as the years passed. Looking back on his life from an adult perspective, he would often claim that his life had been happy until the age of thirteen and that it had all started to turn bad from there on. Was this because he had rose-tinted glasses for the days of no responsibilities? Fond memories of living with his grandmother? Or a later feeling of being lost after the close guidance of church? Even now with the advent of global warming, the summers of our youth seem to be always sunny in the mind's eye – the summer holidays were always bathed in sunshine. 'Most people look back on their childhoods with more fondness than their early twenties or their teenage years which are pretty horrendous,' said Edwards. 'As a child, you put your head on the pillow and fall asleep with no worries. From being a teenager onwards it's pretty rare that you don't end up staying awake half the night thinking about bullshit.'

Richey's parents decided to move from the house that had been the family home to a modern bungalow across the valley in a cul-de-sac off a steep hill that runs up from Blackwood High Street. It was on the High Street that Graham and Sherry Edwards ran their hairdressing business. Richey didn't change schools – it just meant he had further to travel to and from school – but he suddenly had the library within walking distance and the bustle of the High Street just under his nose. I know this because I cruised around the area. It was early afternoon on a weekday when I found myself sitting in my car outside the Edwards' family home. The descriptions were right. Up a steep hill from the centre of town then down a steep cul-de-sac to the modest – but not too modest – bungalow at the bottom. A car was parked outside; I surmised that Richey's parents would probably have both retired by now. Should I go and knock on the door? No, I'd promised myself all along that I would try and act with integrity on this project, just as I tried to do on all of my other ones. After all, what would I say if I found myself staring his mother in the eyes? 'Hello, I'm just here to quiz you about your long-time missing son, don't mind if I come in do you?' No, I'd had the feedback from the family already so why try it on and do nothing but cause them distress? Via the band's management I'd been told that they would never talk to anyone for a book about their son. They did send their best wishes, however, thanking me for my interest. My initial view had been that they would have welcomed any publicity. Surely any chance to keep his name in the public eye would be an extremely thin shaft of hope? But I guess that people have to move on with their lives, no matter how painful the loss. So I sat there trying to take in my surroundings. It would have been a lung-busting hike to the top of the road before a more leisurely stroll down the steep hill into town. As my mind drifted I caught some movement out of the corner of my eye. Someone was at the window. Making sure I avoided eye-contact, I self-consciously put the car into gear and broke the enveloping silence with a hill-start to facilitate my escape.

I was in the region for a few days and later drove into town. True to form, it started to drizzle. I wondered if it ever stopped. When I thought about this place in my mind's eye, it was always 1992. Shell-suits and semi-mullets walked the streets, with the occasional lumberjack shirt open to reveal a Mudhoney T-shirt beneath. Blackwood today is not quite the one-street town as reported of old, but almost. Now, it has the obligatory provincial 24-hour Asda. A small retail park has been added at the end of the winding High Street, which includes all the usual retail suspects. It took me three minutes to drive, slowly, from one end of the High Street to the other, and that included stopping at every pedestrian crossing. The town was very busy for a Tuesday morning. I noticed that all the signs, no matter how trivial, were bilingual. But I wondered who might read only the bottom halves, especially for something like the parking costs behind the supermarket. At the 'Top End' of the street sits the Red Lion pub, scene of early Manic nights out. Every window is now bricked up: not the most appealing of drinking venues. Next door is the much-vaunted Miners' Institute.

Where once the Edwards had the only hairdressing salon, there are now no fewer than six hairdressers nestled together at one end of the street. Perhaps people have more haircuts in Wales now than they did fifteen years ago? As I wandered past the most established one, I saw it was empty of customers but had two bored-looking teenage girls with streaky hair waiting around. Nicky Wire once recalled that the Edwards' shop had been burgled eight times, even though the only thing to steal was shampoo. The local kids only did it because they had little else to do. Across the road is the Blackwood library, once the employer of Nicky's brother Patrick and often the haunt of all four band members. I popped in to look up some local history, but apart from a couple of picture books and some fading postcards there was little to go on and they had nothing on Neil Kinnock.

Despite my seeing Blackwood in the summer time, I just couldn't think back to Richey walking these streets without anything but rain in my mind. As he ascends the hill back to his parents, the rain is swirling down gutters and overfilling the storm drains at the base of the hill. Why does a place I've hardly touched in reality give me these feelings? 'That's been the truth since we were fifteen years old,' said Nicky Wire. 'All I can remember is being melancholy. I've never said I was desperately unhappy. The truly unhappy people of this world are usually the ones who end up suicidal or living on the streets.' Richey Edwards certainly felt that way. 'It's just our natural mood,' he said. 'We've always been like that. You've got the ruins of heavy industry all around you, you see your parents' generation all out of work, nothing to do, being forced into the indignity of going on courses of relevance. Like a fifty-year-old miner, worked in a pit all his life, there's not much joy for him to go and learn how to type. It's just pointless. And that is all around us, ever since we were born.'

Once the house move had been completed, the closest Methodist church was the Central Methodist Church. This imposing building had been erected in 1898 to a gothic design that was seen as extremely modern at the time. Its massive wooden organ with metal pipes rising behind the tiered choir stalls, with balconies along either side, three columns of pews and purple glazed brick would have been intimidating to a young child. But now he was old enough to speak up, Edwards refused to attend any more. 'He's always had this thing about it,' said Nicky Wire. 'I've never really talked to him about it, but he's always made out that it really pissed him off and fucked him up.'

'I went to church three times every Sunday until I was thirteen, when I was big enough to refuse,' Edwards explained in 1992. 'Then it was football. But when you've got an eighty-year-old preacher screaming at you by name if you're late, you fucking sit there and obey, like blind sheep. Next to him, liberal teachers just didn't compare. At school, you walk around like, "Who gives a fuck?" By thirteen, most of us could recite, parrot-fashion, huge chunks of the Bible. I still like a lot of Isiah, I've got some of it in my notebook. In [the Manics' song] "Crucifix Kiss", we quote Luke, Sermon 6: "And if one of the occupation troops forces you to carry his pack one kilometre then carry it two." I've always found that attitude moronic. What's the fucking point? Religion's the reason why areas like this or Liverpool continue to be oppressed, because of a false sense of community stops them rising up.'

Edwards' reaction to traditional schooling and being forced into religion struck a chord when he started reading the works of French poet Arthur Rimbaud. Rimbaud's father had also served in the army, and he had a strong religious upbringing; he also rebelled against classical schooling. Edwards said that qualifications were not a true measure of intelligence and that the most important lessons were not on any syllabus. He would grow fascinated with Rimbaud as his teens progressed.

•

Maybe it was because younger children need less complicated things to stimulate them and keep them happy. An empty field or a group of trees could provide endless possibilities for play. As teenage years progressed, however, it was suddenly very easy to be bored with nowhere to go. Blackwood, like many small towns throughout the UK, suffered from drink-related violence – especially at weekends. It seemed that more teenagers were turning to drink and letting out their frustrations on the Blackwood High Street on a Saturday night. In the 1980s, the town inhabitants were increasingly struggling with the loss of industry and the hard economic environment. Things were certainly becoming grim.

Richey Edwards could understand why the violence was happening around him and where the boiling frustrations came from, but he himself pulled away from it. Never a violent person, he was much more likely to retreat into his own thoughts, which caused problems of their own.

In 1982 James Dean Bradfield was singing in his local church choir, but at school he was known to be tough and the other kids didn't mess with him. When the news was saturated with the Falklands War, he began to have thoughts of a military career – even when the war had cost the lives of thirty-nine Welsh Guards. It was, in part at least, because of the Falklands War that the Tory government was re-elected for a second term in 1983. In July 1981, headline riots in Toxteth and Brixton – but also in Hull, Preston and Birmingham – showed the growing ripples of discontent running through the country. In January 1982, unemployment reached three million for the first time since the depression of the 1930s. Despite this, Labour still managed to lose the June 1983 General Election, signalling the end of Michael Foot's reign as party leader. Foot was replaced by Blackwood MP Neil Kinnock the following October. 'Everything Neil Kinnock stands for is everything that my grandfather would have spat at,' said Edwards. '[His] desperate craving for power at any cost. Labour were told by a right-wing press that they had to move towards the centre. But they should have gone more extreme.

In areas like Blackwood, Labour's always going to win even if a cheese sandwich stands for election.'

It was in this growing climate of anger and disgust that Richey Edwards started his final year at Oakdale Comprehensive. He was growing ever more bitter at the education system, too. 'Comprehensive school was the most depressing time for all of us,' he said. 'They either write you off or fit you in. If you're not academically gifted, it's, "Fuck you." If you are, it's, "The banks are coming in next week for a talk, and we think you should go."' Whatever he was going to do in life, working in a bank was not on the agenda. Not ever.

When the newly elected government announced a forthcoming series of pit closures, it had to know that there would be a backlash from the mining unions. They had already backtracked after similar strike action had been promised in 1981. When a national miners' strike was started on 12 March 1984, everyone knew this would be a desperate struggle with the entire UK mining industry potentially at stake. Three days later, 150 of 170 mines were on strike with union leader Arthur Scargill whipping up militancy on picket lines across the country. In South Wales, almost 99 per cent of the miners remained on strike despite deepening economic despair.

Like everyone else in South Wales, the future Manics were affected by the strike as it stretched across 1984. The news was filled with stories about the strike, and fighting continued both verbally and physically. Nicky Wire, as would become his wont, spoke out about the events to Q magazine years later. 'Streets divided,' he said. 'If a man went back to work his house would be covered in paint. Fair enough. I'm proud that the Welsh were the last miners to go back to work. Quite cool.' What wasn't 'cool' were the lives lost on the picket lines, the families split by the strike, the taxi driver who was murdered for taking a strike-breaker to work. The strike was many things, but cool wasn't one of them.

The turmoil and fall-out from the strike prompted Nicky Wire to write his first political piece – a poem/lyric he titled 'Aftermath '84'. Sean Moore played his trumpet on NUM marches. 'The strike was all around us and it was on TV every day for a year,' explained

James Dean Bradfield. 'When the Yorkshire miners started turn-coating I'd find myself shouting at the telly, "Scab! Scab!" We felt the working class had let themselves down just as much as the government had. So we came to feel we were part of a culture that didn't exist any more. We wanted to believe in something and couldn't find anything to believe in. We wanted to attach some newfound intelligence or some newfound theory to the place and the class we came from. But we were always confused, always contradictory, always very suspicious. Suspicious of the smell of the burning martyr.'

Richey didn't comment directly about the strike but he was scathing about the Labour party. 'Neil Kinnock is our MP,' he spat. 'His constituency house is in the same street as James' – and he's such a tosser. Party politics always seemed irrelevant to us. We got obsessed with cultural politics – it seemed more relevant, the real issues like how futile life is, how fucked up modern society is. In terms of music, we just went back and rediscovered the great bands. Everything else seemed boring and worthless. Dance music passed us by. The clubs in Newport are just about drinking and fighting – there's no "One Love" vibe there.'

Edwards now turned to the writings of Marx and Lenin to go alongside his growing interest in rock stars, as a consequence of what he was seeing on the streets of his own town. In the summer of 1984 he took his O-Levels, gaining ten straight 'A' grades. He decided that taking A-Levels and moving on to university was his way out of Blackwood, and signed up to begin at Crosskeys College that autumn. 'Blackwood is a shit hole,' he said. 'The only way to escape was to create your own reality.' Richey Edwards seemed, in the early interviews he gave, to be portrayed as being shaped by a nondescript little British town with little hope and nothing to do. He talked of the depression woven into the fabric of South Wales but there were hundreds, if not thousands, of similar places existing across the Isles in the 1980s. Coal mining had ended in South Wales but this had also ended in many other parts of the country or else it had been steelworking or shipbuilding. The manufacturing industries were disappearing, leaving the unemployed to fend for themselves. Edwards saw that using his education was his ticket out of this perceived hell.

On the miners' picket lines, the pitched battles continued. There was fighting outside parliament in June, and when the High Court ruled the strike unlawful it only fanned the flames. The strike eventually ended on 3 March 1985, just under a year after it had begun. In the Blackwood region, twelve pits were closed by the end of the dispute causing local unemployment to skyrocket to 80 per cent. A form of regeneration would eventually come in the shape of soul-destroying light-industry jobs paying minimum wages on short-term contracts that people would take because they were desperate. Seeing the crushing of the older generation made a mark on them all.

•

The speed of modern life can be troublesome and frustrating. I think the internet is squarely to blame. People expect instant answers. Emails, it seems, should be replied to before I've finished hitting the 'Send' button. How the heck did someone research a book in 1983? Hours at the library, writing letters, waiting months to get a reply, before moving on to the next one. It would drive me mad. I wrote to Crosskeys College in advance of my trip to South Wales, asking – a long shot, I know – if anyone still there remembered a student called Richard Edwards. I explained who I was, what I was doing and what had happened to Richey after he left Crosskeys, just in case they hadn't read the news. I got a letter back a few weeks later. The nice lady wrote, 'If Mr Edwards could contact the college, in writing, to give his permission then we may be able to help . . . '.

Steve Gatehouse started his A-Level studies at Crosskeys with Richey in September 1984. He'd taken his O-Levels at Blackwood Comprehensive and had been unaware of Edwards until then. Before long, they grew to be friends as members of the self-styled Ian-McCulloch-clones gang that populated Crosskeys in the mid-1980s and also included Sean Moore in their ranks. Floppy fringes and long overcoats were the order of the day.

'Richey and Sean were a year older. They were the two weirdos,' explained Nicky Wire. 'People would look at them because they had strange hair and wore odd clothes. They were into Echo & The Bunnymen before us, and Richey was into Nick Cave.' Echo & The Bunnymen were the first band that Edwards went to see with Sean Moore and James Dean Bradfield.

'Richard very much kept himself to himself,' recalls Gatehouse when discussing the first year of their A-Levels. 'He was, however, always pleasant, polite and good conversation. An early indication of how disciplined he could be, and which caused much amazement and mirth at the time, was when he was asked out by a much-lusted-after female McCulloch look-alike. He politely declined, explaining that he wouldn't have the time for dates until he had finished reading the complete works of some author or poet.'

On one level the story might just prove how shy and inexperienced Edwards was with members of the opposite sex. Nicky Wire remarked that they were 'retards' when it came to girls and that most people assumed they must be gay, although Wire started seeing Rachel (who he'd later marry) at the age of sixteen. Wire and Edwards could often be quite nasty to classmates in order to prove their intellectual superiority, so this story is also totally believable: Edwards was intent on giving himself a well-rounded cultural education to go alongside his academic one. Reading as much he could, often on the 156 bus from the bottom of his hill to college and back. Between lessons. At lunchtime. 'We put into three years everything that took the Rolling Stones twenty,' Nicky Wire later claimed. 'It's just the way we are; we are modern people.' Edwards almost couldn't read the books fast enough. George Orwell. Albert Camus. Tennessee Williams. William Burroughs. J. D. Salinger. Warhol. Debord. Kerouac. Ginsberg. Larkin and Rimbaud. But he also loved a good book on the history of rock. Greil Marcus (*Mystery Train*), Charles Shaar Murray (*Crosstown Traffic*) and Albert Goldman (*The Lives of John Lennon*) were just some of his favourites.

The Richey-Edwards-Reading-List™ could almost be viewed as compulsory for some A-Level courses. A quick web-search will locate pages devoted to listing the books he read and talked about in interviews. Indeed this author spent many hours exploring and going back to the books that Edwards had felt important. Digging into the obsessions of one's subject could be a way of invading their thought processes, and to some extent I think this approach proved fruitful. But in other ways it proved contradictory and frustrating.

To begin with, all of the future Manics immersed themselves in the Beat Generation. 'I'm Catholic and I can't commit suicide,' said Jack Kerouac. 'But I plan to drink myself to death.' Allen Ginsberg and William Burroughs would also be read and reread with a reading of Ginsberg's 'Howl' later being used on stage.

Richey, well versed in the H-blocks, immersed himself in several texts that addressed autobiographical musings on incarceration. One of these, *Borstal Boy*, was by Brendan Behan who originally went to England to be an IRA bomber and later explained that, 'I'm not a writer with a drinking problem, I'm a drinker with a writing problem.' His book covered three years in detention and the characters he met while locked up. In *Miracle of the Rose*, Jean Genet considered a prison spell he served late in the 1920s, while Kafka's *The Trial* saw Josef K one step away from being locked up.

When I became involved with some advance discussion about my research for this book I was attacked on some internet forums for writing about someone's pain and hurt. I responded by using Kafka, a Richey favourite, who said that 'I think we should read *only* the kind of books that wound and stab us.' And I didn't even think that my (this) book was going to wound or stab anyone. But some of the ones I was reading did just that. In Dennis Cooper's harrowing *Frisk* I read about the 'perfect fodder for interest in sexual death'. Edwards would later tell *Select* magazine that, 'Sex and death are closely linked. Sado-masochistic imagery, bleeding . . . I find it attractive, I find it . . . sexual.' This was taken to the extreme in Octave Mirbeau's *The Torture Garden*. These themes were also bubbling under in another of Edwards' favourites, J. G. Ballard's *Crash*, which mixes sexual perversion drawn from the act of crashing cars and the representation of humankind's ability to destroy itself by use of something that it created itself. Another Ballard classic, *The Atrocity Exhibition* (which also provided the title for a Joy Division song on *Closer*), was gobbled up by Edwards and, in an unusual framework, told of a doctor at a mental hospital having a mental breakdown. Edwards was such a fan of this book that he would use a snippet of Ballard reading from it on a Manic Street Preachers album in 1994.

Some books proved to be a waste of my time, but others – such as *The Bell Jar* – caused my cup of tea to grow cold while I turned page after page. Then I went back and read some of them again. Edwards was drawn to the pain evident in the writing of Sylvia Plath, and in particular *The Bell Jar*, which mirrored his own imminent step into the adult world. Richey had devoured Bret Easton Ellis' *Less Than Zero* on its UK publication in 1986, possibly inspired by the widely publicised quote from *USA Today* that called it '*The Catcher in the Rye* for the MTV generation'. Salinger's withdrawal from public life was a source of constant fascination for Edwards; writers' real lives were often just as important to him as the books he enjoyed – if not more so. He would have known this, too: just a brief flick through the names reveals things that can be pulled out and held next to Edwards' legacy. I think that it serves to hold up some of these now, just at the point in the story when Richey was accelerating his reading, and to let them hang in the background as his own story unfolds. Was Edwards influenced so much by these books and authors that they changed the direction of his life? Or, was he inherently like these characters and so therefore drawn to them for that reason?

Malcolm Lowry was a self-destructive favourite who had been a heavy drinker and who'd slashed his wrists and later committed suicide with the use of sleeping tablets. James Baldwin had turned his back on religion during his teens and suffered in adulthood because he was black and gay in 1950s' America. His book *Another Country* fused several elements that Edwards was interested in. Set in Greenwich Village during the 1950s, it is based on the lives of musicians and writers. The jazz drummer at the centre of the story becomes involved in an abusive relationship that leaves his girl in a mental hospital and him considering suicide. In a harrowing passage, he eventually walks to the centre of a cold and windy George Washington Bridge before throwing himself off.

In later life, Edwards was drawn to Japanese writers but as a teen he read his share of Russian texts. Dostoevsky's *Notes from Underground* was one of Edwards' preferred books; its unnamed narrator seeks pain. This is now regarded as being one of the founding works of existentialism, inspiring the form of other Edwards staples such as Joseph Heller's *Catch-22* and Ralph Ellison's *Invisible Man*. Another link in Edwards' tastes was found with the discovery of Ellison being inspired to become a writer after reading Eliot's 'The Waste Land'. Ellison's *Invisible Man* concerned a young African-American man's search for a place in a society that ignored him.

What do all of these books tell us? Edwards was intelligent, he was interested in mental health, suicide, disappearing, existentialism, outsiders, rebels and revolutionaries. In the end, it might be that – even after close research – we confirm only what we already knew: any life is merely the sum of many tiny interactions that build up a picture. So and so was born here, he went there, he read this book, he watched this film, then he was gone.

•

As College progressed, Gatehouse and Edwards started venturing out to gigs further afield as their music tastes expanded. Alongside Echo & The Bunnymen and Joy Division, Edwards was interested in The Smiths, That Petrol Emotion, The Housemartins and the C86 crew. 'Richey often quoted The Wolfhounds,' recalls Steve Gatehouse. 'We were also into The Weather Prophets, Primal Scream and The Wedding Present – we bought *George Best* together from Derrick's in Swansea and also saw and met them at The Mars Bar in Cardiff. He also made me a compilation of McCarthy and Wire, who he loved. He regularly bought indie fanzines and discovered The Darling Buds before me. The first of the many times I saw them was with Richey. We also went to see The Smiths together at the Newport Centre, when Morrissey was dragged off stage and the gig was cut short.' As Edwards grew more obsessed with music – he was musically inept, so could see no way into it for himself yet – he would go on ever more difficult trips to see bands, once driving all the way to Nottingham on his own to see The Jesus and Mary Chain. He was involved in some social circles, however. One of his group of friends at the Red Lion started dating a girl by the name of Rebecca Williams. She and her group of friends were soon aware of this 'beautiful but under-confident bloke', as she puts it. He seemed quite comfortable talking in female company and seemed completely unaware of how attractive the girls found him. He was also quite open about his vanity. 'He would amuse us by constantly asking our opinion about his appearance and his chances with various girls,' says Williams. 'I remember him wearing flowery neck scarves in an attempt to cover spots on his neck and incessantly asking me if they were visible.'

•

In the autumn of 1985, Richey was approaching his eighteeth birthday as he started his second and final year of A-Levels and was joined at Crosskeys by James Dean Bradfield and Nicky Wire, who had matched Edwards' haul of ten O-Levels. These were intelligent lads, well read outside of their syllabuses and striving, no *aching*, to get away from the town of their birth. The world was waiting for them and they were going to show everybody just who they were and what they could do.

James had been teaching himself to play the guitar and had mastered the Stones' album *Exile on Main Street*, while Sean Moore was taking an A-Level in music and was playing the trumpet in the South Wales Jazz Orchestra. 'We just wasted so many days playing [*Exile on Main Street*],' said Edwards. 'On songs like "I Just Wanna See His Face", we didn't really understand what Mick Jagger was saying but they were the biggest rock band in the world, you know! The thing was, on this album they sounded so lonely. I know our situation was completely different but it just seemed to completely represent what we were feeling. The songs are just so sad and lonely. They had everything at their disposal and they just didn't know what they wanted to do with it. We had nothing at our disposal and we didn't know what to do with it either! It's a complete contradiction but it was like, we're rotting away in a bedroom and so were they. They could have any groupie, any drug, any drink and it didn't matter and that's when we started getting really disillusioned. We were trying to work out what would make us happy and I think everybody has felt that at some point in time.'

When they did get out of their bedrooms they would sometimes meet up at the man-made Pen-Y-Fan pond, which was filled with slimy green fish and claimed a couple of swimmers' lives. Still, it was a communal escape for the youth of the area – the venue for school fights, outdoor parties and drinking. Many times it was the scene of a loss of virginity on the nearby slagheaps, the constant dirty reminders of the recent sour history. 'They try to put grass over the slag heaps,' explained Richey, 'and every time it rains they turn into muddy slides – the landscape is swallowed by a huge slap of blackness.' Today, they've been levelled; a neat removal of two hundred years of history.

'James and Nick quickly became part of our little group of indie kids, goths, punks,' recalls Steve Gatehouse. 'Nick was chatty and funny and usually wearing his "Cheshire cat grin", even when he was suffering some typical teenage crisis. James was a drama student, which seemed unusual as he was one of the most reserved individuals I'd ever encountered. However, he had a quiet self-assurance, always looked cool-as-fuck and, when he did speak, usually came out with a great one-liner.'

'For the first eighteen years of our lives we were living in an environment where there's nothing to do,' said Edwards. 'We'd just go round each others' houses, talk, read and play and that's it, like twenty-four hours the same every fuckin' day.'

The gang started experimenting with ways of expressing themselves. Nicky Wire had been doing a little bit of writing since the age of twelve; his best piece was still the strike-inspired 'Aftermath `84' and James Dean Bradfield thought it was brilliant. He and Wire started doing some writing together. Meanwhile Richey Edwards inscribed a mammoth 24-page poem called 'Another Dead Eleven O'Clock'. Later, he, Wire and Sean Moore attempted a play called *Tearproof*. 'Sean wrote a lot of the play, and James was doing drama at the time,' recalls Patrick Jones. 'We entered it into a play-writing competition but we didn't win. It was about a gay boy who was very delicate and quiet and ended up being killed by a group of people who were all in a band together, actually. It was crap. At the end, the last image of him is covered with moths on stage. I might have to borrow that again.'

In 1986 they also saw a chance to have a go at the music business. Steve Gatehouse had formed a band called Funeral In Berlin with friends Nick Curtis and Craig Bruzas. A show at the Crosskeys Workingman's Institute literally changed lives. It seemed like the entire college turned up that night, as over two hundred were in the crowd – including Edwards, Bradfield, Moore and Wire. Steve Gatehouse admits that it wasn't such a success because the band had a large local following, but more because the 'alternative types' had little else to do in the area. The band played a half-hour of Mary Chain-esque noise before smashing up their equipment. 'We caused the kind of rumpus that the Mary Chain themselves were causing in London,' says Gatehouse. 'The members of the workingman's club's committee were not happy! You'd have to come from such a place as the South Wales valleys at the time of the miners' strike to appreciate the effect such an event could have on our teenage minds. Only a few years previously, the Sex Pistols had been denounced as Satanists as they attempted to play in Caerphilly.' The gig was the talk of the college on Monday morning. Nicky Wire told Gatehouse that the gig had been an epiphany for him and that he, Moore and Bradfield had immediately decided to start a band of their own. They borrowed some gear from Colin Mills, a mutual friend, and drafted in local punk Miles 'Flicker' Woodward, who'd been in Nicky and James' year at school. Woodward was all black-leather-studded jacket and spiky hair, a real old-school kind of punk. The earliest rehearsals took place at the Bradfield house with Woodward on bass, Wire on guitar, Bradfield singing and playing lead guitar, and Moore standing up to play two drums just like Bobby Gillespie in The Jesus And Mary Chain. 'Nick was writing lyrics, and he'd given them to James who could already play guitar quite well,' says Woodward. 'We put them to music and started to tape them. I took a tape home, listened to it and thought, that's quite good. A bit like Billy Bragg [but it was] just basic three-chord punk played on crap guitars with crap amps.' Richey Edwards was watching from the sidelines, unsure how he could contribute.

This early Manics line-up recorded some demos during the early part of 1986 (nth generation copies of which are still in circulation), and, without Richey Edwards, on 5 February they played their first ever gig at the Railway Inn, Crumlin, as support to Gatehouse's band.[5] Richey Edwards wasn't around to witness the Manics' first show, and he rarely saw them until around 1988, but if he had been there he'd have seen a raw, antagonistic display. The show took place in the basement with the sound system rendering James Dean Bradfield's vocals almost obsolete, but he did exhibit a strong stage presence. 'He had a real "Fuck you" attitude,' recalls Stephen Gatehouse. 'They covered "Teenage Kicks" and the night ended when somebody threw a pint glass at the wall and, instead of smashing, it just embedded itself in the wall. A pint-glass-at-the-wall game ensued. No joking, the place was soon an inch deep in beer and broken glass. Anybody sensible legged it, leaving the promoter to face the wrath of the landlord. Again, like the Crosskeys Institute gig, two shit bands had acquired the notoriety of The Jesus And Mary Chain in the valleys. You had to be there!'

•

A-Level results day, August 1986. A local TV crew are outside Crosskeys College filming a few vox-pops for the early evening news. Students are hugging each other and dreaming of their now-confirmed university places. Or otherwise. The camera focuses in on a serious-looking chap.

'What did you get, Mr Edwards?'

'Three As.'

'And what were you expecting?'

Mr Edwards looks right into the camera and, completely deadpan, says, 'Three As.'

For Edwards, the perfectionist, this still wasn't good enough. He wanted – no, needed – to be the best and a simple grade wasn't enough to confirm this, even to himself. Despite the outward arrogance, Edwards was actually full of self-doubt. 'When I got my A-Levels, I got straight As, but I thought they weren't as good as other people's straight As,' said Edwards. 'They would look at me as if their As were better. We didn't get percentage marks, so three As weren't enough. I wanted to know I'd got, like, ninety-five per cent. Three As is meaningless unless you're arrogant enough to think you're as good as them. Which I'm not. I need to see it written down to know.' He repeated a similar tale to Villa 65 Dutch Radio: 'I've always felt the need to prove myself against other people. I mean, I'm quite a weak person physically, and I think in school, I wouldn't say I was bullied but you do feel scared sometimes, or frightened, and the only thing I thought I had that was different from other people was the fact that I was actually quite intelligent. I like reading and passing exams or whatever. But even things like A-Levels – say somebody else got straight As – I would not feel as good as them, because I didn't know what percentages we had. I wanted to know that I had ninety-eight per cent and they had ninety-five per cent. It wasn't enough. I felt next to somebody with the same qualifications as me, I would not feel as good. You don't even know what it means. So you're constantly trying to get better and improve all the time.'

With thirteen exams now taken, all passed with A grades, he was living up to his self-imposed high standards. That summer Edwards passed his driving test, was allowed to use his parents' car, and – by all accounts – became more sociable. He drove Wire, Bradfield and Moore to an Echo & The Bunnymen gig in Gloucester, where Moore got drunk, abused Ian McCulloch after the show ('Give me your fucking autograph, you cunt!'), and then threw up in the car all over the front passengers on the way home. Richey's sister Rachel was also into travelling to gigs. She'd sometimes report back about bands she'd seen in Cardiff. Richey was happy to play the part of non-drinking driver. It gave him a role and purpose within the social group, easing any self-doubts or crisis of confidence. Occasionally they'd go by train, sleeping in the station before getting an early train home, or they'd get the last bus home from Newport.

It wasn't all gigs and parties, however. More often than not, they'd be at home reading or watching TV. In 1986, there was a mini ten-years-on-from-punk revival and retrospective. Channel 4 broadcast a documentary on punk, presented by the late Tony Wilson, using footage from his decade-old TV show *So It Goes*, which he'd filmed for Granada with Clive James. This was the first time that Edwards, and the others, had actually seen punk footage.

'That was the first time we'd seen The Clash because we'd never really been interested in them at all,' recalled Richey. 'When we saw them on this programme, it just started with this terrible noise and they were crap! It was just perfect! We got their first album and played it over and over again. At first we couldn't really understand it, but as time went on it meant more and more to us. Even though they were huge in America and all that stuff, they never lost their authentic English roots.'

The snarl of Joe Strummer and the stencilled slogans excited them, the Sex Pistols blew them away and they immediately had to search out VHS copies of the film *DOA*, which became instant and much-repeated viewing.[6] '[*DOA*] was the biggest culture shock we'd ever had!' said Edwards. 'When we started reading about them and learnt more about their history, they got better every day. They're probably the most untouchable band of all time. To put on a Pistols record after coming back from the pub really shook me out of my apathy. After deadening myself with alcohol all night, I'd put that on and it just made me feel ashamed.'

This belated discovery of punk set the cogs whirring in Richey Edwards' mind. Not only did he relate to the bands musically and politically, he realised that they weren't great musicians. Hell, just take a look at Sid Vicious for a start. Maybe there would be an opening for him after all. But first, he was off to university to get his degree. Preferably a First Class honours degree; preferably top of his class.

**H**e had prepared carefully for today. He wanted to make sure that any loose ends were tied up in advance of his departure. He'd recently visited his parents for the last time, but of course he hadn't spoken a word of his plans to them. His father had complained about his now non-stop smoking habit. He'd also intended to have a new tattoo before he carried out his plans, but a lack of time meant he had to abandon that part of the operation. He had, however, handed over the last of his writings at the last moment. While he'd been making his final preparations, no one would have known what he was planning because he seemed happier than he had been for quite a while.

Today is 25 November 1970 and here at the Eastern Army Group Headquarters on Ichigaya Hill, Tokyo, Japan – in room 201, to be exact – General Mashita is tied to a chair. Standing by is Student Captain Masakatsu Morita. Young Koga is also here, Old Koga, too. The shouting and screaming from outside the door has settled down now. Leader Yukio Mishima strips off his clothes, until he is wearing only a loincloth. Then he kneels down.

Today Mishima had risen early. He shaved carefully then applied some make-up to his cheeks and lips, made sure his series of sealed letters to family, friends and publishers were in order, and left a note on his desk: 'Human life is limited, but I want to live for ever'. Then he contacted a journalist and TV reporter, telling them where to go because something was going to happen.

When he had dressed in the uniform of Tate no Kai, complete

with sword, he was collected in a car by three of his student cadets. He told them to read notes that he had prepared, explaining that they were not to kill themselves. He had also put some money in the envelopes towards the legal defence that they would later be obliged to provide. Mishima took along a brown attaché case containing four books: three were his own – *Spring Snow*, *Runaway Horses*, and *In Defence of Culture* – plus a copy of *A Philosophy of Modern Revolution*. He planned to leave these books at the scene, the scene of his suicide.

Yukio Mishima, which means 'mysterious devil bewitched with death' (his real name, Kimitake Hiraoka, was changed as his father disapproved of his writing), was small of stature but he'd given himself a rigorous training regime, maintaining that physical and mental strength were of equal importance. He also deeply believed that he should follow the ancient Japanese rituals and traditions. He had prepared meticulously for the day. When the car arrived at the army base gates, the guards knew he had a meeting pre-arranged and recognised his face. They were waved through and parked near to the parade ground before entering the HQ building. After play-acting through some preliminaries, they tied General Mashita to his chair with some rope and blocked up the doors to his high-ceilinged office, threatening to kill him if the guards attempted to force their way in. Mishima had wanted to entice a military coup but his speech from the general's balcony drew nothing but jeers from the soldiers below. He returned to the office and prepared for the end.

Once on his knees, Mishima drew his knife with his right hand and plunged it four inches into his stomach then pulled it across from left to right. The ritual of what had to happen next had been well prepared. Morita had been given the task of removing Mishima's head, but there was a particular form to this act, too. He was required to carry out a single, accurate chop. He wasn't to send the head bouncing across the room but to cut through the neck from behind – but not to completely sever it, a flap must be left intact so that the head would drop forward onto the chest.

With Mishima bleeding profusely and in a lot of pain, Morita stepped slowly forward, adjusting his grip on the sword nervously. Mishima had keeled face-forward onto the floor from his kneeling position. Morita swung, but missed badly and sliced Mishima across his back. He swung again and missed completely. Then, as panic began to set in, he swung again and chopped into the neck at the wrong angle. He then struggled to dislodge the sword and finish the job. Old Koga stepped in, removed the sword and removed Mishima's head in a single swipe, an arc of blood spraying across the room and decorating the air-conditioning unit on the far wall.

In his book *Temple of the Golden Pavilion*, Mishima used the character of Mizoguchi to discuss suicide in reference to the nature of beauty, needing to answer the question, 'What is beauty for?' Mishima did not hide his real self behind his writings but poured his innermost soul into them as he self-analysed his own demons, something he described as 'dissecting himself alive'. 'He's very much in Richey's mode in terms of mutilation and depression,' said Nicky Wire. 'I respect Mishima,' explained Edwards. 'He had sensitivity in his work and it fitted in with his life. His work is absolutely beautiful! Full of kindness and beautiful music. And he built up his body – he had a really strong physique. He was tremendously sensitive.'

# IV

## VAGUE LITTLE CUTS
*1986 to August 1989*

It's only about thirty miles west from Blackwood to Swansea, but as far as Richey Edwards was concerned it might as well have been on the Moon. Dylan Thomas said that 'Swansea is the graveyard of ambition', and by the end of his course Edwards would have the academic life crushed out of him. At eighteen years old, he didn't see university from the same perspective as most of his Fresher contemporaries in September 1986. After enrolling on a Political History degree course, with vague thoughts about becoming a lecturer, he was billeted in the Mary Williams Hall on the Swansea campus of the University of Wales. The hall was a ten-storey block with Edwards being given a room on the fourth floor. His single room was basic but comfortable. A bed, wardrobe, desk and wash-basin were provided. Bathroom facilities were shared per floor (about twenty people). Edwards' floor was all-male, although the block was mixed. He shared a kitchen per floor, with only breakfast being provided in the cafeteria.

Richey's views of his fellow students couldn't have been more stark. 'I used to get woken up constantly,' he ranted, 'by pissed-up students coming home thinking it would be really funny to rampage up and down the corridors knocking on everybody's door and deciding to have a party in the kitchen at one in the morning. Pathetic!' Apart from dressing up as a sperm for a rag-week event, Edwards was far from your average first-year student. During the week he'd wander around in his slippers after lectures before making sure he was in bed after *Minder*, ready for a new day of learning. It was his willingness to learn that really set him apart. 'I despised those people who sat in the bar going, "Ooh, I was really rebellious today, I didn't go to one lesson!",' he said. 'I thought university would be full of people who wanted to sit around and talk about books and it wasn't like that at all. It was full of people who wanted to sit around and do as little as possible other than have as much fun as they could. But I never equated university with fun. I thought it was about reading and learning, but for most people it was about getting laid.' This was another non-typical student trait that set him apart as he continued to outwardly show little interest in girls, apart from one girl in his second year. In that respect, he left university just as he'd arrived – still a virgin.

'To hole myself up in a tower block with hundreds of people I had nothing in common with was a really bad experience,' he said. 'I think if I'd been able to have a flat of my own, my memory would've been very different because I've never been good with very many different people. I've always surrounded myself with just a very few people.'

It was during his early days at university that Richey started drinking as a way to blot out the world around him. 'I started drinking in my first term at university,' he explained. 'It was something that I'd never allowed myself to do, but it was just a question of getting myself to sleep. It was so noisy, and I needed to get to sleep at a certain time and wake at a certain time, and drinking gave me that opportunity.' As well as drowning out the noise of drunken students, it allowed him to stop thinking about things too deeply and to get uninterrupted sleep – what he called a 'blank' sleep. Again, this showed his unique take on life: he would drink, but – unlike the rest of the student body – he preferred to do it alone in his room. He made few new friends at Swansea, preferring to keep in touch with friends at home and other Blackwood natives now at Swansea. He'd write fairly regularly to Nicky Wire and James Dean Bradfield, who were in their final year of A-Levels, and to Steve Gatehouse, who was working in Blackwood. 'When I finished my week's work on a Thursday, I'd go to Raffles in Port Talbot with him to an indie club to watch bands such as The Primitives, The Soup Dragons and The Bodines,' recalls Gatehouse. 'Then I'd spend the weekend with him in Swansea, shopping for the latest indie releases and watching bands in the Union bar.'

Another of Edwards' favourite books was William Burroughs' *Junky* (titled *Junkie*, in some editions). It seemed to sum up his university experience perfectly. Old Bull Lee, as Kerouac famously referred to him, had met Allen Ginsberg at Christmas 1944 and when the two began corresponding, Burroughs' letters included chapters of what would become *Junky*. In these, he wrote of his disgust at the American education system: 'I majored in English literature for lack of interest in any other subject. I hated the University and I hated the town it was in. Everything about the place was dead. The university was a fake English set-up taken over by the graduates of fake English public schools. I was lonely. I knew no one, and strangers were regarded with distaste by the closed corporation of desirables.' Burroughs became a major influence on Edwards and was all over the Manics' debut album. He might also have appealed to Edwards because of lines such as, 'I'd once got on a Van Gogh kick and cut off a finger joint to impress someone who was interested in me at the time.'

Inscribed on the inside back cover of my battered, second-hand copy of *Junky* is a fading shopping list scribbled in pencil. The list reads:

2 Orange juice
Lemsip
Soluble aspirin
2 oranges

Was the book responsible for this list? Did the contents provoke an illness or was it a severe hangover? Was it a subtle joke by the book's previous owner?

•

Back home in Blackwood, the fledgling Manic Street Preachers were working up a nice little collection of original songs and experimenting with playing live. Through the winter of 1986–87, they penned around a dozen songs such as 'Whiskey Psychosis', 'England is a Bitch', 'Just Can't Be Happy', 'Anti-Love', 'Eating Myself From Inside', 'Love in a Make-up Bag'. One could be forgiven for thinking that these titles had more than just a tinge of Edwards about them, but they were all written without any of his input. Another song would survive to be recorded later, 'R P McMurphy', while two others – 'Go Buzz Baby Go' and 'Behave Yourself Baby' – would later be picked over to add sections to 'Motorcycle Emptiness'.

While they hadn't yet got themselves into position to headline an actual show, they did try a bit of live performing by busking on the streets of Cardiff. An attempt to play as a full band was abandoned when Sean Moore gave up trying to get his drums across the city. Further attempts saw just James Dean Bradfield (often topless) and Nicky Wire belting out Clash and Sex Pistols covers. What the Saturday afternoon shoppers were thinking is unrecorded but it was clear that musical aspirations had overtaken any literary ones.

During his first year, Richey had often travelled home to Blackwood for the weekend and now – as he returned for the summer holidays – he would see a marked improvement in his friends' band. He spent his time earning some summer spending money by mowing lawns for the council. Rebecca Williams and her friend Sally Killian remembered seeing Richey out and about in Blackwood that summer. 'Richard took summer work strimming hedges and he did reduce us to giggles when he told us how he'd strimmed through dog shit and it had splattered all over him,' recalls Williams. 'The men had sent him home early, because he stank so badly.'

Nicky Wire had just taken his A-Levels and spent the summer practising with the band. Richey, ever keen to help out, was driving them and their equipment around but had no direct input yet.

Favourite drinking spots during the summer of 1987 included the Red Lion at the end of Blackwood High Street, with its ultra-loud jukebox seemingly stuck on an endless loop of The Alarm's 'Spirit of '76', and further afield it was the Cuckoo down the road in

Risca. Richey hadn't yet started wearing much make-up but Nicky Wire was more proactive in the semi-cross-dressing stakes. 'We were lucky,' said Wire. 'I don't know why, but we were more on the fringe, regarded more as eccentrics than anything else. We weren't victimised. We used to go into the Red Lion in Blackwood in the full regalia, clothes and make-up, and we were never beaten up, but there were always comments, "Poofter" or "Queer", but that was a teenage thing.' The students and underage drinkers would down pints of cider-and-black, eat Golden Wonder crisps and talk about books, music and who was going out with whom. The local rugby and football types were more likely to fall into the street, fighting, at the end of the night. The closest any of the Manics crowd came to trouble was when Nicky Wire was arrested for drunkenly trying to steal an old Ford Escort on the way home from a nightclub. He was given a conditional discharge.

For daytime meetings the crowd would gather at one of the cafes in town, sometimes The Square, but more often at Dorothy's on the High Street. They'd sit around reading Kerouac or rummaging through Woolworth's carrier bags to discuss the latest vinyl purchases over cups of tea and more packets of crisps. If Wire, Bradfield, Moore and Woodward were missing from one of these lunchtimes they were most likely sharing a bag of chips before an afternoon of practising in the Bradfield sitting room. James was working in bars at night, keeping himself fit by running miles around the town and practising, practising, practising on his guitar. By now they had decided on the name Manic Street Preachers, having finally voted against being named Betty Blue. Richey said it was a great name, and so much more original. This confirms that later stories about Richey coming up with the name for the band are untrue.

The sound of the band at the time was described as a mixture of Pop Will Eat Itself and Primal Scream, and they asked local girl Jenny Watkins-Isnardi to sing with them. James Dean Bradfield had always wanted to be the band's guitarist rather than guitarist *and* lead singer, but as no one else could fulfil the role it became his by default. The band were all big fans of Blondie and the idea of an all-male band fronted by a girl was gaining popularity in the late 1980s with The Primitives, The Darling Buds and Transvision Vamp all using the formula. Watkins-Isnardi's first audition came when she was asked to sing to Wire down the line from a call box. The second audition was in Wire's bedroom, where she sang the Strawberry Switchblade song 'Since Yesterday'. She was eventually allowed to join the band for practice, which seemed to be a lot of hoops to jump through to rehearse with a band that had yet to really get out of the living room.

Another early show was played, again with Funeral In Berlin, at the Little Theatre in Blackwood. Miles Woodward circulated photocopied flyers, shaved his head and tried to pierce his own ear before the show but succeeded only in making a right mess of his ear lobe. Most of the crowd consisted of goths who only wanted to see Funeral In Berlin play, and by the end of their set the place all but emptied. The Manics took to the stage and belted out 'God Save the Queen' before getting cans chucked at them and a chair smashed into the house piano. All watched from the wings by Richey Edwards. The band was banned. Miles Woodward had had enough and wanted out. Nicky Wire tried to make him change his mind. They turned back to busking in Cardiff instead, this time with Sean Moore playing a tambourine. They made two pence in three hours on St Mary's Street.

'Everybody thought we were crap,' recalled Miles Woodward. 'There was a lot of abuse at the gigs. We used to like a lot of the same groups, but the others were also into indie while I liked a lot of heavy metal and American punk. They were going more pop; I just wanted to go more hardcore.' Woodward would leave the band soon afterwards. 'I do feel very proud to have been a part of it. Mates do have a bit of a joke with me when a song comes on the jukebox, saying that it could have been you, but I'm not that bothered. They were great times, I suppose. The best times I've ever had. That feeling you get from being in a great band, it really did feel like us against the world.'

Nicky Wire was overly ambitious from the start. After seeing The Alarm play in Cardiff he promised that the Manics would be

'a million times better than that!' He was convinced that it wasn't
a case of *if* they made it big but *when*, and when they did, he told
Watkins-Isnardi, he was going to kill himself and go out, in the words
of The Alarm, in a blaze of glory. By now, he'd written the new
song 'Motorcycle Emptiness'. When he got his A-Level results he
realised that he could have got himself a better place than the
course at Portsmouth Poly afforded him by his predicted three D
grades.

In her book, *In the Beginning*, Jenny Watkins-Isnardi recalls
meeting Richey while he was home for the summer of 1987. She
writes of one evening when he held court in the pub talking
about the withdrawal of J. D. Salinger and the death of Marc Bolan
and other rock stars. He was heavily into the myths and legends
of literary and rock 'n' roll deaths, suicides and disappearances. He
also bemoaned his lack of funds to see bands and the fact that
he thought the other students were 'scum'. By the end of the
summer, Watkins-Isnardi drifted away from the band, Wire headed
to Portsmouth and Edwards went back to Swansea. As he usually
did, Richey had one last stop to make before leaving Blackwood
– the Pot Noodle factory on the edge of town. He'd call in and buy
a sack full of rejects to last him as his staple diet for the next term.
This time he was out of halls and was in a shared house at Uplands
in Swansea, a short walk from Singleton Park and the university
campus.

The letters that Edwards continued to send to Steve Gatehouse
provide an insight into his second-year life. He'd been getting
questions from the careers office about what he thought his future
direction might be. He previously considered going into teaching
but now his thoughts were focused on the music industry. He
hadn't quite worked out how he could achieve that aim, but he did
plunge sixty pounds of his dwindling grant funds into a second-
hand guitar. He told Gatehouse that he had to buy it despite having
no idea how to play it because he didn't want a life of 'What if?'.
The money spent on the guitar meant his other social outgoings
were seriously cut back. He decided that seven pounds was too
much to pay to go and see The Pogues and a planned trip to see The

Godfathers was also cancelled. While he was spending more time in his room he was excited about a radio documentary he heard about Joy Division, calling Ian Curtis' suicide 'the greatest loss in musical history'.

He also took some delight in reporting the latest brawls between 'townies' and students, often centred on Cinderella's nightclub. 'Last Saturday at Cinders (I was there!) there was a riot between our rugby team and townies,' he wrote. 'It ended up with a townie in intensive care – MEATHEAD AND BOOTHY (in hall with me last year) kicked his nose into his brain. Bastards. So since then they've been [sic] some serious repercussions. The next Saturday there was no one there and so the townies simply started beating students in the street. I don't blame them though.'

Mid-way through the autumn term of his second year, Richey was joined in Swansea by Nicky Wire. Wire's stint at Portsmouth Poly had lasted just a matter of weeks and he described the experience as 'a Club 18–30 holiday'. His mother, Irene, put in some calls to Swansea, where Patrick Jones had studied previously, and secured him a transfer to a politics course. Wire, like Edwards, abhorred much of student life, yet – unlike his friend – he didn't throw himself into his studies, but took the opposite approach. Wire rarely attended classes, preferring to spend his time at the golf course or the pub slot-machine, and running up quite a debt while doing so. Wire hadn't exactly inherited his parents' work ethic; he would end the course with a 2:2, and only then after Richey Edwards completed some of his coursework for him. During one Christmas break he took on a job as a postman but lasted for just three days, and his father even had to help him finish his round. Wire was always proud to talk about being working-class, he just didn't like the 'working' part of it.

It was only now that Edwards and Wire really became close friends, much closer than they had been before. 'It's from this time on that, to me, Richard became "Richey",' says Steve Gatehouse. 'He formed a close relationship with Nick and was disillusioned with his fellow students. He confined himself to a close circle of friends and rarely socialised.'

With this further withdrawal, it therefore came as a surprise when Richey wrote to his friend of a girl that he'd become besotted with. 'It's true what you said about Capricorns being later starters in life,' he wrote, before explaining that he'd spied this girl at the student doctor's surgery (although he didn't expand regarding why he was there). He described her as 'mega' and admitted that he'd compromised his principles to attend the student ball in the hope of seeing her there (he'd skipped the event in his first year). He did see her, but she was with a boy, so Edwards consoled himself by downing a bottle of vodka. He ended the night on his knees, puking, and as she left with the boy, Edwards could only watch while vomit dribbled down his chin. 'I really would die for this shining beacon in a sea of mediocrity,' Edwards wrote to Gatehouse. Later the same week Edwards came across the girl in a nightclub; she was without the boyfriend and Richey was without the bottle of vodka. He says he managed to make an impression but she left him on Mumbles pier at two a.m. and he never met her again. Rebecca Williams remembers the events well. 'He would go to Cinderella's on the pier on a Tuesday night,' she says. 'Like most of us, he'd get sloshed. When sozzled he became even more adorable. He would make a beeline for Sally [Killian] and me in the hope that we could help him pull. He developed a major crush on a girl in my halls at one point. Her name was Ceri. She was a veritable Patsy Kensit lookalike, petite, pretty, alternative, but not in a heavy duty way, just enough to appear cool. She was very sweet, basically. Unbelievably, she wasn't interested in him and turned him down. I seem to remember him giving her flowers. The worst part was that she ended up with a boyfriend who looked like Chesney Hawkes.'

While Richey's drinking at Swansea had increased, his eating had dropped away – as had his weight. By the summer of 1988 he was being described as skeletally thin, but despite his frail physique he was starting to describe himself as the Manic Street Preachers' roadie. This essentially meant that he'd occasionally helped Nicky Wire carry his equipment around Swansea. He'd been spotted back at the Crosskeys College canteen working on a flyer for the Manics. His meal that day consisted of a cup of hot water with some lemon juice squeezed in. One of his favourite meals was what he called 'white noise' – a baked potato with rice and sweet corn. Of course, he also ate his fair share of Pot Noodles.

•

By the time of their first ever demo sessions in June 1988, the band were a three-piece. Local Blackwood musician Glen Powell had a small set-up called Sound Bank Studios. Powell had once played with Jimi Hendrix in New York. The band booked in to record 'Suicide Alley', a song about nights out at the Newbridge Rugby Club disco, which inevitably ended in violence between the metal fans, rugby players and alternative types. 'When I first met them they were very Clash-based,' recalled Powell. 'I helped them get that stereo guitar sound.' Only Sean Moore and James Dean Bradfield played on the first songs, with Bradfield adding all the different guitar parts. Over a few weeks they demoed a number of songs that would later surface on their debut album. 'They were a good bunch of boys really,' adds Powell. 'Even though they used to look really aggressive. If they owed me £20 for a session, the next time they came in they'd put it down on the table before anything else. You could trust them.'

An issue of *Impact* magazine[7] from the autumn of 1988 gives us the first glimpses of the band. In a piece penned by Patrick Jones and titled 'On The Edge', he bemoans the lack of any music venues in Blackwood while meeting several local bands, including On The Edge, Stoned Lazy and the Manics. The band are referred to as a three-piece and mention is made of them busking on the Blackwood High Street, although an accompanying photograph shows Richey with the other three seated at a cafe table in the same outfits that would grace the cover of their first single: tight white jeans and leather jackets. The letters page is an entertaining read, with one letter from Nicky Wile [sic] of Swansea. The letter is really just a teenage rant/advert for the Blue Revolution group of writers and their forthcoming play *Teaproof*. Elsewhere, 'Seany Dee' and 'Jamie Kat' (Moore and Bradfield, to me and you) wrote in about the Blue Generation, mentioning that Ritchie Vee (Edwards) and Stevie-boy Gee (Gatehouse) are among their number. It's hard not to smile at their trying-too-hard plug for their forthcoming gig at Newport: 'Steal car, hitch a cloud and motor on down to the beat of the street.' The final letter worth mentioning came from David Geary of Blackwood. Writing about Nicky Wire, he says, 'Granted he is a talented guy and his band is good but he is completely full of shit . . . knowing what he's like it's really annoying to see him getting coverage in *Impact*.' The future Manics were up against it in many ways. Luckily they had supportive families, which helped to send their children to university, but musically the bands of choice for most of their own age group were hard metal and pomp rock. With a community that was more interested in Bon Jovi and Black Sabbath, the Manics' punk sensibilities were anathema. These music fans were the same 'townies' who would see Richey and Nicky walk into a pub and wonder what planet they'd just dropped off.

For Richey's final year and Nicky Wire's second year, they shared a house on King Edward Road in Swansea. 'He was the most dedicated student,' Wire told the *NME*. 'I remember sitting in his room eating a Fray Bentos pie and chips he'd cooked me, reading *NME*. Another time we almost poisoned ourselves. We were in this little room with only half a window open and we were spray-painting these white T-shirts for the band, and realised we felt really ill from the fumes.'

James Dean Bradfield kept in close touch with Edwards and Wire in Swansea and Edwards would often visit him back in Blackwood. 'When I'd go and visit Richey and Nick down in Swansea University, Richey would be there at the weekend with all the Sunday papers, kneeling on the floor, circling things and cutting them out,' said Bradfield. 'He was a classic careening-around-his-subject kind of student. He was really earnest at the end of the day; he'd say, "My Mum and Dad worked hard to get me here and I'm not going to piss it up in the Uni Bar."' Bradfield was still working in bars in the evenings and practising during the day. He'd now learned Guns N' Roses' *Appetite for Destruction* from start to finish. Apart from the politics of Big Flame, McCarthy and Gang of Four, Edwards hated most current bands but fell in love with the strutting of Axl Rose and Slash. 'Bands were written about in the music press as if they would change your life,' he said. 'You'd go and see them, and there would be twenty people there, and the bands would be fucking shit. Every song, total and utter rubbish. We just found it sad, forlorn. Then we would go home and look at our old videos of The Who and The Clash, and that meant so much more to us.'

'At the time we'd only really been playing old records and it just seemed there was nothing much going on. There were millions of little indie bands that had nothing to say and people would say "Rock music is dead", but whenever we went out, everybody was wearing metal T-shirts. In the provinces, rock music never dies at all. Rave and acid culture is very much a city-based, middle class kinda culture. Of course there's a lot of working class youths into raving and fashion but at the same time there's at least half as many people from the same generation into rock bands. Basically, *Appetite for Destruction* was the first time we realised that rock wasn't dead. We had the Stones, The Who and The Clash and we'd basically given up on hearing a new rock record that we'd really like. When we heard this it was just so instant and exciting. All these little indie bands just used to stand there and look so crap. We wanted to look as exciting and pretty as them! People accuse rock bands of all kinds of different things but take a record like "Welcome to the Jungle" and it said more about the way we felt inside than a thousand so called intellectual, articulate bands.'

During the Christmas break, Richey and James set off for a night out in Newport to celebrate Richey's twenty-first birthday. Early in the evening they stopped by a McDonald's for some food. Reports differ as to what actually happened next and how it was precipitated but a group of local lads numbering between ten and fifteen either burst in and attacked them 'for what they were wearing', although it was usually Nicky Wire who dressed the most outrageously, or just for the heck of it or (if you believe the version in *In the Beginning*), because James picked the fight and came off worse. What we do know for sure is that Bradfield ended up with a broken jaw, while Edwards was knocked down and took some kicks and punches but was OK. The fall-out was that Bradfield had his jaw wired and couldn't sing for six months. 'On a Friday or

Saturday night, mindless violence is just the acceptable thing,' said Edwards. 'Fifty-two weeks of the year, you go to a pub and put a glass in somebody's face.'

During this Christmas break, Richey began to feel alienated from the circle of friends that he'd had since the Crosskeys days. The following spring he wrote to Steve Gatehouse and complained that everyone hated him for being associated with the Manic Street Preachers and that they disagreed on his views about bands and music. This rejection of his ideas was still eating away at him months later. In his final year he was moving on from bands such as Hanoi Rocks, which he'd loved the music of even if he didn't like the band's Dionysian lifestyle. 'Listening to them now brings back lots of memories,' he said. 'Everyone else used to be out at the pubs getting pissed and we'd be locked away in our bedrooms playing these records. They just made a noise that we really liked. It was purely for the music, not for their rock 'n' roll lifestyle. That's why Public Enemy made such an impact because although Hanoi Rocks summed up our youth, it never really said that much, we just loved them. There was always something missing and when we heard Public Enemy we realised what that was. We realised we had to do something.'

1988's *It Takes a Nation of Millions to Hold Us Back* really hit a chord with Edwards. 'This record came at completely the right time in our youth,' he said. 'There was nothing really saying anything at the time, nothing really contemporary anyway. At first we were put off by all the sexist bullshit and were never quite sure how to take the band, but once we got this record it really blew us away. I mean, a song like "She Watched Channel Zero?!" with lyrics like "Her brain's controlled by a twenty-four-inch remote" just summed us up. We were spending all of our days stuck in front of a TV with nothing to do and this really hit it home to us.'

Back in Swansea, Edwards was on the last stretch to his finals despite the distraction of living with Nicky Wire who was more interested in the band than his studies. Richey started helping out with some lyrics for the new songs, even though he wasn't actually a member of the band yet. 'People can't understand,' Wire told

*Esquire* in 1998. 'Sitting in a room writing lyrics together. It was an unbelievable sensation. I was having a bit of a rough time, women-wise, and we'd just sit around listening to dodgy records and writing songs together.' Before his finals, Richey wrote to Steve Gatehouse that the batch of new songs included 'Motorcycle Emptiness', 'Sunglass Aesthetic', 'England is Still a Bitch', 'Ruthless', 'Whiskey Psychosis' and 'Colt 45 Rusty James'.

Edwards still considered it a privilege to be able to sit in a nice library and read books all day. He would sometimes go out for dinner with his lecturers, wearing a strange combination of a jumper and leather jacket. He still struggled with acne and was taking medication for his skin.

During his final year Richey had to choose a 'special subject' that would contribute to a large portion of his final mark. He chose a course entitled German–Soviet Relations in the Inter-War Period, which was run by Dr Eleanor Breuning, who was also assigned as his personal tutor. 'We taught a special subject which was very intensive and he took my special subject,' says Dr Breuning. 'So I got to know him quite well. Single honours students almost always had the special subject tutor as their personal tutor. He was a very good student, and what we used to do in our capacity as personal tutors was to have a one-on-one interview at least once a year, with all of our personal tutees, and then write a little report. What one did was ask them things like, "What's your home life like?", "What are your ambitions for the future?", "Do you have any problems with your work at the moment?", and "What are your extra-curricular interests?". I remember very clearly that he said he was into fanzines. Now, I knew what a fanzine was because I'm very interested in the language of popular movements, so I wrote all of this down and it was then reviewed by my professor, which was normal, who put a query mark in the margin; he obviously didn't know what a fanzine was! He didn't tell me straight out that he was involved in popular music, just that he was into fanzines and I think he almost deliberately lived two lives, one of which was his life as a student, into which he threw himself very fully. He was always on time with his essays and I would have said he was a top-of-the-range 2:1 student, a good, diligent, polite, pleasant student, but I think he kept his other life rather apart from all that. I remember he was slenderly built, quite thin-faced, but very normal in his dress; he didn't stand out at all from the student body. You can never tell how they are going to turn out, all you can do is buff up their minds a little bit.'

Edwards had to take eight papers as part of his finals and was examined on all of the subjects that he'd studied in years two and three of his course. The special subject contributed 25 per cent of his final grade. 'Obviously you couldn't expect a group of six or eight undergraduates to have both German and Russian,' explains Dr Breuning. 'So for the purpose of the course I put together a portfolio of selected documents, which I had translated for them. So they were studying raw documents and we would go through these together in my office in our very small group. I would explain how a historian would interpret the material and set it into context and [Edwards] was really into the course, he understood what was going on, and quite responsive. I can see that he would be annoyed with his fellow students, why they didn't buckle down with their books – he must have felt something of an outsider.'

He was so dedicated to his studies and his aim of a First Class degree that he took control of every aspect of his life that he could. He managed to slow down his vodka drinking and his eating to the stage that he was sober enough to revise at night, but everyone around noticed how his weight had dropped. He also started to exhibit other forms of self-control. James Dean Bradfield was visiting during Easter 1989 as Richey was doing his final weeks of revision. While sitting around a table Richey almost unconsciously reached over and picked up a compass, which he used to score his forearm over and over, drawing blood. Bradfield was shocked at the display and the sight of his almost emaciated friend but didn't say anything. 'The lowest I've got down to is just under six stones,' Richey later admitted. 'That was my third year at university, that was the skinniest I ever got, during my finals. But again, that was all about control. When it came for me to do my finals, I suddenly realised that I can't go in to do my finals pissed.

So the way for me to gain control was cutting myself a little bit. Only with a compass, you know, vague little cuts, and not eating very much. Then I found I was really good during the day. I slept, felt good about myself, I could do all my exams. I got a 2:1 so I wasn't a one hundred per cent success, but I got through it, I did it. I remember James came down to see me in the Easter holidays before I did my finals. I wasn't very healthy then. But I did alright in my exams.'

Despite saying that he 'did alright', Richey was devastated that he didn't get a first. It was the only time he hadn't come away with the top grade in an exam. 'Being Richey, anything he believed in and wanted to do he dedicated himself to it until he had mastered it,' recalls Sally Killian. 'I remember how ill he looked during his finals, he worked so hard [to get a first]. Anything less wasn't good enough.' Before his exams Richey had written again to Steve Gatehouse, saying, 'Only one thing to know about exams – if you know you're intelligent, why worry? To consider failure during a three-hour exam is to admit you are intellectually inadequate. That has been the basis of my academic life.' Now, it was the summer of 1989. Richey had failed to reach the top for the first time in his academic life. Was he now, by his own definition, 'intellectually inadequate'? Did he consider himself a failure? He had no job, no clear idea about a career. He was twenty-one years old and weighed six stones. What was Richey Edwards going to do with his life?

# V

## STRAIGHT OUTTA BLACKWOOD

*September 1989 to December 1990*

Shortly after lunchtime on Friday, 22 September 1989, Richey Edwards climbed in behind the wheel of a hired van and started a trip around Blackwood. He collected Nicky Wire, James Dean Bradfield, Sean Moore and all of their equipment, except for Moore's drum kit, which didn't fit in the van, especially as they had a bunch of friends crammed into the back for moral support. Then he set course along the motorway to the Severn Bridge, over into England and along the M4 to London. Edwards had never been to London before. In fact, he'd hardly ever been to England and wasn't sure how to get across the Severn Bridge. He made it across and the journey became one that would be familiar to him over the next few years.

On this trip the destination was a Victorian pub on Portland Street called the Horse & Groom, where they would be supporting a long-forgotten band called The Claim as a result of their concerted letter-writing campaign. The slot had been booked by writer Kevin Pearce, who Richey Edwards had been writing to for some months. His persistence had finally paid off. Ian Ballard was one of the few who paid £2 to get into the upstairs room and see the nine-song Manics set. 'There was no stage,' says Ballard. 'They were just playing through their little amps. It was a bloody row, to be honest, but they were all jumping up and down in white gear with slogans painted on them. It was one of those gigs you went to where you thought, "God, this is really good."' Afterwards, Ballard asked if they wanted to do a single with him. They said they'd think about it.

Another curious bystander at the gig was Saint Etienne

keyboardist and then *Melody Maker* writer Bob Stanley. Stanley, who would write the first live review of the band in the national music press, remembers the show well. 'We were laughing,' he says, 'but only because it was so unexpected. There was obviously something there, because the tunes were so good. After the first number, they said something to the effect of, thanks, that's the most applause we've ever had. We were totally won over.' Stanley's live review ended with the words, 'Given enough rope they could become champions' – a cheeky Clash reference.

A few weeks before, the *NME* had finally got around to reviewing the 'Suicide Alley' single. 'Retrogressive, exciting and inspired. You'll probably hate it,' wrote Steven Wells. Only a few copies of the single were up for sale, with most being sent to writers. Steve Lamacq was sent one and immediately recognised the Clash-inspired sleeve picture of Wire, Bradfield and Moore in their leather jackets – a photo taken by Richey Edwards. The three hundred copies of the single were stored under the Moore–Bradfield bunk bed and placed into flat-packed sleeves and sent out when required. A few were sold locally at Dorothy's Cafe on the Blackwood High Street, without the shop taking any commission. 'They were really supportive of the band at the start,' said James Dean Bradfield. 'They made us feel like members of the Beat Generation.' A small ad was also placed in the back of *NME*, which was how Ballard had got a copy.

'At the end of his studying days, when it looked as if the band could actually make a go of it, Richard asked our opinion: what should he do – train to teach history, or go for it with the band?' recalls Rebecca Williams. 'We advised the band, simply because we thought if it didn't work out he could always still train to be a history teacher. We kept in touch, on and off. We would go on sort of dates, very occasionally, but we never had a proper relationship. I think he simply felt comfortable with girls he knew. We are talking one extremely sweet-natured bloke, basically.' Many Welsh bands seemed to think that a rep from Warners or Sony would spot them playing a show in the valleys and that the only cultural advantage of being based in London was being able to get the *NME* a day early. Richey Edwards was strongly of the view that you had to play shows in London if you wanted any chance of success. It wasn't just label reps that you had to impress, but it was important to make friends with writers and promoters to get a little buzz going and your name known. God knows what he'd have done if MySpace had been available in the 1980s. Prior to the Horse & Groom gig, Richey Edwards had been working hard to make some connections in the English capital. Radio 1 DJ John Peel, John Robb at *Sounds* and Steve Lamacq of the *NME* were just some of those who received Edwards' missives and a copy of the band's debut single. The initial letter to Lamacq had ended with the question, 'If we do some London dates, would you come?'

They played in London several more times before the end of the year, including poorly attended gigs at the Rock Garden and Shepherd's Bush Opera on the Green. By the time Steve Lamacq got to see them play live at the Bull & Gate in London, they'd already had some favourable write-ups. But, in an almost empty pub, he wasn't impressed: 'They sounded spindly and looked like they'd come out of a box marked "punk rock action figures".'

Edwards continued his mail-outs, writing to journalists, editors, record labels and other bands he admired. One of his favourites was the Aberdeen band Jasmine Minks and their singer Jim Shepherd. One of Edwards' letters to Shepherd explained how the Manics had taken inspiration for their name from the Jasmine Minks' album *One Two Three Four Five Six Seven, All Good Preachers Go to Heaven*, which was obviously a large stretching of the truth because the band had been named before Edwards was really involved, but this didn't detract from the correspondence they struck up. 'He was just like this mad agitator,' recalled Shepherd. 'The way he put things across to me, the music didn't actually live up to it. I always thought it was like Stiff Little Fingers, it was old hat. But the way he spoke about South Wales and the mentality there, it really spurred me on, and lots of other people, I'm sure. He'd just stop in the middle of a letter and there'd be two pages of poetry before he came back to the point. Obviously his brain was buzzin'.'

Other recipients of his long, sometimes rambling letters included

Kevin Pearce of the *Hungry Beat* fanzine, to whom he wrote of the loneliness and desperation he'd experienced in Swansea and of the rush of excitement he felt from certain bands, prompting him to say 'He had enough energy to fuel the nation.' The exchange of such letters was the catalyst that helped evolve Edwards from being a shy teenager into the mouthpiece of the band that would be any publicist's waking dream.

Since his teenage years, when he'd really become an avid *NME* reader, he was aware of which writers favoured which types of music and were influenced by which bands. He used these years of reading to good effect and knew which writers would be open to the band and his style of letters, but it didn't prevent him from going after everybody. 'I'd put in endless literary quotes,' he said. 'It was incredibly pretentious really, really dumb. But, as time passed, the letters became more and more surreal. We knew that most people would just hurl the whole package in the bin. So we actually sat down and had a discussion and decided that there was only one way around it. Everybody . . . and I mean everybody in the London music business, would be approached. We simply reasoned that somewhere, somehow, it would land on the right desk at the right time.'

At a Manics show at the Square Club in Cardiff, a visiting Londoner said afterwards that the skinny, beautiful roadie should be on stage. By December, he was. Edwards became the band's second guitarist, adding a bit of noise behind the accomplished playing of James Dean Bradfield. Now he was 'officially' a member of the band and not just its press officer, spokesman, minister of information, roadie, lyricist and chauffeur. Edwards was mainly an onstage presence, rather than a musician, because he was throwing Clash shapes and the poses of all the classic rock guitarists even though he could barely play the instrument himself.

With the quartet now finalised, they were ready to really press forward. A few ground rules were set, there and then: no taking drugs, no writing love songs and no getting married. As well as their own rules, they had unwritten ones to fight against in the wider world. Being a rock band from Wales was definitely not cool.

'We were a Welsh rock band, and in the eyes of some people then that was the very worst thing in the whole world,' said James Dean Bradfield. 'We were totally a product of our environment but we had to prove we weren't The Alarm.' They had ideas well above anything The Alarm had accomplished. Bradfield admitted that they started on the basis of delusions of grandeur. They were perhaps the first band in history to make a round of the major banks, asking for a loan to get started. They trooped in with a copy of the *NME*, which they held up to explain why all of the current bands were rubbish and why they would blow them all away with a little bit of financial backing. Not surprisingly, they were turned down every time. But this summed up the band completely. They were unlike your 'average' group: their logic was different to a lot of people's and their self-belief bordered on the manic (pardon the pun). While the decade-ending charts were full of hedonistic dance-rock crossovers and acid house, the Manics' idea of hedonism was to have a few cans of beer and some fish and chips. Ian Ballard would witness this difference first-hand when they followed up on his invitation to visit him in London.

Ballard had started up Damaged Goods in 1988 as a punk reissue label, run from his East London home. Before Christmas, the Manics kept their promise of getting in touch with him and paid him a visit. Rather than go to the pub, they discussed things over games on the Sega Megadrive. The two parties agreed to release a single and take it from there. 'Basically, I was being auditioned to see if I could do their single,' recalls Ballard. 'James and Richey did most of the talking – they were very straightforward and down to earth.

'He [Richey] must have read books from day one while the rest of us were watching telly. He's very intelligent; I think he finds it difficult talking to people who aren't similarly educated. He'd sit there quoting things and I'd be nodding, thinking, I don't know what you're talking about.' Although they were eager to get a 'proper' single released, they didn't want to rush it just for the sake of it. They also realised that Damaged Goods was only a stepping stone, and Richey continued writing letters and trying to secure the band support slots. To an extent, this worked: the band gained slots supporting the likes of Mega City Four and Cranes. The trade-off to playing these shows was that they were losing money every night. They wanted to accelerate their 'career', so they started thinking about getting themselves a manager. They started asking around their music business contacts for any suggestions. Steve Lamacq mentioned that ex-*Record Mirror* writer Philip Hall had set up a PR company called Hall Or Nothing in 1986 and had experience of working at Stiff Records. Hall Or Nothing were already starting to make a name for themselves, handling the affairs of The Stone Roses, Beautiful South and The Sundays. Hall was willing to give the Manics a chance and said he'd make sure he made it to their next London gig. When they told him that they didn't have one, he agreed to travel to Wales and see them there – quite an unusual thing to do.

In the meantime, Ian Ballard paid for the band to have two days at the off-the-radar Workshop studio in Redditch. It was enough time for them to record four songs – total cost: £186. The Workshop was chosen because it was cheap and it was one of the only studios that Ballard knew. These were the first sessions that Richey Edwards had participated in. His main contribution was to ask producer Robin Wynn Evans to dub into the mix the sound of a guitar being smashed. Evans replied that if that's what Edwards wanted he should smash his own guitar, which he did.

Ian Ballard was enjoying the Manics' punk sensibilities at a time when punk was the most unfashionable genre anyone could think of. 'They had basically slagged off most of the big bands around at the time, which was great; things were pretty safe at the time,' says Ballard. 'A lot of people really hated them, people were asking me why I was doing a single with that bunch of arseholes. I just said they were a great band, I liked them.'

The *New Art Riot* EP was not released until 22 June 1990, but it furthered the band's reputation. The title track attacked British culture and the aristocracy, covered the NHS, terrorism, and suicide, and invited listeners to 'Kill, Kill, Kill'. And all in a little over three minutes. The whole EP was over in eleven minutes – full of slogans and rhetoric. Loud, fast, energetic. Made you want to hear more. The first thousand copies were each stamped 'Made in Wales'.

Ian Ballard sent 29-year-old Philip Hall an advance copy of the EP and re-ignited his interest in the band. Hall and his brother Martin drove over to Wales. The band had set up for a practice at the Newbridge school and were feeling the pressure of having someone drive over from London just to see them in a sterile, empty room. Nicky Wire somehow managed to give himself a smack in the nose with his own bass while they warmed up and by the time the Halls walked in, his white shirt was covered in blood. James Dean Bradfield was so shy he initially walked out. Despite this dodgy opening, the Halls decided to stay anyway and were impressed enough to take their interest further.

Soon afterwards, Richey wangled a show back at the Rock Garden in London. Among the sparse crowd were Saint Etienne's Bob Stanley, who had convinced Heavenly Records bosses Martin Kelly and Jeff Barrett to go along with him, and the Hall brothers. When Nicky Wire had finished smashing up his bass and the gig was over, the band was approached by the Heavenly brass about signing a deal. Initially, Richey thought they were taking the mickey and told them to fuck off. But when their credentials were established, the band said yes. Richey had written to Jeff Barrett and sent them a demo tape. 'It was passionate, it was on fire, it wanted to change the world and it really excited me,' said Barrett of the letter. 'Unfortunately their demo tape didn't do as much for me.'

'There were about fifteen people there,' says Martin Kelly when recalling the Rock Garden show. 'They played the most amazing set ever. We were completely blown away.' Heavenly and the Halls then had a meeting and agreed that they should all work with the Manics together. Hall would become a passionate champion of the band, by all accounts a true gentlemen in a usually ungentlemanly industry.

Richey continued his one-man press offensive. To Steven Wells: 'You can't expect anyone who comes from where we come from to like The House Of Love. It's so boring that everybody just stays in and gets drunk and you don't want to bear Guy Chadwick droning on about love and stuff. We look like nothing else on Earth. A car bomb kiss-off to *The Face*. Politics and adolescent cheap sex. Fuck the rotten edifice of Manchester. Too safe in dressing like a bricklayer. Too boring. Too macho, males afraid of themselves. That's why we look up to the images of Kylie and The Supremes and not bald-fat-ugly-glutton-filth Inspiral Carpets. They make us vomit.'

'Richey was the one who came out with the best quotes; he was the most lucid,' says Bob Stanley. 'I got the feeling that he was the driving force. He was very intense, very inspiring. Plus, he looked like a star. He was very quiet and seemed very intelligent. You know that thing when you can't tell whether something was really funny or really brilliant? That's what the Manics were like when I first saw them live. Richey first got in touch with me. He wrote, "Dear Bob, inspire me, Richey."'

Edwards and Stanley struck up an eighteen-month correspondence that led to Stanley writing up their first interview in *Melody Maker*. The interview took place in a pub and he noted that none of them were drinking. Afterwards, he offered them a floor to sleep on but they preferred to sleep in their van. Richey joined the Saint Etienne fan club and made a T-shirt for Stanley that read 'REVOLUTION FLOWER'. When the Manics later toured with Saint Etienne, Stanley and Pete Wiggs wore homemade T-shirts with 'Ballroom Blitz' and '48 Crash' stencilled on them, but the Manics thought they were taking the mickey.

The Manic Street Preachers finally signed up with Heavenly Records at the end of August. As well as being a label, they handled the press campaigns for bands such as the Happy Mondays and Primal Scream – both targets for the Manics at the time. 'I'll never forget the look on their faces when they walked into the office and saw all the Mondays memorabilia on the walls,' smiles Jeff Barrett. The Manics were not ashamed to regale anyone who would listen with their opinions, but would go directly against these so-called beliefs when it suited them. The Heavenly connection allowed the band to play more London gigs, but they were still often playing for less than thirty minutes a night and then driving back to Wales.

Heavenly booked the band into the Power Plant studio in London to record ten new songs in four days at the end of October. The label then planned to pick out the best tracks for use as future singles. They then sent the Manics out to play some more dates before Christmas. On 1 November, they opened for the Levellers – a band that Richey Edwards had despised for a while. He liked their followers even less. Here was another in a long list of Manics, and Edwards, contradictions. Edwards was more than happy to speak out about how much he hated a band, but then the Manics would go and play a show with them anyway. For all the protestations and worthy interview snippets, a few pound notes helped to smooth over any objections. Edwards' main point of contention with the Levellers was that their 'crusty' fanbase was mainly populated by middle-class types who wanted to play at being dreadlocked Caucasians with a dog-on-a-rope. 'You could go to any Levellers concert and stand in the middle and shout "Jeremy!", and seventy-five per cent of the audience would turn round,' he ranted. 'You can tell they're middle-class poseurs because they wanna dress down like scummy people. The working-class tradition has always been to want to be clean. All my Dad's friends want to do when they come home from the pit or whatever is have a wash, have a shave, dress up and go out.'

Two weeks later, in Manchester, they opened for a baggy Heavenly band, Flowered Up, and went down like the proverbial lead balloon. These support slots were getting the Manics out and about but the fans of the main acts they were supporting didn't know what to make of them. Sometimes they'd walk out to a taped reading of Allen Ginsberg's 3,000-word poem 'Howl'. What a happied-up crowd made of an intro tape from the Beat Generation that talked about being fucked up the ass and blown by sailors is anyone's guess. The Manics didn't care if they were labelled as pretentious; in fact, they were happy to admit that they were. Their main objective was to do things that other bands didn't.

Better support slots were found in the form of Saint Etienne and Scottish Big Star wannabes Teenage Fanclub. Richey Edwards' lack of guitar-playing expertise was generally hidden by the fact that the band played fast and loose – his frantic background strumming didn't spoil any exquisite musical moments. The Manics spent most of November on the road before the Heavenly Christmas party showcase at the Camden Underworld on 13 December. Saint Etienne and Flowered Up were also on the bill. It was a triumphantly drunken end to the year. Richey Edwards was bladdered and when an unnamed, thirty-something press officer dragged him away to a toilet cubicle he didn't resist. Unlike his claims to have lost his virginity at twenty-one, he was two weeks shy of his twenty-third birthday. When word got out about what had happened, James Dean Bradfield was livid. He tracked down the unnamed woman and confronted her, saying, 'Do you realise what you've done?' The last shred of Edwards' innocence was gone.

In the 1970s, it was the Glimmer Twins: Jagger and Richards hanging all over each other. Inseparable. In the 1980s, it was Morrissey and Marr. In 1984, a *Record Mirror* cover presented a well-coiffured Johnny Marr with a pink-and-white-polka-dot-shirted Morrissey draped over him. In 1988, Morrissey got it *all* off his chest on the front of the *NME*. These music covers became iconic to the constant readers of the 'inkies'. When the Manics started to give regular cover appearances in the 1990s, they knew both the importance of them and their history. Wire and Edwards became the Glamour Twins because of their semi-outrageous dress sense and heavy reliance on the latest beauty products.

Of the six times that the Manics were featured on the front of the *NME* up to October 1994, the entire band was included only three times. Once it was Richey with two other bands, once was Richey and Nicky, and once it was Richey alone. It was very clear who the music press thought the real star was – the pin-up boy for the 1990s.

In their first *NME* feature, the band was photographed outside Buckingham Palace to give another nod to the Sex Pistols.[8] Richey used the session to parade about in a home-made shirt with 'London Death Sentence Heritage' stencilled across the front. He also used red tape to attach a page from a London A-to-Z street map to the shirt. The stencilling was haphazard, with ink splattered across his chest. It all looked like a bloody mess from ten yards away.

The May 1991 *NME* cover of Nicky and Richey was photographed by Kevin Cummins. 'This was their first *NME* cover,' he says. 'I bought the gold sari cloth to give it a trashy glam look – although it's since drawn comparisons to the paintings of Egon Schiele, with the gold backdrop and the slightly twisted bodies.' The cover image showed the two band members on their backs, gazing up at the camera. Wire has his right arm around Edwards' shoulders and Edwards is pressing it to his chest. Both have panda-eyed make-up. Wire is in a leopard print shirt, open to below his nipple, while Edwards has a black crocheted top. Before the shoot, they'd decided that they should both have a collection of love-bites on display and so the night before they had gone nightclubbing to try and get some. Wire succeeded but Edwards didn't, much to his own disgust. In the photo studio, Kevin Cummins wrote 'Culture Slut' across Nicky Wire's upper chest in lipstick. Edwards, upset about losing the love-bite competition, was determined not to be upstaged. He produced a school geometry compass and wandered over to a mirror, where he scratched 'HIV' into his upper chest. But he forgot he was looking at his reflection so what he actually wrote was 'VIH'. It still made the cover.

He'd already done the writing-on-himself routine for a very early session with Joe Dilworth, where he'd used a more conventional writing implement – a pen rather than a sharp spike – to write 'RIOT' across his chest. He knew exactly how he could reach and influence young minds through the music press, just as he himself had been influenced. But it was dangerous as well. For *Smash Hits*, he wore an 'I'm Too Dead' T-shirt and told the readers, 'Our manifesto is: "Don't do it kids." Never get past the age of thirteen.'

'Sometimes you get caught up in the mythology that there's nothing but darkness surrounding the Manic Street Preachers,' said Nicky Wire, '[but] what struck me about the early days is that we usually had smiles on our faces. Having been friends from the age of five, we were incredibly confident and comfortable together. We also had an evangelical spirit that made those first six months to a year better than anything that's come since. Not that we weren't nihilistic.'

# VI

## DESTROY THE HIERARCHY
### *January to July 1991*

With my son safely on his way to nursery with my wife, I took the opportunity to flop back into bed for an hour or so. I had been up with him since just after five a.m. and I had been working until after midnight the night before so I didn't feel guilty. I was just nodding off when the doorbell rang. The postman. He delivered a video-shaped parcel. In it was a video – and a note: 'These gigs take me back,' it read. 'I wish the Manics were still like that.' What did that mean? What were the Manics like almost two decades ago? I put the tape in the machine and wandered off to get some cereal.

The year 1991 was a year of musical hand-over. It saw the death of 'baggy' and the birth of grunge. In critical terms, My Bloody Valentine's *Loveless*, Nirvana's *Nevermind* and Primal Scream's *Screamadelica* were the musical leaders of the year. R.E.M. went acoustic with *Out of Time* and Bryan Adams managed to keep '(Everything I Do) I Do it for You' at number one for an astonishing sixteen weeks. The Gulf War was the big news during the early months, but in this dress rehearsal for the 'real' Gulf War, Saddam was left in power.

By early 1991, the Manics had written to enough journalists and pestered enough PR agencies to have their name known in various circles. Richey Edwards would write to anyone and everyone, from the most famous rock journalist to a humble fanzine editor. In fact, fanzines would prove to be one of the best ways for the band to generate a buzz. At one point the running joke was that the band had more fanzine titles than fans. Even when a 'zine was specifically about the band, there were some that used the Manics' cut-and-paste, stencilled styling as their 'look'. One of the professional writers who had picked up on their early vibe and was on their side – at a time when a lot of writers were after their heads – was John Robb. Punk hadn't exactly been *de rigueur* during the late 1980s; in fact, it was probably at its lowest ever ebb. It wasn't considered 'cool' to be punk in any way, or even influenced by it, as the Manics and their Clash sensibilities obviously were. Lancashire lad Robb had started out playing bass in The Membranes[9] before becoming their lead singer. During the 1980s, he started freelancing for the likes of *Melody Maker, ZigZag* and *Sounds*.[10]

Robb was a prime target in Richey Edwards' letter-writing campaign. 'One day I got sent a demo with a letter,' explains Robb. 'The letter was very polite except it said something about not liking The Wonderstuff and The Wedding Present. It also mentioned my band The Membranes positively – he had obviously done his research. Thinking about it now, they must have done some work to get my address! This was in the pre-internet, pre-*Facebook* era and it wasn't that easy to get people's addresses. The music papers didn't give them out to anyone. I remember getting it and being surprised by how polite and how naive, in a good way, that it sounded. It was very charming and made out that the band had selected me specially, but I'm sure they said that to the other handful of journalists who were into that kind of music at the time.'

Robb was impressed with the demo and interested in meeting the band, so he wrote back to Edwards saying just that. Being complete unknowns it was difficult to break the band in any of the music weeklies, but Robb spent the next few months dropping their name here and there. His persistence matched that of Edwards and eventually he was able to give the band its first big media coverage in *Sounds*. 'Intermittently *Sounds* would have space available for upcoming bands,' recalls Robb. 'It was the best music paper by a mile and the only one genuinely interested in bands if they were interesting musically on the outside of what was going on. In the late eighties, playing lipstick-mascaraglammy-punk-rock was totally out of fashion, so the Manics were very much swimming upstream – that's one of the reasons that I loved them straight away.' Indeed, 'swimming upstream' is a phrase that summed up the band in early 1991. Many people took one look at a photo of them and instantly dismissed their mixture of old-school punk and anti-fashionable tight clothes. When people could be persuaded to listen to them, there was a danger that the Manics seemed so far from the mainstream that they would similarly be dismissed out of hand. Robb, however, kept talking them up and his editors gave him a little bit of leverage. Richey Edwards could still barely play his guitar, but that was an irrelevance to him: conveying his message was more important than being able to strum his instrument.

*Sounds* heard that the band was about to release 'Motown Junk' on Heavenly and thought that the time was right to introduce them to a wider audience. An interview was arranged at Jeff Barrett's office, although this eventually took place in the Manics' van parked outside. 'They were very eager to do an interview, which was rare in those days as most bands were not that arsed about doing press,' says Robb. 'The band was a weird mixture of very quiet and very vociferous. Richey seemed quite shy but very clever. He did most of the interview. The rest of the band would join in now and then and embellish what he said. The interview was a fantastic tirade against modern culture; it's still one of the best interviews I've ever done. Richey was fantastic – he spoke clearly and made loads of sense. The van was cramped and we sat on all the gear. Richey was hunched down as I was sat on an amp. He had mascara on and black spiky hair that was spiked with soap, and he still had teenage skin – kinda not acne but rough skin! The band were broke at the time and their glam-punk look was very homemade-looking, which made it look even better. Richey said the most outrageous things in this quiet, softly spoken, polite voice, which made it even more intriguing.'

When Robb submitted the piece, his editors were suitably impressed by what Edwards had to say and the band was given the cover and a two-page spread inside. This was an unusually large amount of coverage for a new band. 'Sex, Style and Subversion From MANIC STREET PREACHERS' blared the cover in late January. Underneath the headline was a Steve Double portrait of the band under the graffitied slogan 'Generation Terrorists'. Richey was wearing his white, long-sleeved 'Kill Yourself' T-shirt. This introduction to a wider audience proved Edwards' importance to the band. He'd tagged a journalist, worked on him, and now had two pages to put across his manifestos, and he achieved all this in a polite, quiet, understated way. The blaring headlines about sex and subversion were very different from the actual Richey that journalists sat down and talked with, often over a cup of tea. The *Sounds* cover was the first real victory of his media assault. While Edwards was only 25 per cent of the band, 60 per cent of the article's quotes were by him. Even at this stage, Robb had deduced that this band was different as Edwards talked about the Manics' plans and ambitions, what they wanted to achieve and what they stood for. A good chunk of the other new music coming through either didn't want to change anything or was just interested in having a good time. Richey, on the other hand, was talking about being the best band in the world, about changing homophobic attitudes and disrupting the social hierarchy.

'People say why don't you try and write a love song, you should reflect people's feelings,' Edwards told Robb. 'But everyone I know has been pissed off at least once and we reflect *those* feelings.'

The *Sounds* issue hit the shops within days of 'Motown Junk', helping the single edge just inside the Top 100. It was a start. Richey and Paul Cannell[11] had come up with the idea of the picture sleeve featuring an image of John Lennon and Yoko Ono with a gun to their heads, referencing the line in the song which said 'I laughed when Lennon got shot.' This was the overt 'Generational Terrorism', a systematic rejection of the previous generation's heroes. With Edwards again showing his grasp of pop-culture history he was very aware of which figures and movements he wanted to be aligned with and which he wanted to quash. In his mind, the Stones were cool; The Beatles were not. Keef was still shooting up. Lennon got shot. Good.

Heavenly had paid for 'Motown Junk' as one of the ten songs recorded back in October at the Power Plant studios in Willesden. The band used the same room where Rod Stewart had recorded 'Maggie May', much to Richey Edwards' pleasure. The 'Motown Junk' 'revolution' intro sampled Public Enemy, while the outro sampled The Skids – from one extreme to the other in the space of a couple of hectic minutes. Rather than trash the memory of the great Detroit hit-factory of the title, the song spat at its imitators that were slithering all over the charts – the likes of Simply Red and Wet Wet Wet. It was also a loud two-fingered salute to the current rages of 'Madchester' and 'aciiiiiid', despite the former being all over their own record label.

As it transpired, Jeff Barrett vetoed the single's Lennon cover and Cannell had to quickly come up with an alternative. He settled on a burned watch, scorched into a permanent sixteen-minutes-past-eight by the Hiroshima bomb, denoting the time of detonation. The picture sleeve wasn't the only change inflicted on the band: one of the B-sides had originally been called 'Ceremonial Rape Machine', an anti-monarchy rant that the pressing-plant employees had refused to work on. It was changed to 'We Her Majesty's Prisoners', which was evidently more palatable to the workforce.

During the busy week of the *Sounds* cover and the single release, the band also got its first real TV coverage when the BBC's *Snub TV* programme aired.[12] The band also used footage from this show to make up a promotional video for 'Motown Junk'. The clip featured the live footage with studio music dubbed over the top. Richey was in his ubiquitous 'Kill Yourself' shirt with, as usual, tight white jeans. Sean Moore sported a very Madchester-esque pudding-bowl haircut. Edwards took the opportunity at one point during the song to step forward in front of James Dean Bradfield and strum away right into the cameraman's lens. No wonder people assumed he could play.

•

Philip and Terri Hall were married in 1990 and moved into a house on Askew Road in Shepherd's Bush. In January 1991, they took an unusual step and invited the Manics to move in with them. Driving back and forth between London and South Wales was becoming a drain on their energies, especially with the increasing frequency of their London appointments. They weren't earning any real money yet so the option of renting somewhere wasn't very attractive. Neither was the prospect of spending up to a year sleeping on floors, couches and in shared beds, but at least it was free. This gesture was a measure of both how much Philip Hall liked the band and how much confidence he had in them making it big. They turned out to be perfect house guests. They would clean the house from top to bottom and cook the evening meals. Richey Edwards generally shared a room, and bed, with Nicky Wire. The bassist would therefore bear the brunt of Edwards' complaints, rants, theories and bad jokes. He also had to deal with the morning after a boozy night: not just his own hangover but also the stench coming from the other side of the bed. 'I woke up with the vodka seeping out of Richey's skin,' he complained. Despite the occasional boozy nights out, Edwards was very polite around the Halls, and for much of the time you'd have hardly noticed that he was even there. But when you did, it could be disconcerting.

Terri Hall soon got used to seeing a row of Babysham bottles in her fridge, rows of stencilled white shirts hanging in her bathroom and four pairs of white Levi's in her laundry basket. What she didn't get used to was seeing Edwards nonchalantly cutting his arm while everyone was sitting around watching TV. If one of the band spotted him doing it they quietly hinted that he should stop, until one day he was stubbing cigarettes out on his arm and Philip Hall had a word with him. He said that it had to stop while he was living in someone else's house, and it did.

Living with the Halls eased the transition from South Wales, but getting used to life in London was a culture shock to Richey Edwards. He regularly phoned his mother and would always keep in close touch with her when he was away on tour. A decade later, Edwards would have been a prime candidate for a reality-TV *Osbournes*-type show and his exploits could have been a real eye-opener. 'Up here people seem to put a lot of work into things we never thought about when we were growing up,' he told *Top* magazine. 'Like being seen to wear Calvin Klein underwear, to be seen to be doing the right thing. I'd never even heard of bottled water before I came to London. Back home you've got to really search for your Evian!' Having only really experienced Swansea and Blackwood, London could have presented itself as a mire of dubious nightclubs and excruciating temptations, but having five people around him – who he trusted implicitly – smoothed over any potential problems. This wasn't like being holed-up in a tower block of students that he hated, and Philip Hall became a pseudo-older-brother who could dispense advice about anything and everything.

Edwards wasn't shy about enjoying the nightlife with his bandmates, however. '[I remember] sleeping in the same bed as him for six months when the Manics moved in with Philip Hall in Shepherd's Bush,' Nicky Wire later told the *NME*. 'I'd sleep on one side of the bed, him on the other. He'd say stuff like, "I think I have an orange growing in my stomach, Nicky! I can feel it!" because he used to drink so much vodka and orange.'

With the new single out in the shops, the band started the hard work of playing small shows to try and promote it, and themselves. Often the gigs were in unusual and unlikely places. In January they played at the Royal Holloway College, which Richey Edwards mistakenly thought was a public school. Journalists and music business types took a strange delight in watching the Manics' early London shows, often treating them as circus sideshow or a laboratory experiment. Was this strange-looking gang of Welsh oddballs just another Sigue Sigue Sputnik? Was this cartoon-Clash a parody or joke? Most shows split the audience down the middle. Richey didn't mind this at all: a negative reaction wasn't a problem to him so long as they got a reaction of some kind. He was adamant that rock had gone too soft and someone needed to stir things up. It was a job that he was only too willing to appoint himself to. With press and TV coverage behind him, Edwards was quickly growing in self-confidence with the media. He was truly averse to much of the music around at the time and felt that the Manics really were going to be the best band in the world, to be the only band that really mattered and to be a band that could change things. If he couldn't be part of the best, he'd rather not be part of a band at all. As usual, it was all or nothing for Richey Edwards and he was going to make sure it was all.

'Richey looked you right in the eye when he spoke,' says John Robb. 'Somehow, he was really in your face. It was almost like he'd worked out the interview beforehand. He'd rehearsed it. It was like he had a blueprint on how to be the ultimate rock 'n' roll band. He wasn't a massive extrovert, but he was obsessed with rock 'n' roll. He was a shy guy and it was almost as if rock 'n' roll made him reach out and talk to people. The way he talked was half positive and half with a complete disgust of the music industry.'

The band was like a tight-knit gang. They went out together, they stayed in together. Bradfield and Moore were more than happy to let Wire and Edwards do all the talking, but they were all serious about how they wanted to go about things and the two spokesmen accurately conveyed the feelings of all four of them when it came to interviews. Moore barely said a word during interviews and would make his excuses and leave whenever he could. Bradfield seemed as shy off the stage as he seemed confident and confrontational on it, despite looking like he'd pick a fight with anyone. Wire was more openly antagonistic towards other bands, while Edwards always had a point to put across, even if he did tend to drift into nefarious tangents. During the year, Edwards and Wire would start making ever-more outrageous claims about the plans and hopes they had for the band. These sometimes changed but the general line was that they were going to record a double album, sell sixteen million copies, headline Wembley stadium, and then break-up. 'No one has ever sacrificed themselves,' said Edwards, ever-mindful of getting a reaction. 'If we become huge and just throw it away, that is a big statement.' Big statements were important to Edwards. Anyone could make small statements, but big ones took balls. Big statements really meant something, and that was everything.

So out they went. Edwards had decorated the interior of their pale blue mini-van with a collage of icons, actors, models, rock stars and literary figures. He was also doing the driving. Looking back at the list of venues you can easily see that this was a band prepared to start at the bottom and work their way up. The work ethic instilled by their families was there for all to see. They weren't afraid of paying their dues, but they wanted to get it over with quickly and move on up. They had worlds to conquer. The Stoke Wheatsheaf witnessed the start of the tour proper, followed by shows at the Duchess of York in Leeds, the Adelphi in Hull and the Charlotte in Leicester. Then they played the Zodiac in Oxford on 7 February, which is where my grainy old VHS tape kicked in as I settled down for some breakfast. The nth-generation copy isn't very easy on the eye but the band are visible enough, giving it their absolute all to a pretty nonplussed crowd. Even the front rows were fairly static and hardly a head was nodding as the band ripped out 'You Love Us'. Thirty minutes later, the set was over in a hail of feedback. All the posturing, sweat, jumps and kicks had done little to win over the crowd. But obviously someone had had the foresight to think it would be worth filming for future reference. Zigzagging back and forth across the country, gigs were played at the Coventry Stoker, Brighton Basement, Aldershot Buzz Club and Taunton Priory – among other venues – before the band's first overseas trip, to Paris.

Richey Edwards had never left the British Isles before and consequently didn't own a passport. The day before departing, he had to buy a temporary visitor's passport and the band set off for a Heavenly showcase at La Locomotive, alongside Saint Etienne and Flowered Up. Things were moving quickly for Richey Edwards. He'd hardly left Wales for the first twenty or so years of his life, but now he was living in a city of ten million, had travelled up and down the country and was venturing overseas, all the while with the spotlight increasingly picking him out, waiting for his next polemic. The Paris show saw the Manics trash the stage at the end of their set, smashing the club's neon sign in the process. Edwards showed little interest in exploring the French capital and didn't venture far from the bus. For someone so bright, he'd never taken to languages and was unwilling to experiment.

Back home, the band literally went the length and breadth of the country to whip up some enthusiasm. Grey days spent on the motorway didn't matter to Edwards. They were heading towards something better and this was just a temporary means to an end. This was the start of the rock star life he'd wanted, his ticket out of Blackwood, his way of making a difference in an otherwise horrible world. The tour visited the home turf of Swansea and led up to Glasgow in the north and Southampton in the south. In between, they were filmed again at the legendary Marquee club in London on 13 March. Here, they got a much better reception, with Richey resplendent in white jeans, boots and a flimsy blouse with Marilyn Monroe prints all over it. With his dark hair and make-up, he almost looked like Liz Taylor in *Cat on a Hot Tin Roof*. Edwards' looks and dress sense were now starting to get him singled out from the rest of the band. He was gaining a growing number of admirers in the press and amongst fans. The Manics' biographer Simon Price described him as 'the most beautiful man I had ever seen' and Caitlin Moran described his brown Bambi-eyes as 'beauty beyond lust'. As the group toured more extensively, it became common knowledge that Edwards and Wire weren't averse to inviting groupies and fans back to their shared hotel rooms. Interviews the morning after the night before would sometimes start with a discussion of the previous night's after-show events. Simon Price reported seeing Edwards take two girls back to his room and commented that he was a quick learner, having lost his virginity only recently. It was also reported that Wire would be shagging in one bed while Edwards was across the room shagging in his. Sometimes they'd swap partners. Sometimes Edwards would just read a book. Wire was drinking and sleeping around more than Edwards in the early days. In an early morning hotel room interview with James Brown, Edwards said, 'I'm never embarrassed by his [Wire's] behaviour, because it's never long enough to get embarrassed about it!' Wire's wild excesses could not continue indefinitely, however, as he was later diagnosed with Gilbert's Syndrome[13] and had to give up drinking. He also later reunited with his girlfriend Rachel and his touring shenanigans came to a halt, leaving Edwards to sometimes party alone. Edwards had never had a steady girlfriend and he wasn't about to start now. He preferred the quick attentions of groupies to avoid any emotional attachment, and this would continue through the Manics' tours. After a while, Edwards grew tired of this: it was reported by Stuart Bailie towards the end of Edwards' time with the band that younger fans would get the 'slumber party treatment', with Edwards talking about make-up tips. Hugging was just about out of the question.

Edwards could be almost naive in his openness to interviewers. His polite, considered responses were sometimes more shocking because of the calm with which he delivered them. He would often agree to questions about his sex life, but appeared to take a perverse pleasure by saying how bad it was. He also played with the facts about losing his virginity. He told Holland's *Villa 65 Radio*, 'When I lost my virginity it was a definite act, I was twenty-one, everybody for years and years had been fucking around me saying how brilliant it was, and I felt like, "I'm not happy, maybe it is this glorious event that's gonna change your life." And so I just deliberately went out and sat in a pub, drank until somebody came up and said, "Do you want to come back to my house?", and we went back and we fucked. It was very clinical and the next day I felt really bad. I didn't like it, and that kind of shook my perspective on things.' Edwards, ever the historian, was never shy about rewriting his own past, whether it be the naming of the band or when he'd lost his virginity. Self-image was everything to him – not just physically, but emotionally as well. He had to be seen to be doing the right thing, the cool thing, even if the reality was a little bit different. At the same time, his complex personality was exposed by his self-deprecating interviews about his sex life and manhood. When many others would have simply laughed off certain lines of questioning, Edwards would do the opposite and be brutally honest.

When *For Women* magazine asked him to be their centre spread he commented, 'Public nudity is repugnant, private nudity isn't much better. The human form is ugly compared to, say, a leopard or a seal.' On another occasion he said, 'I have no desire to expose my genitalia. Too small.' For a 1993 questionnaire in *Select* magazine, he answered:

Most intense erotic experience – never had one

How do you rate yourself sexually – poor

Most regrettable sexual experience – every one

Edwards had serious issues about the human form and especially his own looks. This went beyond simple vanity and as his own body shape became an issue he would start excessive exercise regimes, but it was never enough. He also told another interviewer that his ideal body shape for a woman was extremely skinny, 'so you can see the ribs'. It wasn't a particularly healthy view to express.

Richey was sceptical about relationships and this bled into his view of mankind as a whole. 'Men and women just aren't compatible. Men are too selfish,' he told Sylvia Patterson. 'But it doesn't really matter because it won't be long before we're all wiped off the face of the earth anyway. In three generations' time seventy-five per cent of the animal species of the world will be wiped out! And it's all our fault! We've only got five generations of man left if you ask me and maybe it's just as well – mankind is the worst thing that's ever happened to this planet!'

•

Next up, was a whistle-stop tour of Ireland. The hundred or so kids that crammed into a 'fucking skittle alley-cum-smack house' (according to Nicky Wire) to see them in Limerick saw a great little show, but then in Coleraine only a handful were present so the band trashed all of their equipment. In Belfast, they got a tour of the Falls Road to see the political murals. Wire summed up the time to *Hot Press*: '[It was] frightening but at the same time amazing to see first-hand. Our tour manager nearly got swept away at the Giant's Causeway. It didn't matter 'cause back then we were bulletproof.' The Irish fans were quite receptive, but in England the shows could quite often be confrontational. Bottles and cans would rain down onto the stage and verbal sparring would go back and forth between band and audience. There was more trouble at the Manchester Boardwalk, where the opening act actually turned on the group: the quickly forgotten band First Offence called the Manics a 'bunch of faggots' and left the stage to a tape of 'Motown Junk' with chicken noises played over the top. After a couple of 'gay' comments were shouted at the stage, Edwards and Wire decided to antagonise the hecklers by really camping it up. 'Our *first offence* is to be beautiful!' shouted Wire, before Edwards lay down on his back and allowed Wire to straddle him in simulated sex.

At the start of May 1991, Heavenly issued 'You Love Us' as the next single while the band continued to tour. They weren't afraid to go back to venues they'd played earlier in the year and were gradually building up a larger and larger following. The thinking behind 'You Love Us' was that the fans would love them eventually, even if it wasn't love at first sight. 'Camus said that, "If God does not exist, then I am God",' said Richey Edwards. 'That was our philosophy.' The band, and by default Edwards as the unofficial spokesman, were in danger of being seen purely as a bunch of loud-mouthed yobs with nothing tangible to say. A few neat slogans weren't going to go very far if the music wasn't worth hearing. Edwards, who had been revelling in his new-found freedom to create and lambaste, was aware that things could take a turn for the worse if they didn't keep a high public profile.

Simon Dudfield made 'You Love Us' the single of the week in the *NME*, writing, 'I'm sure everyone wants to be in this band, living out their sordid rock 'n' roll fantasies. They just won't admit it.' Indeed, very few did admit to wanting to be like the Manics. Richey Edwards created the sleeve for the single with another of his collages.[14] Unfortunately, he hadn't cleared permission for any of the iconic images he'd chosen – Bob Marley, DeNiro in *Taxi Driver*, Robert Johnson, Marilyn Monroe, The Who, Beatrice Dalle in *Betty Blue*, and more. Minor threats of lawsuits soon followed, but Heavenly tidied up the mess.

These legal issues were just the first problems in a mini-avalanche of bad press and controversy that Edwards would be at the centre of over the next couple of months. Still very much a rookie to this game, Edwards was not always sure where the boundaries were. In the next incident, he stepped closer to a rumpus with Steve Lamacq. 'By the time of the follow-up, "You Love Us", we'd started to fall out in public,' recalled Steve Lamacq in his autobiography, *Going Deaf for a Living*. 'They had a dig at some bands I liked; I had a dig back, making some rather unkind comments about them in a review of another band called Bleach. In retort, they dedicated "Starlover" to me at their next gig. It was all a bit petty, but I guess it must have been serious stuff at the time.'

On Wednesday, 15 May the Manics' tour reached the Norwich Arts Centre. On paper it wasn't likely to be any more than a run-of-the-mill show. The only slightly unusual thing was that the *NME* were sending along – guess who? – Steve Lamacq and photographer Ed Sirrs to cover the show for the next issue. Unless you follow the career or life of a public figure quite closely, there will usually be one thing that person did or said that is always brought up in relation to them. It's the one thing that they never shrug off; for many people, its the first thing that they think of when the person's name is mentioned. For Richey Edwards, his life-defining moment was about to happen.

There have been lots of rumours about what really went on that night and why. It was reported that the band were watching a Nottingham Forest game on TV in the hotel bar before the show, but in fact Forest never played on that date. It was said that Steve Lamacq phoned for the ambulance, but he was just standing there stunned and shocked. It all started when Lamacq agreed to travel to Norwich and review the show because he thought the band had been getting sycophantic reviews and wanted to give, in his opinion, a more balanced assessment of where the band were at. James Dean Bradfield kept away from Lamacq from the start – a mixture of shyness and distrust.

The show itself was uneventful, even disappointing. The hall, a converted church with tombstones forming part of the floor, was half empty and the crowd were not especially excited by what they were seeing. Edwards didn't want a big negative write-up about the show, so he took matters into his own hands.

'The difference between me and Richey,' said Nicky Wire, 'is he always wanted to be understood and I prefer to be misunderstood. I don't feel the need for people to love and respect me. Richey really did. He couldn't take strength from the fact people didn't like him.' It was this need to be understood and believed that led to a lengthy conversation with Steve Lamacq after the show. Edwards most likely knew that the gig review wasn't going to be that great. He caught Lamacq's attention afterwards and asked if he could have a word. Towards the end of their chat, Edwards gave an impassioned statement of what he thought the band was about. While doing so, keeping steady eye contact with Lamacq, he produced a razor blade. After pulling up the shirtsleeve on his left forearm, he began cutting into his own flesh. As he continued talking, he carved the slogan '4REAL' into his arm to back up his words about not being a fake. Lamacq later said that the first, deepest, cut must have really hurt, but Edwards showed no signs of pain and remained calm throughout. Lamacq kept glancing down at the unfolding drama but Edwards' voice and general demeanor was mesmeric. The points he was making to Lamacq, let's face it, were pretty unimportant in the grand scheme of things. They were just a rock band. It wasn't more important than life or death, was it? Richey Edwards seemed to think it was. It was the most important thing in the world.

When Richey had finished cutting, the pair continued chatting for a couple of minutes as Lamacq became increasingly concerned about the mess of blood and open wounds. Eventually Lamacq suggested that Edwards do something about his arm before he damaged the carpet. When Lamacq moved away and spotted Philip Hall he told the manager that he should check on Edwards. Moments later, Hall dashed past on his way to phone for an ambulance. Lamacq headed outside for some air and a cigarette.

Richard Lowe interviewed Richey about the incident for *Select* magazine. 'It never occurred to me he may be fucked up,' said Lowe. 'He seemed really level-headed. But running through the Manics was this "life is futile, life is crap" idea. He really believes that. Everything for him is sad, he's not a happy-go-lucky person. He takes everything seriously, not just music. That's his problem. He feels personally burdened by everything horrible in the world. It upsets him and hurts him. That's the sort of person he is.'

Photographer Ed Sirrs was on the scene and took the now-famous blood-soaked photos. 'I have children myself, so I felt sorry for him, and went a bit fatherly, but he seemed completely unconcerned,' said Sirrs. 'I've been criticised for taking advantage of his distress but, in fact, he volunteered to have the pictures taken. In effect, he hijacked the situation and salvaged something from a lousy gig to give his band some credibility. They knew they'd never get another major *NME* review after such a dire performance, so he had to do something. And a week later they'd signed a deal with Sony.'

To some degree, the incident must have been a premeditated act by Edwards. He might well have had a razor blade with him on tour – he was always having a little cut of his arms, here and there – but he would have been unlikely to carry it around with him at all times. It may be that he'd collected it before meeting Lamacq, 'just in case'. Edwards had seen a situation that might have gone out of his control, so he'd wrestled it back and taken control so that the poor-quality gig was overshadowed by his show of 'authenticity'. It was a price that he was more than willing to pay.

Nicky Wire accompanied Richey to Norwich General Hospital, where seventeen stitches were needed to close Edwards' wounds. Feeling that his self-inflicted cuts shouldn't cause pain to anyone else, Edwards insisted that all the other patients went before him. Then the next day, ever sensitive to others' feelings, he phoned the *NME* to apologise to Steve Lamacq. The writer was out but Edwards left him a taped message saying sorry for upsetting him in any way.

The next issue of the *NME* ran a news piece about the cutting with the soon-to-be infamous shot of Richey's arm reproduced in black and white, the gig review followed in the 'Live' section.[15] The photographs had been turned over to the IPC (owners of the *NME*) legal department before a decision on usage was made. Lamacq ended his piece by saying, 'What wouldn't we give for a new political pop band back in the charts? Someone who'd go further than just being worthy. But the fact is I'm not sure the Manics have everything under control at the moment.' He was partly right. Did the Manics have things under control? Or more pointedly, did Richey have things under control? He would later argue that his cutting was exactly his way of keeping control over things, but it wouldn't always be that way.

In 1994, Nicky Wire was more subdued about the incident and said: 'None of us realised quite how symptomatic it was of the shit that was going on in his head. We've been friends since childhood, so I knew he wasn't doing it for the attention, but I never appreciated the extent of his despair or how far he was prepared to go in trying to relieve it.' But fourteen years later it was almost as though Wire was trying to backtrack over the reality of the incident when he spoke to the *NME* about it. 'I still think it's an absolutely brilliant artistic statement. I did at the time and I do now,' he said. 'I don't think you can equate that with self-harm or disappearing or whatever. It was a statement. There was a point to it. And it showed how much the band meant to him. When we were sat in the hospital with the nurse treating him, we both actually felt a little bit guilty at wasting NHS time. Thing is, I still can't believe it wasn't the cover of the *NME* that week! I remember talking to Richey afterwards and him saying, "I did all that and it wasn't the cover?"'

•

The following night's show in Birmingham was understandably cancelled, but the tour soon continued amidst a deluge of articles, features and graphic colour images. All of this was a great boost of publicity for the band and their new label, and Richey Edwards had provided it. Instead of being on the verge of drifting out of sight before they'd even made it, they were now big news and big business.

Philip Hall had masterminded a big money move to Columbia, which was part of the Sony empire. The official signing was on 21 May and reports suggested that a massive ten-album deal had been agreed for £250,000. Tim Bowen was the key figure at Sony and had been the man that had signed The Clash back in 1977 – something that connected with the band. Heavenly were disappointed to be losing the Manics so quickly, but must have been expecting it. The photo that appeared in the music press showed the Manics seated in the Sony boardroom while Paul Russell, the Sony UK chairman, and Tim Bowen, Sony MD, used both hands to shake with the four band members. Richey was using his left hand to shake with Bowen and so his fresh bandages were in full view. There was nothing hypocritical about signing to a major label; in fact, Richey had made their aims clear right from the start. They wanted to be the biggest band in the world, and – with all due respect – they sure weren't going to achieve that by staying on at Heavenly.

The new deal meant the severing of the Manic Street Preachers' links to Heavenly. The label website states that the arrangement had been beneficial for all concerned: 'Although only at the label for a short period, it was long enough to provide a shot in the arm for both parties – the band achieved the notoriety they craved and the label put itself well and truly on the map.' The Manics did right by the label and paid back to Heavenly the £6,000 that the label had lost on the band.[16] That night the band played a triumphant gig back at the Marquee to celebrate.

Although they'd never considered themselves to be an 'indie' band, the fact that they had signed to a major 'corporate' label before their first album had even been recorded did make the band prime targets. As soon as the ink was drying on the Sony contract, the 'sell out' accusations started flying. Indeed, at the Marquee show they broke one of their own rules and came back to play an encore. Strike one.

'The whole indie mentality that grew from punk onwards just seemed so bullshit to us,' said Richey, 'because the most subversive, really important group in the world were Public Enemy, and they were on Columbia. The level of corruption on an indie label is just on a smaller scale.'

The national press also started to take an interest in this major-label band, after these yobs from Wales had landed a quarter of a million. The *Daily Mail* asked 'Is Rock Music Destroying our Children?' alongside a picture of the '4REAL' incident. But rather than being a danger to society, Richey Edwards enjoyed his first pay cheque by embarking on a spending spree for designer punk T-shirts and a portable CD player. This was the first time in his life that he really had any amount of disposable income.

The combination of Fleet Street outrage and Sony-related hype led to a heightened sense of anticipation and danger in advance of the band's next one-off gig, one which they had agreed to play before signing to the major label. This was the May Ball (even though it took place on 22 June) at Cambridge University's Downing College. It's hard to think of any event less likely to be on the Manics' radar, but again, money talked. Back in 1991, the £150-a-ticket fee was a steep price to pay for a Manics gig (it still would be now) and the students had obviously been reading the band's press cuttings in the lead-up to the show. The college rugby team was brought in to act as security in case the group decided to smash up the house equipment. The Hall brothers and other guests were resplendent in their tuxedos, but the evening's entertainment didn't last long. With the band playing in a large tent, the crowd were almost willing something outrageous to happen. When Richey Edwards dared to rest his foot on one of the stage monitors the stage crew wildly overacted by pulling the plugs and declaring the show over, even though they'd only been playing for a few minutes. The band members couldn't believe what was happening. One 'security guard' appeared, brandishing a tent pole, while another guard arrived with a vicious-looking dog. The band was 'escorted out', but not before James Dean Bradfield had floored a member of the rugby team with a punch. The police were called and it made the pages of the *Daily Star*. The *NME* called it the 'Cambridge F**k Festival'.

Proving that the band were a mix of extremes if nothing else, their next press coverage was in the pages of *Smash Hits*. An August issue had Dannii Minogue on the cover and featured posters of Extreme, Seal and Cathy Dennis. The cover mentioned 'Manic Street Preachers' right next to 'Vanilla Ice'. Inside, Richey discussed the Cambridge fiasco: 'We started playing our set and before we knew it there was blokes on stage pulling the plugs and wielding sticks.'

Before the summer was out, another new song, 'Stay Beautiful', was released as a single and was officially listed as a Heavenly/Sony single. Steve Brown was a trusted producer who had worked with such varied artists as Elton John, ABC and The Cult, and was brought in by Sony to work with the Manics on the song. They met up for the introductory sessions at Manor Studios in Oxfordshire. If all went well, then Brown would work with the band on their debut album that autumn. 'Stay Beautiful' became the band's first single to break into the Top 40. The Walter Stern video was inspired by *Twin Peaks*. The band was filmed performing in a red room with silhouettes moving around behind red curtains, with red-lined corridors and zebra-print floors. As coloured paint starts dripping into the room, the band are splattered like a moving Jackson Pollock work – an imitation of the famous Stone Roses picture.

The occasional shows they played here and there through the autumn were hit and miss. Sometimes, they had been playing gigs to as few as two hundred people. They didn't get a lot of radio play for their singles, either. They might have bitten off more than they could chew: the £250,000 being invested by Sony would need some instant return. All they had to do was get around to writing that legendary double album that would sell sixteen million copies. It was all too easy, wasn't it? As Richey told *Smash Hits*, 'We play rock 'n' roll and we live rock 'n' roll. Rock 'n' roll is our lives.'

# VII

## NOTHING TO CLING TO
*August 1991 to December 1992*

Black Barn Studios in Surrey offer just that: a black barn. Close to the M25 near Woking, and set in picturesque countryside, this was the high-priced setting for the Manic Street Preachers' first album. The sessions were expected to take eight weeks but ended up lasting almost three times that as the recording costs rose from a planned *maximum* of £400,000 to over £500,000. The band had enough material from their teenage years to record eighteen tracks for the album, which had the planned title of *Culture, Alienation, Boredom and Despair*. Steve Brown arrived to start work with the band in August 1991.

Richey Edwards was going through a rough period and living the rock star's life a little too much for his own good. With the band working in the studio, he had nothing to do and the safety net of his constant companions taken away from him. His guitar playing had shown no signs of improving and he'd shown no interest in wanting to spend time practising. Left to his own devices, he was starting to show signs of losing control. The now-defunct *Select* magazine reported that, 'In the studio Richey indulged in every kind of abuse. He cried a lot. And although he seemed able to sort himself out again quite easily, James was more worried about him than he had ever been before. It became common knowledge around this time that Richey had told James that if the band ever split up, he would have nothing left.' Edwards' insecurities were heightened with the band in the studio because, quite simply, he'd done his bit. His lyrics were complete and he wasn't playing guitar in the studio. Practising his guitar was out of the question: it had no musical use to him.

Matt Olliver was working at Black Barn. 'They're just really lovely people,' he said at the time. 'As far as I can tell, they don't do any drugs. They read a lot, and they play computer games.' Olliver was called upon early in the sessions to act as a driver one time when Richey had been drinking and so couldn't drive. Guns N' Roses were issuing two albums on the same day: *Use Your Illusion I* and *Use Your Illusion II*. Edwards managed to talk Olliver into driving him, in his bashed-up old mini, to Tower Records in London, which was opening at midnight to sell the albums straight away. Then they rushed back to play them. 'We stayed up all night playing those albums,' said Nicky Wire. 'It was really bad, because the first side of *Use Your Illusion I* is terrible, and we were like, "Fucking hell, what's gone wrong?"'

The studio was relatively secluded, so Edwards had nowhere to go unless he was driven into London. From his earliest involvement in the band, his role was very different to most rock stars. He wrote the words, some with Nicky Wire, some alone, and the pair added and made suggestions to each other's work. The lyrics were then passed on to James Dean Bradfield and Sean Moore, who wrote all the music. Edwards was not involved with the music writing, nor was he deemed good enough to actually play or sing on the album. So in the studio he just wasn't needed. In the pre-contract days, he'd made himself useful by at least chauffeuring the others around but even that role was now fading away. When news leaked out that Edwards hadn't played a single note on the album, there was a mixture of amazement and anger. Was he faking it?

'Why is everyone hung up on an ugly piece of wood and metal and strings?' he countered. 'I can't play guitar very well, but I wanna make the guitar look lethal.' That was Edwards to a T: vain as ever, he just wanted to *look* good. This attitude led to his being sometimes unfairly compared to the likes of Sid Vicious and Bez. 'This guy out of [Manchester band] The High came up and started talking to me about an interview he'd done just about his guitar and equipment; when I told him I wasn't interested and that James plays my guitar on the record he went mad,' recalled Edwards. 'He was going, "There ought to be a union to stop people like you"'. That kind of reaction was clearly over the top. It wasn't as though Richey was doing a Milli Vanilli and duping the fans into thinking he could really play; he was quite open and honest about his place in the band. Indeed, he revelled in the fact that he couldn't play. Taunting others that he looked good on stage simply *holding* a guitar was a source of pleasure, at least for the time being. Again, his image was everything. Image was important to the band as a whole, but the other three could just about back it up when playing live. Nicky Wire was the least proficient musician, but James Dean Bradfield was developing into a mesmerising lead guitarist and Sean Moore was a solid if largely anonymous drummer.

As the sessions dragged on, Sony decided that they needed to keep the band in the public eye with another single. With the album taking longer than expected, the band had gone almost six months without releasing anything new. The choice for the new single was the double A-side of 'Repeat' and 'Love's Sweet Exile'.

The Manics headed into London to appear on the late-night Channel 4 show *The Word*. They practised a run-through of the relatively safe 'Love's Sweet Exile' to pacify the show's producers, but they thrashed out a version of 'Repeat' live on the show. Edwards was resplendent in a red blouse, with James Dean Bradfield outshining him in a gold one. The band was surrounded by over-enthusiastic, look-at-me-I'm-on-TV moshing. The single confirmed the Manics' gradual progression and edged into the Top 30, boosted by a slick video. With the Sony budget behind them, the band could really go to town with their videos – a natural extension of their visual image that was being cultivated through their photo shoots and stage show. Although Richey played little or no part in the recording studio, he was front and centre when it came to a video shoot. Edwards had already hinted at the band's favoured icons in 'You Love Us'; now he started the literary education of the

Manics' fans with the video's opening sequence, which featured a stark, black quote on a white background:

> 'Then came human beings,
> they wanted to cling but there
> was nothing to cling to'
> Camus

As the song began, the camera panned across Edwards' 'Useless Generation' tattoo as the drums started, before a mélange of homoerotic black-and-white footage of Richey Edwards and Nicky Wire all over each other. Topless and lipsticked. Eyelinered and clutching. Edwards accosts the camera, leaving a lipstick smear on the lens. A large metal crucifix hangs across his bare chest. Then he's in a gas mask. Then the footage turns negative with cheap psychedelic special effects edited in as the background, just like the typical backdrop to *The Word* every Friday night. Edwards and Wire were always experimenting with their 'look' and neither was averse to some make-up and a blouse, something that Bradfield and Moore always looked like they were tolerating rather than enjoying.

While Wire outdid Edwards by going the whole way and wearing dresses, Edwards managed to outdo his partner in the make-up stakes. He could carry off a see-through blouse much better and, anyhow, Richey Edwards had always been in touch with his feminine side. Back at Oakdale Comprehensive, this had been apparent. Jonathan Medcroft was in the same school year as Richey and recalled, 'He was kind of androgynous even then. There were early signs of anorexia. I mean, in Wales you don't find that high cheekbones occur naturally . . . you need to starve yourself.' Richey himself told the *Melody Maker* that he wanted his band to sound like the Sex Pistols but to look like Duran Duran, who had worn plenty of make-up in the early 1980s. He answered questionnaires about his favourite make-up (Rimmel eyeliner) and explained that when he put up pictures of Kate Moss, who he'd seen in *The Face* in 1989, it wasn't because he wanted to sleep with her; he wanted to *be* her. His Liz Taylor haircut was a homage to the actress. The press even ran stories about Edwards wanting to save up enough money for plastic surgery to turn himself into Diana Ross.

The final stages of the recording sessions were documented by Edwards in a brief diary commissioned by *Select* magazine. It revealed the day-to-day activities of this guitarist that didn't play his guitar. Edwards' average day started with a breakfast of bottled water, tomato and cheese, before a car would arrive from CBS/Sony to drop him off in Fulham. They he'd attend to the band's fan mail. Some days he would take the company credit card, get chauffeured into London, spend money and come back that night covered in love bites after visiting Soho strip clubs. One of the places he'd often visit was The Ship pub on Wardour Street. It was there that he was spotted by The Damned's Rat Scabies, who told Mick Middles, 'I do recall this guy, a geeky rock 'n' roll guy. One of those people who you would always sort of see around yet never quite know what he did. Looking lost and famous.' He was getting more famous and he was also in danger of getting lost. He was going through a phase where he wouldn't spend free time buried in a book, but he'd wander, spend money from the band account and generally waste his days away. The worrying thing is that he was well aware of his slide, but didn't seem to want – or be able – to do anything to halt it. Edwards knew that the constant spending and deliberate time-wasting was taking a toll. 'I know that if I get to the end of this year I'll have no dignity left at all,' he said. 'It's all gone. I live in a big fantasy world. All I do is get into the company Mercedes, drive to London, drive around for five or six hours then come back to the studio. It's sad.' He'd often end the day drinking even more to block out the world and allow him to get to sleep. Being a rock star wasn't turning out to be as challenging or exciting as he'd dreamed back in his Blackwood bedroom.

On a day that James Dean Bradfield made Edwards practise, he wrote that it 'Spoils my day.' He'd much rather spend his time reading the latest *Silver Surfer* comics and playing on his Megadrive. 'It treats me better than most people do,' he said about his gaming console. 'Also I think how shit everyone is who still owns a Nintendo. It has been my duty to practise six hours a day. Fuck my guitar.' The new-found ability to buy whatever he wanted when he wanted it, within reason, wasn't as great as he sometimes pretended it to be. Deep down he knew it was a way of hiding the emptiness of his life. 'The more toys you get, the more empty you feel,' he admitted. 'The only time you're really happy is when you're really young before you want anything.'

Richey's love of comics stemmed from his childhood, the time when everything was good in his life. This might also have explained his obsession with computer and video games. Richey: 'You know the myth of Stagger Lee, that he would kill for a Stetson? The Manic Street Preachers would kill for a Sega Megadrive.' The man who wished he'd had a never-ending childhood would spend hours playing games. 'In a video game you can murder, maim, and impoverish thousands, you can create and destroy whole populations,' he explained. 'Put four people playing guitars next to that, and it has to be boring!' He would often mention in interviews what his latest game purchases were or how well he was progressing at a certain game. 'It took me a couple of weeks to do it: to get to the end and kill Doctor Robotik,' he said. 'I should be interested in learning to play guitar, but *Sonic the Hedgehog* rules my life. I find that very sad.' Other favourite titles included *Decap Attack*, *Kid Chameleon* and *PGA Golf*. The others liked to play, too. In Japan in 1993, Edwards declared that he could 'beat anyone on Sony games. Anyone. Anywhere,' and explained that James Dean Bradfield 'likes the fighting games' and that Sean Moore had spent 24,000 yen on games during the trip (about £120).

'We had our Sega Megadrive when we were down the studio making [*Generation Terrorists*] and we were spending hours a day playing because it's so engrossing,' Edwards told Q magazine. 'But it's so sad that the best human minds on the planet are just trying to invent characters like Sonic the Hedgehog.' Almost as sad as some of the best minds in pop music spending more hours playing with them. Edwards' razor-sharp mental agility was being blunted by the shunning of a classic read for another hour in front of his gaming console.

•

Back in the studio, while the others were recording, Edwards would drink, chew his nails and occasionally cut himself. He decided to decorate the studio with collages and took on the responsibility of the album's artwork, on which he referred to himself as Richey James. Once the idea of the Guy Debord sandpaper sleeve had been discounted, he began visiting London galleries for inspiration. The Charles D'Offay Gallery, the Spink Gallery and Ryan Art were some of his favourite places to view. Many of the pieces that caught his eye had religious or pop icon imagery. He was interested in getting permission for Bert Stern's defaced photograph of Marilyn Monroe, Andres Serrano's *Piss Christ*, Rodin's *Je Suis Belle* (*I Am Beautiful*), Clarence Laughlin's photograph *Spectre of Coca Cola,* Grunewald's *Crucifixion* and Dali's *Christ of Saint John of the Cross* were all refused permission or priced too highly for consideration.[17] Instead, he settled on the idea of using his own tattoo. He'd had a rose inked onto his upper arm with the slogan 'Useless Generation' written below. For the new album title, this slogan would be airbrushed over to read *Generation Terrorists*. Veteran rock photographer Tom Sheehan took the photo of Richey's arm and the cover was finalised. Another photographer to visit the sessions was Tim Jarvis, who took band portraits with a backdrop of Richey's collages behind them. Edwards was caught leaning back into a corner, in his sleeveless, black printed T-shirt and uniform tight white jeans. His '4REAL' scar was still visible below the 'Useless Generation' tattoo. His look was all eyeliner, dyed black hair and assorted metal bangles with a cross on a string around his neck. By his side was a small table littered with empty Smirnoff bottles, which were full of dead and dying yellow chrysanthemums. The walls behind him were plastered with Axl Rose, the Stones, Warhol and assorted pop art images. There hung Jean Harlow, Sophia Loren, Katherine and Audrey Hepburn. Paul Newman and Liz Taylor. Bardot, Lydon and Henry Miller. Collecting these images on a wall was a very teenage thing to do. It could be argued that the cut-and-paste technique was all the Manics had behind them at the time. A band that had looked through the history of rock and ripped out the bits they liked best and tried to emulate them, but – as the world would soon discover – without doing a particularly good job of it. Along with his video-gaming obsession, reading of comics and literal cut-and-paste aesthetic, Edwards was exhibiting all the signs of simply wanting to prolong his childhood. These traits seemed to have grown while the band was working on the album and were another sign that Edwards was already becoming disappointed with the rock star life. Childhood had long been known to be the time of life he'd enjoyed best and now he was almost regressing to it.

On the last day of the Black Barn sessions, Wednesday, 4 December, Edwards got up to collect the day's music press and then went back to bed for the day, not even bothering to pop his head into the studio. He eventually got up to watch the *Six O'Clock News*, then began ripping down his collages. He carried out the scraps of paper and deposited them on a pile with his clothes and other items that would remind him of the sessions. Then he set them alight, while playing Hanoi Rocks' 'Don't You Ever Leave Me' on a constant loop to accompany his ritualistic bonfire.

Edwards was more excited about the location for the mixing of the album – London's Hit Factory, which was where The Clash had produced their debut album. While mixing, the band was invited to stay at Steve Brown's Wandsworth mansion and Richey Edwards was given a bed under framed pictures of Wham! and The Cult, with whom Brown had previously worked. Edwards participated just as little here as he had done at Black Barn. 'It is tiring staying in bed all day,' he commented. The solitude of being in one's bedroom alone was attractive to Edwards, however, and he had already started to mention his admiration for J. D. Salinger and his withdrawal to his 'bunker'.

One of the claims that the Manics made, and actually kept to, was that their debut album would be a double LP. The eighteen-track collection (the US version was cut to fourteen tracks) was a decent, if broadly unspectacular debut. If they had exhibited a little more quality-control and released a ten- or twelve-track album, it would have been tighter. This was basic punk-glam-metal-rock, with not a love song in sight. Listening back now on CD, the ebbs and flows of the album are lost somewhat compared to the four sides of the original vinyl version, which open up with 'Slash 'n' Burn', 'Love's Sweet Exile', 'Another Invented Disease' and 'Damn Dog' respectively.

Richey Edwards took great pains to pick a literary quote to accompany each song on the album's inner sleeve. For the concerned listener, these often helped decode what the song was actually about, and – with four sides of vinyl to fill – he'd been able to cover a lot of ground. No one else in rock was pushing fans towards books. Edwards carefully chose quotes that helped capture his thoughts about culture and his feelings of alienation, boredom and despair. This was a complete package for disaffected youth. This was the album that Richey Edwards would have wanted to be able to buy two years before, when he wanted some hope that others felt like he did and felt that flaunting intelligence was not a bad thing. The classic dual-guitar opening attack of 'Slash 'n' Burn' used a quote by e. e. cummings to reveal that Edwards was presenting a stunted treatise on the scorched-earth policies used in the Third World. Many of the album's lyrics were abstract. 'We took the abortion language of the *Sun* and turned it to our own means,' explained Edwards. 'Anyone of our generation isn't conditioned to think about one thing. You're always flicking TV channels, always switching radio stations. For us to sit down and write a song about something would be so forced.'

'Born to End' was a nihilistic, if noisy, effort with Arthur Rimbaud[18] rambling on about his purging of all human hope. The nineteenth-century dead poet was another hero that had been added to Edwards' list of suicides and vanishings. The fact that Rimbaud threw everything away at a young age, just as fame was about to overwhelm him, struck a chord deep within Edwards. It was the perfect gesture, as far as he was concerned. That Rimbaud managed to re-invent himself away from the limelight after doing so was the cherry on top.

'Motorcycle Emptiness', with Sylvia Plath looking for help and finding none, comes next. This was one of the Manic Street

Preachers' older songs and the words had been a real collaborative effort between Edwards and Wire. They'd sat around Wire's bedroom and literally worked through it together, line-by-line. Despite the suggestions of the title this wasn't a helmet-less ride across an American desert, but a song about living a comatose life. Musically, it didn't fit in with the rest of the album – Richard Cottle's keyboards helped to give it the cinematic edge and almost two decades later it's still one of the band's best songs. During one take of 'Love's Sweet Exile', an inebriated Richey Edwards was goading Bradfield into playing ever-faster guitar solos. 'Go on, play the fastest guitar solo you've ever played, play millions of notes,' he chided. Bradfield did just that, but afterwards admitted, 'I'm ashamed of myself.'

'Little Baby Nothing' was an ambitious idea, which Richey managed to pull off. The lyric was a female take on the male exploitation of women and required a female singer for part of the vocals. Kylie Minogue was considered but, after they had failed to come to an agreement, Richey got in touch with Traci Lords, the ex-teen porn star,[19] and sent her the words. She liked what she read and flew in to see the band play at the Diorama in London on 13 December, then added her vocals. The song was one of the better efforts on the album, with an epic, American feel and keyboards that were reminiscent of Springsteen in his 1970s pomp. And surprisingly, Lords could actually sing. Apart from recruiting Lords, Richey Edwards' contributions to the song included a day spent trolling back and forth through a video cassette of *A Streetcar Named Desire* looking for a section of dialogue to sample.

The second disc of the album starts to drag and the 73-minute running time is just too long. Overall, the album addressed many concerns about beauty and disgust, escape and suicide. Knowing Richey Edwards' personality, interests and lifestyle, it's easy to pick out lines that describe his life at that time. His drinking to waste time at the sessions: 'A line of vodka tears inside / A shot of boredom helps my mind' – 'Condemned to Rock 'n' Roll'; using his brainpower as a weapon: 'You're gonna pay for my intelligence' – 'So Dead'; and his constant self-cutting: 'Get some pain and I feel alive' – 'Born to End'. The clues are all there.

•

Much was riding on the album. Sony had taken a big gamble and there was no guarantee that it would sell. Small crowds at their gigs was one problem; that their videos had failed to make a significant impact on the music channels was another. Outside the music press and its devoted readers, few people in the country actually knew who the band were. There was also the small matter of having rubbed up various music journalists the wrong way, and others in the 'community' not knowing what to expect of them when they were interviewed. Through 1992, one by one the members of the press who met them realised that they were in fact polite, well-spoken young men and not raging, hotel-room trashing weirdos. They also had to deal with a measure of mickey-taking. 'Taff Alert!! Hey, hey, it's the Janet Street Porters,' said one headline. A spoof analysis of the album claimed that the song titles included 'Motorcycle Sluts on Methadone' and 'Motorcycle Lipstick Holocaust Victim'. At the end of 1991 they'd also been called the 'Bash Street Kids' alongside the question, 'The Most Hated Band in Britain?'

The album would most likely have received better reviews if they'd kept their mouths shut during the previous year, but they would also probably have received fewer reviews, too. Isn't any publicity good publicity? For many critics, the release of *Generation Terrorists* was just what they had been waiting for. The Manics were going to fall flat on their faces and they would be the first to say 'we told you so'. 'You promise the greatest album ever, then what do you do?' asked *Select*. Despite the album being given a lukewarm reception, reviewer Richard Lowe gave it '3/5', pointing out that the Manics had introduced lost values back into the world of rock: arrogance, mouthing-off, dressing-up. 'It's a shame they're not good enough to pull it off,' he closed. In the more sympathetic *NME*, Barbara Ellen was given a full page to review the album. She wisely pointed out that the LP was 'destined to be panned severely, both for a variety of very good reasons and a plethora of silly sulky ones'. It was finally given a maximum '10' with the caveat 'People who steer too close to the sun often get their wings melted . . . so stuff the marking system.'

The split in opinions was highlighted on the 15 February *NME* front cover, which asked 'Do you really, sincerely love THE MANIC STREET PREACHERS (or do you want to kick their heads in?)'

During 1992, the likes of Jimmy Nail, Wet Wet Wet and Right Said Fred all topped the UK singles chart. It was no wonder that the grunge movement heralded the return of guitars. The Manics' contribution was to release a re-recorded version of 'You Love Us' and embark on a year of frantic touring and self-promotion. Edwards spoke out against criticism of the band reissuing a single and explained that they'd only pressed three thousand copies of the Heavenly version and that this was long sold out, plus the band had re-recorded it with Steve Brown. The Manics had also been given a healthy budget of £40,000 to film a new video for the song, and the enigmatic 'Wiz' directed it. It featured black and white footage of the band – especially Wire and Edwards – heavily glammed-up. Edwards was shown strutting around and pouting like some prima donna with a feather boa, gold lamé shirt and a ton of make-up. The set was a cross between a fashion show catwalk and live stage with a back-screen showing oversized portraits of communist leaders, Malcolm X and other political figures. Some out-takes from the filming included Edwards strutting down the catwalk with his guitar being pulled along behind him – a direct comment on himself being eye-candy in the band rather than an actual musician. He also wore a wedding dress, with a hand grenade in his mouth – a not-so-subtle comment on his views about marriage. Footage that wasn't cut out included Richey writhing around on the floor, suggestively rubbing his chest while stuffed into the top of his unbuttoned trousers was a mini TV showing an atomic bomb exploding in his underpants. For the filming, Edwards had stashed a bottle of sherry behind his amp and by the end of the shoot, was, in the words of Nicky Wire, 'Gone!'. When Edwards and Wire rubbed together, cheek-to-cheek, their white-stencilled blouses matched up to spell out 'suicide babies', while they fed each other oysters and generally played the homoerotic card again. The video ended with the fashion photographers rushing the stage. As the stage empties, the giant words across the back-screen read 'FAKE'.

The band showed up again on *Top of the Pops* to promote 'You Love Us'. Unfortunately the BBC studio crowd didn't love them and stood around, slightly confused at the spectacle before them. *Generation Terrorists* was released a couple of weeks later, reaching number 13 in the album charts and building up sales of 300,000. Given that the band had been talking about selling sixteen million and then breaking up, this nevertheless fell short of expectations. As for ending the tour at Wembley stadium, well, that didn't quite happen either. Instead, the first leg of the tour was scheduled to terminate at Northampton Roadmenders. Having made the headlines with their initial predications of success, the band weren't afraid to backtrack in the press. 'Our ego has always been way ahead of our bounds,' commented Nicky Wire. 'We have no sense of proportion at all. But we still think it'll happen.'

'We read all the classic rock books, which make everything out to be so fast,' added Richey Edwards. 'You're meant to explode, but that never happens.' Already he was learning that rock stardom wasn't all it was claimed to be – another realisation in what would become a long list of disappointments making up the fabric of adult life. Going out with a bang was good in theory but the reality was somewhat more prosaic.

The tour included venues such as polytechnics, small clubs and large pubs in various suburban locations. In concert, the *Generation Terrorists* songs were given a 'metal' edge in terms of their sound, as showcased at the Astoria in London on 20 February when a Japanese TV crew filmed the show. Audiences were growing compared to the previous year and Richey was often singled out for attention. He seemed to attract the more alternative fans, and even gothic types. He was getting his own sub-cult of largely female admirers. They'd arrive at gigs with '4REAL' written on their forearms in marker pen and enter venues early to crowd around the front of his side of the stage. As the tour progressed, so did the band's media profile and Richey's cult. In Germany, a female fan drove into the tour bus and abandoned her car just so that she could get Richey's autograph. The band's set would usually be over in less than an hour, cramming all nine singles and an occasional cover version into their frantic performance.

Edwards and Wire could also be found at after-show parties discussing make-up tips with teenage girls. 'We get loads of girls at our gigs,' said Edwards. 'We get criticised for that because people think that's too poppy, "Oooh, you've got girl fans", so we can't possibly be serious. That is so patronising because these people are saying that girls aren't real fans, like they can't possibly like or understand the music and they're not going to have fifteen pints of lager, have a big mosh down the front and have a curry on the way home. And they should be at home reading *Jackie* and thinking about blokes. It's crap! In terms of sensitivity and intelligence, girls understand so much more than men. How that can condemn fifty per cent of the population of the entire world is completely beyond me.'

The high proportion of female fans also meant that there were more women willing to hang around stage doors and after-show parties as well. For someone like Richey, this ensured that he had a never-ending line of willing partners for a night. 'I interviewed him in a motel in Birmingham and I saw them play at Birmingham University,' recalls John Robb. 'In the interview him and Nicky talked about life on the road and the way they would have girls in the same room; one would fall asleep whilst the other had sex – they talked about it in an almost detached way, it seemed quite rock 'n' roll but not in a demeaning way.' Edwards also told Robb that his never-ending queue of willing partners meant he could 'fuck the girls to fill a void'. Edwards was drinking plenty by this stage, but wasn't dependent on alcohol. He didn't smoke and the band had kept their initial pledge to avoid drugs. Richey would spend ages getting himself made-up before a show: it was like going out for a glammed-up night on the town, but he'd have to interrupt his night by standing on stage for ninety minutes in the middle of it before the partying could recommence.

Edwards was careful to remain detached from the girls in these encounters, as he saw the route of relationships as a downward spiral to a life he just didn't want. It became an issue that would eat away inside him. Later on he would say he wanted a relationship because he saw those around him settling down and being happy, thinking that a steady girlfriend might make him happy too. But for now he was convinced it was the worst thing that could happen to him. 'Once you fall in love, or get your girlfriend pregnant, or fall into credit, you've got no chance, you've got responsibilities,' he said. 'There's no way you can ever do anything. Once you get reduced to a couple, alone together between your four walls with your TV set, you're cut off.'

He told *Melody Maker*'s Sally Margaret Joy that 'Love is an impossible concept', and she witnessed him take two girls back to his room because they told him they'd shagged members of Dogs D'Amour the night before. He was quite open about his promiscuity. In a joint interview with Nicky Wire, he talked about taking a girl back to his room after a show: 'the little voice in the night, "I'll never see you again, Richey"', 'Yeah, I've heard that.'

•

The Irish Recorded Music Association awards, or IRMAs for short, are effectively the Irish equivalent of the BRIT Awards. In April 1992, the Manics were invited at short notice to attend this live TV event. The day before, they had done a *Smash Hits* photo-shoot but then instead of sitting down for a pre-arranged interview with the teen mag, they had to fly out to Dublin. They invited the *Smash Hits* writer to go along with them. On the Saturday of the awards event, the rest of the band had found the hotel bar and settled in to watch the Wales vs. England rugby match – leaving Richey to handle the interview. Four and a half hours later, he finally stopped talking. The interview covered everything from pop culture, his hatred of Sony ('They signed us up for loads of money for being what we are and now they expect us to start dressing like them and looking as chronically ugly and boring as them with their crap haircuts and no brains'), and his frankly disturbing message for *Smash Hits*' younger readers not to reach their teenage years.

That night the band played 'You Love Us' and ended the song by smashing up their kit, to which co-host Gerry Ryan made a sarcastic comment. At the after-show party, James Dean Bradfield thought that Dave Fanning, the other host, had made the comment and the two almost came to blows. Bradfield, the rest of the band,

and their accompanying Sony contingent were unceremoniously kicked out by the bouncers. The party had already featured some childish but harmless messing around, with Nicky Wire bursting the table balloons and Richey Edwards depositing three bottles of wine in an ice cooler and then tipping it onto the floor. After they were thrown out and returned to the Berkeley Court Hotel, things got worse: Nicky Wire was ejected from the bar for wandering around in only his boxer shorts and later Richey got into a fight about Catholicism with some random businessman staying in the hotel. This was out-of-character behaviour for Edwards because – no matter how drunk he was – he would usually rather stand at the bar and engage in political or ethical conversations as well as shooting the breeze about some brand of eyeliner or the latest single by so-and-so. Perhaps, in this instance, religion had touched a nerve.

Back on the road, a few dates in Europe preceded the first big trip to North America. The tour started in Montreal before moving down the USA's East Coast then across to California, but they only took in a handful of major cities. At New York's CBGBs, they were witnessed by *Rolling Stone* writer David Fricke, who pointed out the contradictions of the Manics but who could also perceive the promise hidden under the hype. 'Are the Manics the only ones who don't see the irony of railing against the economic fascism of NatWest, Barclays and Lloyds while enjoying the generous bankrolling of Sony?' he asked. 'You Love Us? Not Hardly. At least not yet.'

In Los Angeles, the band arrived in the wake of the riots that had exploded after the Rodney King verdict had been delivered and tensions were still running high. The *NME* were following the Manics' American tour and put the band on the cover once they reached the West Coast. 'To Live and Dai in LA' said the headline in reference to the riots. The cover photo, taken in front of the Disneyland sign, showed Richey Edwards looking like a crazed monk or a boxer in his white hoodie and shades, pre-dating Slim Shady by years and adding a chain around his neck, hanging to his navel, and a dozen or so metal bangles on his left wrist. Local radio station KROQ was playing 'Slash 'n' Burn' in relation to the riots, but Edwards pointed out that it had actually been written about third-world economics and deforestation policy.

The highlight of the mini-tour was the show at the world-famous Whisky A Go Go. Members of the Red Hot Chili Peppers, Guns N' Roses and Bon Jovi were curious enough to attend the show. But rather than revel in the attention, Richey was depressed about what he was seeing in the USA and his self-abuse was escalating. Stuart Bailie was a first-hand witness to Richey suffering an allergic reaction to tequila: it caused his arms to swell and turn pink, highlighting the multitude of fresh burns, scars and lesions – something he called the 'road maps of anger turned inwards'.

The band visited Disneyland for the *NME* and then drove through post-riot Compton. During an interview, Edwards started idly unfolding a paperclip and then began slowly and almost absent-mindedly gouging the palm of his own hand. After a few minutes the interviewer had to stop the recording, upset with what she was witnessing.

Part of the 1992 tour had The Wildhearts[20] opening for the Manics. It was noted that Edwards was either quiet and withdrawn or almost constantly in the presence of Nicky Wire. Wildhearts frontman Ginger: 'I don't recall Richey speaking much on tour – probably because he couldn't get a decent conversation out of many people on the road. One major part of Richey's character was being hyper-intelligent. Journalists couldn't spar with him on words because he would have made mincemeat out of them.' Danny McCormack was The Wildhearts' bassist and toured with the Manics more than once. 'Richey and Nicky were inseparable at one point – you'd never ever see them alone,' he recalled. 'It was like two big leopard-skin jackets walking towards you. I could tell they were a very close band.'

Another non-musical task that Richey took to was liaising with the fans through the band's newsletter. He'd often provide a manifesto statement to be sent out, all capital letters and literary rhetoric. In May 1992, he wrote about life on the road overseas: NOT A BRAIN CELL ON THE WHOLE STREET. LOS ANGELES TURNED

FROM RIOT TO LOOTING TO RACISM AND PREJUDICE. THERE'S
NO DIFFERENCE BETWEEN SELECTED AND DESTROYED KOREAN
BUSINESSES – 1992, AND BURNT OUT JEWISH BUSINESSES – 1933.

He also wrote that Japan was the biggest culture shock, 'just
because it's organised'. In Japan, the band received their biggest
overseas reception yet. Edwards was thrown into a maelstrom
of attention, the likes of which he'd never experienced before.
Fans had made their own Richey dolls and followed the Manics
everywhere, camping outside the band's hotels at all hours. While
they were in Tokyo, the video for the next single, 'Motorcycle
Emptiness', was filmed. With Martin Hall directing, and lacking a
permit to film, the band remained on the move and were shot
in a variety of outdoor settings so as to stay ahead of the police.
Edwards took part by standing motionless, looking like a prettier
Paul Westerberg; denim jacket, shades and tousled hair. Under
the neon *Blade Runner* signs or sitting in his hotel room window
sill, looking down on the city with his knees pulled up to his chest,
Edwards was the song personified, happy to play the part of the
pouting depressed outsider, which sometimes he was.

The posters advertising 'Motorcycle Emptiness' were black and
white photos of each of the band members sitting on hotel beds:
Nicky Wire in leopard print and shades gazing up at the ceiling; Sean
Moore sitting cross-legged, staring straight into the camera; James
Dean Bradfield strumming his guitar; Richey slumped against the
wall with his knees pulled up, either pissed or depressed – or both.
Released on 1 June, the song became the band's best-selling single
to date and breached the UK Top 20. Edwards was playing the part
of rock star and for once seemed to be enjoying it. The Japanese fans
also found his politeness endearing – this was a quality not often
exhibited by visiting Western rock stars. Being mobbed whenever
he went out and having his every whim catered for was bound to
inflate any ego, and in this respect Edwards was no different.

A series of summer festival appearances followed. The Manics
knew that playing festivals was a valuable way to reach a wider
audience. At these events they knew that they could be heard by
people who wouldn't usually attend a Manics show, perhaps because

they thought the band were a bunch of hyped-up wankers. Their mailbag that summer proved that when people actually heard them play live, they could be converted. At Reading the band walked out into the early evening sunshine to a tape of Marilyn Monroe singing 'I Wanna Be Loved by You', just as Richey Edwards' nemesis, the Levellers, were playing in the next field. His July manifesto addressed this in a piece he opened with: 'SOME THOUGHTS ON CRUSTIES WITH CREDIT CARDS. ME, I'M GONNA GO AND WASH, GET CLEAN AND PLAY A CD. WHY DON'T YOU STAY PURE TO YOUR PRINCIPLES AND ONLY RECORD IN MONO YOU LUDDITE THATCHER CHILDREN. YOU ARE BRITAIN'S CULTURAL CHERNOBYL.'

During the summer the band had been approached to contribute a track to the forthcoming *NME* compilation *Ruby Trax*, which was being assembled to celebrate the fortieth anniversary of the newspaper. Forty bands were asked to record cover versions of number one singles from the previous four decades. In a contrary moment, Richey Edwards decided he wanted the Manics to record the 1975 Bay City Rollers hit 'Bye Bye Baby'[21] but he was over-ruled and instead the band chose 'Suicide is Painless', also known as 'The Theme from M*A*S*H'. Recorded at the downmarket Soundspace studio in Cardiff for just £80, the song became the Manics' first Top 10 hit when it was released in September, peaking at number seven.

The accompanying video was simple and to the point: the band was filmed playing the song live in an empty warehouse that had its walls decorated in a multitude of different flags.[22] Directed by Matthew Amos, a series of handwritten slogans are mixed in throughout the film, with a couple of Richey-isms included: 'You can't invent another colour' and 'Pay no more attention to me than if I were a machine – I am little else'. The latter might have had something to do with the band's nickname for Edwards – 'Android'.

The song was added to the band's live set during the heavy touring schedule up to the end of the year. They would often walk onstage to the strains of Ice-T's 'Cop Killer' and cover The Clash's 'What's My Name?'. MTV Spain filmed the gig in Madrid.

Edwards was a shadow at the back of the stage. Dressed all in black he blended into the gloom and during some songs he was hardly glimpsed at all, but elsewhere he was still making waves. In 1994, *The Times* would feature a Caitlin Moran story about meeting Richey in Bournemouth during the autumn 1992 tour. Calling him 'the most untouchably beautiful person I have ever seen in my life', she wrote of him fussing around her and making her tea – ever the charming, polite, valley boy.

The year ended in controversy, with Nicky Wire shooting his mouth off again. An end-of-tour show at the Kilburn National saw Nicky Wire proclaim, 'In the season of goodwill, let's hope Michael Stipe goes the same way as Freddie Mercury.' The R.E.M. frontman had been the target of rumours that he had AIDS, which Mercury had died of complications from in November 1991. Richey Edwards did not comment publicly on the matter, instead offering his final public words of 1992 via his Christmas manifesto. This wasn't exactly filled with seasonal spirit: 'LIFE IS MEANINGLESS. THERE IS NO TRUE LOVE, JUST A FINE TUNED JEALOUSY . . . WE SIT IN STRAIGHT LINES, DO WHAT WE ARE TOLD, LIKE SEATS ON LOCKERBIE, DECK CHAIRS ON THE TITANIC. ALL ACTION IS FORCED. ALL REBELLION IS FAKE.' He was realising that stardom wasn't all that it was cracked up to be and that in many ways being in a band could be compared to any other job. You're told where to be and when, you do a shift, you do a tour, you move on, and you go home on your own. The adulation is for what you represent rather than what you actually are. The girls want Richey Edwards, pretty rock star. They don't even know Richey Edwards, human being. He knew that the next year was likely to be similar to the one just passed, and that the one after this could be much the same. Things weren't the way he had hoped they would be.

The Manics were already getting old. Richey Edwards knew that there was a danger that their fire could begin to die out. Where they used to argue about politics, sport, bands, films, books, anything, they now piled into the van wrapped in their world of Walkmans and handheld video consoles. As Edwards said, it was 'An existential nightmare!'

NOTHING TO CLING TO • 123

'Boredom is the only reason we exist and still exist,' he added. 'We still cannot learn how to enjoy ourselves.' He might not have realised it at the time, but he was actually speaking for himself more than the band as a whole. The others did learn to enjoy themselves, mainly by pursuing relationships and interests outside the band. Richey Edwards didn't, or couldn't, and that would lead to more problems down the line. He was already drinking more often. During the year he'd been asked if he would be bitter and twisted at the age of thirty-five if the Manics didn't work out. 'I've always been bitter and twisted,' he replied. 'It's not going to change with how old I am.'

# VIII

## THIS SECTION IS NOT CALLED FROM DESPAIR TO WHERE

*1993*

Some of Richey Edwards' favourite literary heroes were drunks. By 1993, Edwards was well on the way to joining them. Nicky Wire told *Melody Maker* quite bluntly that he'd seen his bandmate become an alcoholic over the past eighteen months. When Simon Price visited Edwards at the Hall Or Nothing offices in 1993, he was witness to Edwards drinking whisky from a glass being used as an ashtray; Edwards was so far gone that he was oblivious to the ash and knocked it back in one. Richey had steadily increased his consumption since the days of trying to get some sleep in Swansea. Now he drank to get to sleep, drank to avoid having to think about things too deeply, drank to fill time spent hanging around while on tour, drank to have the courage to get on stage every night. He wasn't usually a loud drunk, though.[23] 'I drink alone, which isn't maudlin,' he explained. 'I feel maudlin enough when I wake up in the morning anyway. I get in bed, drink vodka and flick channels. It sounds sad but it's the most pleasurable thing I can think of doing. And Tuesdays and Thursdays you've got *The Prisoner, If You See God, Tell Him* and *Top of the Pops*. I guess I drink three quarters of a bottle of vodka a day. I don't hate myself enough to be bombed out of my brain all day long. I just start at seven in the evening. I like four hours to pass slowly, till I feel my legs are dead and I can hardly move my head. It's a blur.'

Work on the songs for the Manics' second album had started during the previous summer at Outside Studios in Wales. The band had also recorded some demos at Kent's Impact Studios with Dave Eringa, and these sessions had gone so well that they asked Eringa to produce the album. In early January, the band rented a flat in Shepherd's Bush and commuted out for more demo sessions at the House in the Woods studio in Surrey, a Gothic manor that the band would record in again at a later date. The Sony bosses were unimpressed when the band chose the unknown 21-year-old producer, but the Manics were insistent: at the end of the month the sessions for the album proper were booked at the residential splendour of Berkshire's Hook End Manor, and Eringa got the job. Equipped with 48-track mixing facilities, a swimming pool and a gym, and set in luscious, landscaped grounds, this was a top-end set-up that left little change from £2,000 a day.

The band was keen to get the best out of the money being spent and utilise the expensive studio to its full potential. This approach is possibly why the album's songs suffered. Sometimes they used twenty-five microphones on the drums alone. Unlike on *Generation Terrorists* they actually played together in the studio (well, three of them did), rather than recording the individual parts alone and layering them together later. James Dean Bradfield was the driving force behind the album. When he wasn't singing his vocal parts alone in the dark, he worked long hours to push things along in the control room. Meanwhile, Richey Edwards spent his time at Hook Manor reading or laid out on his four-poster bed listening to Rod Stewart's *Every Picture Tells a Story* and drinking. He didn't suffer hangovers because he was drinking steadily all the time, getting ill only when he stopped. Each morning, he'd go for a swim and then work out in the gym. Despite his slight frame, he wanted to hone a textbook physique. He was somehow able to keep to his exercise regime on just one meal a day, usually a jacket potato and some grapes. He could achieve 1,500 sit-ups, and then lift some weights. Toning his body was another form of self-control, along with the restrained eating and the self-cutting. Despite his high intellect, he couldn't escape from the media-constructed image of beauty and body shape. Things did catch up with him eventually and when *Select*'s Andrew Collins visited the studio for an interview, Edwards passed out. He was, apparently, 'babbling to the end of the Smirnoff bottle'. 'Drink was his only recourse,' said Collins. 'It probably would have done him some good to have taken drugs. He never wanted to take E, hated the idea of it, he never wanted to take a drug that made him happy. He couldn't imagine anything worse than a drug that made everybody happy – he didn't think there was anything good in everybody being happy and thinking everyone was OK. He preferred the traditional route of drinking to dull the pain.'

'Ecstasy is too designed to make you happy,' said Edwards. 'People I know who've taken E just want to be friends with everybody. I've got so much more respect for people who stick a needle in their veins. Someone who's drunk a bottle of whisky is more fucked up than someone who's smoked a spliff. But if you're gonna do it, do it properly. Take smack.' Despite this bravado, there's little or no evidence, or even rumour, that Edwards ever followed his own advice. Any drugs he did take were generally prescribed and when he did try smoking a joint Nicky Wire refused to speak to his bandmate for several hours. The band's initial 'no drugs' rule had been pretty much kept to.

When the *Gold Against the Soul* sessions ended, the band insisted that Edwards book himself into a private health farm to sober up before the touring restarted. It was reported that this wasn't something Edwards was interested in doing and he was practically forced into going there.

Musically and aesthetically, *Gold Against the Soul* was a radical departure from the metal-tinged *Generation Terrorists*. The overt influence of Guns N' Roses was fading from the mix. The band's teenage influences were slowly being pushed aside, partly because they were growing up but also partly due to record company pressure that the band should move closer to rock's middle ground. Sony had invested a lot of money in signing the band, paying for the *Generation Terrorists* album and now funding the expensive sessions for a second album. They wanted some return on their money. The Manics' lives had changed so radically over the past two years that it was probably unrealistic to expect their music to stay the same. Some fans were bound to feel betrayed but this wasn't the same group that had first come up to London from Wales. The four small-town boys had grown worldy-wise in a hurry.

'It's definitely more personal,' said Edwards. 'With the first one, 'cos we'd wanted to be in a band so long we were really like hung up, really paranoid, wanted everything to be important, wanted everything to be like sound-bite type slogan. We were very influenced by William Burroughs, we didn't want anything to seem cinematic, we didn't want anything to really rhyme when you read the lyric sheet.'

The problem with *Gold Against the Soul* is that it didn't really challenge anyone or anything. Although their debut album had many faults, at least it was angry. For a band that had burst into the music press with a mega-attitude and lots to say, this new album had little to shout about. It was neither especially good nor especially bad. These different, older Manics were ostensibly dull. But at the time, Richey Edwards certainly thought they had made a progression. '[The album has] better songs all round, better sound,' he said. 'We'd been reading too much William Burroughs when we wrote the last album.' He went on to admit that there were lots of faults with *Generation Terrorists* as a lot of the songs had been written when they were quite young. They hadn't played in previous teenage bands to enable them to get the 'crap' out of their systems, so they were saddled with doing their growing up in public. Gone was most of the sound-bite, scattergun, sloganeering, and this had been replaced with middle-of-the-road safety.

All of the lyrics were credited as Wire–Edwards, but it was easy to see which ones Edwards had more input to. The album's opening track, 'Sleepflower', concerned his problems with getting to sleep, worrying about getting to sleep, sleeping pills, and the morning after. It was all there, wrapped up in James Dean Bradfield's heavy metal riffs. 'Sleep is constantly throughout every lyric I've written from the start,' said Edwards. 'It's a big thing for me because I'm scared to go to sleep because the things I get in my head, I don't like. That's the reason I ever started drinking, to knock me out. I've tried sleeping tablets, but I don't really like them. I like the effect of drinking. I can get a blank sleep, be out for five or six hours and wake up and then do my job.'

Two singles quickly followed – 'From Despair to Where' and 'La Tristesse Durera'. Although Edwards and Wire often worked together on the same lyric, the words of 'From Despair to Where' indicate Edwards writing alone on his bed, revealing that 'there's nothing nice in my head / the adult world took it all away'. The song follows the grunge template of a quiet opening verse that explodes into a loud guitar-driven chorus, giving the song an anthemic quality before the strings and heavy keyboards kick in. 'From Despair to Where' is unique in the Manics' catalogue: Richey Edwards actually played, briefly, on the recording. When the basic track had been put down, Bradfield got Edwards into the studio to add a bit of trashed background guitar work.[24] 'We cleared everyone out and it was just me and Richey and he did pretty well,' recalled Dave Eringa. 'He was nervous and he was like, "Oh, we're going to be here all night, Dave", but he just played it. No one laughed at him. Except Richey at himself, of course.' If nothing else, Edwards could see the funny side of his musical limitations. 'La Tristesse Durera (Scream to a Sigh)' came from Nicky Wire's reading of Vincent van Gogh's suicide letter, in which the painter wrote 'The sadness will last forever.' Set to a gentle Madchester beat, the song tells of growing old from the perspective of an elderly war veteran.

'Yourself' again addresses the question of being able to sleep and being in an 'alcoholic haze' and allows James Dean Bradfield to show off his growing vocal maturity.

'Life Becoming a Landslide' starts off with a woman's perspective of childbirth and progresses to Edwards' long-held view that growing up is the worst thing that happened to anyone – 'I don't wanna be a man' – then flashes back to Edwards' unhappy childhood encounter with pornography, and confirms his view that 'There is no true love.'

'Roses in the Hospital', as many pointed out, was very close to being a cover version of David Bowie's 'Sound and Vision'. There are mentions of scratches on skin and the line 'Stub cigarettes out on my arm'. The song's title was picked out from one of the band's favourite films, *Times Square*.[25]

Elsewhere on the album, 'Symphony of Tourette' could be a sly admission from Nicky Wire, while the title track ends proceedings with a mixture of Mudhoney (well, this *was* 1993) and Black Sabbath.

Overall, the LP jettisoned the band's political rantings and attempted to focus in on something more personal: self-loathing and disgust with the world at large. These were sentiments held close to Richey Edwards' heart. Rather than expressing political opinions, he had become comfortable writing about his own hang-ups and problems. The album was more personal than the Manics' debut, but its personal writing was on the edge and made for uncomfortable listening for those who concentrated on the words. These words were gradually taking more prominence in Edwards' day-to-day world. On the attached press release, Richey wrote that he wanted 'to piss on the floor of Seattle', but in reality the album seemed to be moving towards that sound.

Japanese photographer Mitch Ikeda designed the unusual sleeve image, based on Yukio Mishima's *Killed By Roses*. The packaging contained just one piece of literature, in contrast to the eighteen quotes used on *Generation Terrorists*. The band chose Primo Levi's poem 'Song of Those Who Died in Vain'[26] for the inner sleeve. Obtaining permission to use this delayed the release date by four weeks. Sony were much more careful about this kind of thing after the problems with 'You Love Us' on Heavenly. The band portraits for the artwork were virtually caricatures; James Dean Bradfield in full scream, clenching his fingers, Sean Moore sitting quietly in a corner, Nicky Wire doing his best Sid Vicious impersonations and Richey Edwards slumped in the corner of a bathroom – gazing dejectedly into a mirror, with some Polaroid photographs scattered by his side.

The album entered the UK Top 10, peaking at number eight, but it wasn't helped particularly by its reviews. 'Ultimately, one suspects that the Manic Street Preachers will always struggle to write the songs to match their song-titles,' wrote Keith Cameron in *Vox* (rating: '6/10'). Q magazine, in the days before it was all readers' questions and lists, feature-reviewed the album alongside The Smashing Pumpkins' *Siamese Dream* and U2's *Zooropa* (both of which the magazine liked) and Paul Rodgers' *Muddy Waters Blues*, which was awarded two out of four stars – the same mark Peter Kane gave to *Gold Against the Soul*. Right from the off it was a case of their mouthy past coming back to bite them. 'One album too many for Manic Street Preachers?' *Q* asked. The answer seemed to come back as a resounding 'Yes': ' . . . the cupboard looks to be already distressingly bare,' wrote Kane, adding that the album represented the 'sounds of a band digging in for a long-term career rather than knocking over a few of the statues. When will they ever learn?' Writing for *Select*, Stuart Maconie was more enthusiastic and gave the album a score of '4/5' (let's hope it wasn't him that came up with the headline 'Dai Harder!'), but even he couldn't help mentioning the one-album-then-split routine: 'They said they would split up after one record. They were lying. Good.'

The TV Tour to promote *Gold Against the Soul* began in May 1993. The band's new image was revealed during an appearance on *The Beat*. James Dean Bradfield was sporting a beret/cap, white T-shirt and leather coat, which, with his semi-designer stubble, left him looking like a combination of Bruce Springsteen circa 1975 and a thinner, angrier Zucchero. Sean Moore now had long hair and shades, possibly to hide his eyes from the bad shirt he was wearing, while Nicky Wire wore a white Marilyn Monroe T-shirt and Cobain shades. Richey Edwards probably looked the coolest, which wasn't difficult, with his Brian Jones haircut and open shirt over a black vest. During 'Yourself', he crouched by the back of the set – seemingly with nothing to add – but joined in a with bit of strumming later on. The accompanying interview segment got the on-screen captions of Richey James and Nicky Wire the wrong way around. This was a sure sign that the production crew didn't even know who was who, and signalled the distance the band still had to go to be famous.

These were the days when no TV request would be turned down by the Manics. The ITV children's show *Gimme 5* saw them miming 'From Despair to Where' to a studio of twelve-year-olds and a puppet sheep. Saturday morning magazine show *The Ozone* sent Philippa Forrester to 'discover if the Manic Street Preachers are the most depressed band in the charts'.

'Are you a glum lot?' she asked, getting straight to the point. 'The charts are always full of quite happy, bouncy songs, it's good that people can go out and buy a song that they can get a bit maudlin to,' explained Richey. On *Entertainment UK*, he was asked about the '4REAL' incident yet again, more than two years after the event. The initial excitement of being in a band had well and truly dissipated. Now, it was in danger of becoming just another job. 'The rewards for what we do are nothing,' said Edwards. 'We get to do things like shopping and buy stupid little things, but tomorrow morning we will be bored again. When we first got signed, it was fucking heaven on earth. We thought we were never gonna have two boring seconds again, and it's just not true.'

The routine was set to continue for the foreseeable future: a repeated cycle of touring-recording-promoting-interviewing-touring. The post-album routine was already becoming dull for Richey. Once he'd done something, he wasn't likely to enjoy being put through it again. He was of the view that human nature tended towards reducing everything in life to a routine, and that there was no escape.

The roller coaster started again when *Gold Against the Soul* was released on 20 June. Three days later, the band played a warm-up gig at the Marquee in London and the tour proper started in Leeds on 1 July. The initial summer dates had the Manics headlining a triple bill with Credit To The Nation and Blaggers I.T.A. The controversy started on the first night and – for a change – the Manics weren't directly involved. The two support bands had been hand-picked by the Manics to add an exciting, uncompromising edge to the shows. Unfortunately this boiled over after the Leeds show when a *Melody Maker* journalist was injured after a scuffle with Matt (who was supposedly too cool to have a surname) from Blaggers I.T.A., resulting in some facial injuries.[27] The *Maker* and *NME* stood by their man while the Manics decided not to chuck the band off the tour. Despite keeping Blaggers I.T.A. on the tour, Richey Edwards made his feelings public. 'Morally, it was indefensible,' he said. 'We've had more than our fair share of bad press and stitch-up jobs but no matter what was printed about us, we'd never resort to smacking someone in the face. Blaggers say they want to put the Nazis out of business but I can't think of anything more fascist than using physical violence to intimidate people whose viewpoint differs from yours.

'We gave it a lot of thought and decided that sacking them would in itself be a fascist action. We don't agree with Blaggers, we don't particularly like Blaggers, but we'd be hypocrites if we censored them.'

During the summer, the Manics had more important worries on their mind. Philip Hall had been diagnosed with cancer back in 1992 and now he was undergoing chemotherapy at London's Cromwell Hospital. The band carried on: Dave Eringa joined up to play keyboards on the road and flesh out their sound. Yet despite often having eleven singles within the set-list, they weren't selling out the modest-sized venues. Richey Edwards was certainly not overjoyed to be touring again, especially given that the band was playing another series of festivals over the summer. When asked if he was happy to be back on the road, he answered, 'Er, no.' When *Kerrang!* asked 'What's your favourite moment onstage?' he replied, 'When we walk off.' His growing dislike of touring was exacerbated by playing at festivals. 'We never really look forward to the festivals, just because you never know what it's gonna sound like or what it's gonna be like,' he said. 'You know you get no sound-check, so you've got no idea what it's gonna be like.'

Edwards, like the rest of the band and crew, was given a tour itinery that mapped out the immediate future of his life in segments comprising a few weeks and often in minute detail. The bound, A5 booklet was filled with all the details that the band and crew would need and punctuated with *Far Side* cartoons, letters clipped from newspapers and assorted photocopied ephemera. On the day of the Leeds-to-Manchester leg, the quote of the day was 'Grim? Grim? It's so bad up here they don't even bother begging.' Additional information on the gig at Manchester read,

'Manchester is now renowned for being such a lovely safe place to be, so make sure you leave equipment unattended outside, have lots of money stuffed in your pockets and of course leave the bus unlocked. Flak jackets are available from the Students Union to go to the bus after dark.' Later on, the itinerary informed them, the band would be staying at the Embassy Hotel on London's Bayswater Road. This became the first of several visits there.

The Heineken Festival in Swansea's Singleton Park on 7 August could have been a triumphant homecoming. It was within walking distance of Richey's old student digs, but the reality was that free beer had been given out by the sponsors to the 10,000-plus crowd all day and by the time the Manics came on, the audience was a seething mass of alcohol-fuelled chaos. The stage was littered with broken glass, there was fighting in the crowd and a general feeling of tension and unease. It wasn't quite Altamont, but it felt nasty nonetheless. It didn't take long for Nicky Wire to get hit on the head with a glass bottle and need to be taken offstage for treatment. Tensions continued with the band threatening to pull out completely, but their angst-ridden, venomous set ended with Richey climbing the speaker stack, putting his arms out either side like a Christ figure and diving into the crowd. 'Cans are easy. I've learnt to hit them with my guitar,' said Edwards afterwards about the perils of projectile-dodging on stage. 'And plastic glasses I can catch in my mouth. But bottles are something else. In a way I wish they'd hit me instead of one of the musicians . . . I don't expect roses and petals at my feet, but the amount of grief we get here is non-stop. Anything from Welsh bands complaining about us betraying Wales by not singing in Welsh, to gangs of four blokes in Cardiff pouring lager over me and saying, "What are you going to do about that?" Tom Jones doesn't get it!'

Other festivals passed without any trouble before the band took part in a surprise support act to Bon Jovi at the mammoth Milton Keynes Bowl natural amphitheatre. 'It's not the most obvious support in rock 'n' roll history, is it?' Richey told Hot Press. 'We always enjoy a challenge and playing a gig where ninety-five per cent of the crowd probably hate your guts has a perverse appeal.' It also paid a good amount of appearance money, too. The two shows, on 18 and 19 September, also included ageing dreadlocked punk Billy Idol and soft-rockers Little Angels playing to the crowd of sixty thousand per night. As the first band on stage at three p.m., in broad daylight, it was always going to be difficult for the Manics, but they got virtually no reaction from the crowd and had finished their day's work by four p.m. Once offstage, Richey started downing pints of vodka and tonic and decided it would be a good idea to head out into the crowd to watch Billy Idol, where he was immediately surrounded for autographs. He did manage to stay and watch the show, punching the air to Idol's set in a drunken haze. Later on, Jon Bon Jovi offered a badly rehearsed 'thank you' to the support acts that he'd obviously not watched or even had the decency to check the names of, and he thanked the 'Maniacs' for opening the show. 'When you've agreed to do a gig it almost seems pointless to rebel,' said Edwards. 'We did agree, and played to 120,000 people who didn't want to know who we are or what we're supposed to be. But just seeing our "All Rock 'N' Roll Is Homosexual" T-shirt on a board made it all worthwhile!'

At the end of the month, Richey took the unusual step of donning a suit and tie. The occasion was Nicky Wire's wedding as he tied the knot with long-time girlfriend Rachel. Sean Moore had moved to Bristol with his girlfriend, and James Dean Bradfield was now spending much of his free time in London. Things weren't how they used to be. Life was moving on and changing. Richey was unable to adapt to this. He did have a kind-of-girlfriend, though. She has only ever been referred to as 'Jo'. In his book on the Manics, *Everything*, Simon Price described her as a 'glamorous, stunning model-type from London'. Richey said she was the only person he'd slept with in 1993, 'the one person I've found attractive for two years. But I barely see her and we just talk.' Later, he'd say that he had only kissed her 'once or twice'.

In the mini-diary he kept for *Select* during the *Generation Terrorists* sessions, Edwards was bothered by things that would hardly register with most people. After reading the Sunday papers he wrote, 'Debbie Lang's impeccable boyfriend heritage – David

Bowie. David Essex. Andy Summers. Roger Taylor – is marred by
Climie Fucking Fisher. All this upsets me. Big Time.' Why would the
boyfriend of someone he'd never met be so upsetting? He added
that 'Today I would rather fall in love with a washing machine
than a woman.'

●

In October, the band was back on the road yet again – this time, to
Japan for an exhausting thirteen shows in sixteen days. While the
Far East might have been one of the places that Richey was more
interested in visiting, he was still unhappy with touring in general.
His argument was that he never got the time to really experience any
of the places they were travelling through. 'I never find it exciting
to go anywhere,' he said. 'You get much more true information from
literature than from travelling. Like, if I want to know about France,
I'll buy the book . . . I don't know if that makes me a moron.'

In Japan, the promotional posters for *Gold Against the Soul* and
the tour all focused on Richey. Rather than a band photograph,
the posters were grainy black-and-white portraits of Richey
alone in head-and-shoulder side-profile. As became widespread
throughout the Far East, he was the main focus of fans' attentions
and hero worship. In Japan, he was given a 'suicide doll' with a
note asking when he was going to kill himself.

Martin Hall joined the tour of Japan and witnessed the latest
in Richey's growing list of vices – smoking. Although he'd only
started in September he was already up to a fifty-a-day habit,
saying that when he liked to do something, he did it a lot. He was
also still cutting himself as much as ever, as evidenced on Japanese
TV. 'Richey's a private partier,' said Martin Hall. 'He parties just
as hard – but alone, with a bottle of vodka and a razor blade! It's
not the kind of party you want to be invited to.' The band didn't
really know how to handle the growing list of Edwards' 'hobbies'.
It's thought that they had never really confronted him about his
cutting, preferring to turn a blind eye – after all, it seemed to
help him deal with stress and calm him down. The drinking was
something they'd all done to excess at one period or another and
smoking wasn't really a problem apart from Nicky Wire making an

issue of theatrically wafting away the smoke if Edwards came too close. Edwards had always been skinny and so any further weight loss wasn't really noticed.

The eastern tour was covered on Japanese TV with Richey being interviewed in his hotel room. Sitting on his bed, wearing a grey beret, his exposed arms displayed horrendous scars, cuts and burns – especially on his left forearm – and he wore a bandage on his right wrist. His heavy, dark mascara gave him a haunted look and he'd taken to wearing rock-star Converse sneakers.

Now, my understanding of Japanese is pretty much non-existent, but the clean-cut young man and woman introducing the shows were very enthusiastic and held up a large stack of letters that seemed to confirm the Manics' high standing in Japan. They read out important-sounding letters and postcards about the band. Then suddenly, inexplicably, the girl started talking in English and introduced the band playing live in a small club. Footage of them playing 'From Despair to Where' follows, and the whole place – not just the first few rows – was the stereotypical single mass of jumping bodies with hands in the air. Other clips included the machine-gun strobes of 'Sleepflower', while the girls squashed down at the front knew all the words to 'You Love Us'. The end of the concert sees Richey quietly watching Nicky Wire strip off his shirt and climb on top of James Dean Bradfield's shoulders. As his two bandmates totter around the stage, Edwards rips off his guitar and really launches himself into the audience. It takes four security men to untangle and haul him back out.

Richey and Nicky were interviewed in the foyer of the empty club at the end of the tour. After long questions in Japanese the translations for the boys were edited out and we get to see their English replies with Japanese subtitles on the screen. For English-speakers, it was a case of trying to decipher what the question had been – almost like the Two Ronnies' *Mastermind* sketch. We get to hear that Richey thinks there is no real *reason* to be unhappy in the First World, but there's a feeling that something is missing from his life. Richey chain-smokes through the interviews, and at one point he hitches up his sleeve to reveal a mass of fresh cigarette burns. He had taken to stubbing them out on his arm as well as cutting himself. He gladly proves that he knows the words for scars and burns in Japanese. He explains that the highlight of the tour for him was a visit to the Hiroshima peace memorial and that he thinks 'Japan has the most discipline of any country in the western world [sic]' as he lights up about his fourth cigarette of the interview. When asked to sign off to the camera he says, 'Give thanks and praises to the most high, love Richey.'

Back in Europe, the band visited the concentration camps at Belsen and Dachau on their days off. For Richey, having studied the Holocaust at university, these were especially moving visits. For the rest of the tour he went through a 'bad period', drinking and cutting more than ever. He was said to be necking vast amounts of Johnnie Walker whisky during the day. When they got back to the UK, the band insisted that he check into a health farm again. This was getting repetitious, but no one was sensing any greater danger as yet.

A couple of shows were still to be played before Christmas. On 7 December, the Manics were in Lisbon when they heard the devastating news that Philip Hall had died after a two-year battle against cancer. The rest of the band's 1993 arrangements were cancelled and they flew back to the UK.

'I phoned Hall Or Nothing to check if it would be OK to play a Manics track dedicated to Philip on that night's *Evening Session*,' recalled Steve Lamacq. 'An hour or so later I got a call back from Nicky Wire and we went ahead with a short tribute on the programme.'

Philip Hall's funeral was held on 14 December 1993. This was the first funeral that Nicky Wire had ever been to. Richey Edwards took it all very badly. At the time it was a tragic event, but with hindsight it was a tragic event that signalled the start of a traumatic twelve months for the band – and for Richey in particular. With the loss of Philip Hall, things would never be the same again.

*T*he *Deer Hunter* won five Oscars in 1978. It was more than just another film about Vietnam and the problems of coming home after the war. It was a film that confronted suicide and mental illness. The movie starred Robert De Niro – one of Richey Edwards' key icons, especially after the actor's performance in *Taxi Driver*. *The Deer Hunter* has many memorable scenes, one of the most famous of which depicts a game of Russian roulette played in Saigon. The set-piece – a steeply seated arena inside an old warehouse filled with sweaty men screaming and waving fistfuls of bank notes as the two 'contestants' sit face-to-face across a small wooden table – has been etched into pop culture to the extent that a chocolate manufacturer used it as the basis for an expensive advertising campaign.

The first mention of Russian roulette in the film occurs when the Americans are captured and forced to play it in a waterside hut. After they escape, Christopher Walken's character Nick decides to stay in the city and earn vast amounts of money by managing to stay alive in the Russian roulette circuit. When De Niro's character, Michael, returns from America to find him, Nick's mind has gone AWOL, and he can only concentrate on the game. While Michael watches, his friend's luck finally runs out. These sequences were actually filmed in the notorious Pat Pong district of Bangkok, an area said to have a vice for every taste.

In 1994, the Manics visited Bangkok. With a flotilla of journalists in tow, whacking their expenses on the plastic, Richey Edwards held court in Pat Pong at the centre of the red light district. Among the middle-aged businessmen, sex tourists and curious couples,

Edwards then vanished into the night, returning with tales of young prostitutes and hand jobs. Momentarily, he had lost sight of the big picture and concentrated on a different game. Luckily, for now, he was back in reality, having avoided being strung out for top tourist dollars or being accosted by ladyboys. His own private hell was only weeks away, this dip into the dark side of life an indication of what might lie ahead.

# IX

## BANGKOK

*January to June 1994*

Like many cities with riverside areas or docks, Cardiff started regenerating its run-down waterside areas in the early 1990s. Old mills and warehouses were swiftly converted into wine bars and blocks of apartments for yuppies (they still used that word back then). Other buildings were torn down and new developments shot up. Brigades of high-rise cranes provided a new cityscape like an advancing army of H. G. Wells' Tripods. Back in 1994, these new developments seemed like the future of modern urban living. Atlantic Wharf is a large development in Cardiff comprising living accommodation, business premises and bars/restaurants. Early in the year Richey Edwards and Nicky Wire were having a drive around the new developments, out of curiosity more than anything else, but before they left Richey had decided on a new third-floor apartment almost as an impulse buy in the way most people would purchase a book or a new coat. Wire had been living with his in-laws until buying a house when he had married in the previous autumn. Edwards had been in a similar position. 'I lived with my parents until I was twenty-five,' said Edwards. 'I was never bothered about being a homeowner or anything like that. I saw my flat one day, and I bought it the next, just like that. I hadn't thought about it before. I was just passing by, and Nick said, "Oh, let's go and have a look at these", and I thought, "This is all right." I asked her how much it was, she told me, so I said, "I'll buy it." And I just moved in. I didn't really know what to do, I just paid the bills."

Photos of Richey in his apartment show a taste in interiors that probably indicates someone else bought his furniture for him, too. The floral sofas certainly aren't the kind of thing a mid-twenties male in a rock band would be assumed to buy. His walls were plain magnolia, although later he would decorate them with ever more dense collages and pictures. A wall of books and CDs framed a signed picture mount of Elizabeth Taylor, while another wall featured a large poster for *Apocalypse Now*.

During one of my own South Wales visits I checked into the hotel across the road from Atlantic Wharf. I sat on my bed, laptop on lap, looking at Edwards' old flat. He lived in part of the Admiral's development with each building getting the name of a historic seafarer: Jellicoe, Anson, Nelson, Keyes and Howard. Each block has its own keypad entry system. You can't even buzz the occupants of a particular flat, so I went for a walk around instead. I found the spot where, crouching by the waterside, Richey had his photo taken. The whole area now seems to be a little bit run down. The 1994 new-builds were made to look like old waterside buildings, but it's all fake: you'd find the same glass and plastic in Liverpool, London, Dublin and elsewhere.

After first moving in, Edwards didn't have a telephone installed for several months. He used the apartment and its views of the water for solitude. It was a place where he could quietly read and drink. 'I enjoy being away from people,' he told *Raw Power* magazine in early 1994. Occasionally he'd go down to the quayside and feed the birds. Despite having a fitted kitchen, he didn't figure out how to use the washing machine. Instead, he drove his laundry to Blackwood once a week for his mother to wash.

The loss of Philip Hall hung heavy over the band, and Richey in particular took it very hard. 'The last time I interviewed Richey I did see a huge deterioration in him,' recalls writer and broadcaster Tania Alexander. 'It was shortly after the death of Philip Hall, and Richey just seemed as though he was trying to grin and bear his way through it all. He looked really terrible, but he was still so incredibly polite.'

Things were up and down, however, and *Kerrang!* writer Paul

Elliott found Richey on good form later in the year. 'The last time I bumped into Richey was at a friend's wedding in 1994,' he says. 'He was there with his friend and press officer Gillian Porter. I remember becoming involved in a lengthy argument with him regarding the coverage of rapper Snoop Dogg in the UK music press. I couldn't help feeling that Richey enjoyed playing devil's advocate in the discussion, gently stoking up the argument, although it never became too heated. The discussion ended when a four-year-old girl interrupted us, looking for her mother. This is my last memory of Richey – a rock star you could invite to your wedding. There aren't many of those.'

It was during the first half of 1994 that Steve Gatehouse ran into Richey Edwards for the first time in about four years. 'My dad had just died and that seemed much more important than petty squabbles,' he says. 'Richey was always asking how I was coping and at the time I thought this was partly due to embarrassment on his part – the successful pop star meeting the grieving son. I now wonder if his questions were partly about how to cope with the depression that he was also enduring.' The two soon hooked up their old friendship and had a few nights out together. 'One incident I remember seemed to sum up the disillusion he was feeling with pop stardom,' says Gatehouse. 'We were leaving Metros club in Cardiff when a girl recognised him and literally begged him to take her home. She said he could do anything to her, it didn't matter how he treated her. It was one of the saddest things I've ever witnessed and Richey looked aghast. It exemplified what he'd told me earlier about groupies. At first, it seemed fun but then the levels that girls would stoop to just seemed pathetic, especially to someone who'd always respected women so much.'

These stories neatly encapsulate Richey Edwards. Someone who was upset with life, but who would just as soon enquire about someone else's problems. Someone who would rather try to grin and bear it, than cause a scene. Someone who was incredibly polite and reserved, despite having strong opinions on many topics. The depths that humanity could stoop to – whether it be a girl offering him her body in a nightclub or a bloody massacre in some far away country – saddened him deeply. For now, however, he had to put that behind him as the Manics were heading out on tour again at the start of 1994. The grinding routine was starting up yet again. Alongside The Wildhearts, Compulsion and Eve's Plum, they had sped through Leicester, Southampton, Brixton, Bristol, Hull, Middlesbrough, Glasgow, Liverpool, Cardiff and Sheffield by the first week of February. Then, during a four-week break, Richey finished working on the series of lyrics that would define the band's next album and, to many people, his own legacy.

While previous albums had seen writing duties shared fairly evenly between Edwards and Nicky Wire, this time Edwards had been prolific and would be responsible for around three-quarters of the next album. Wire, newly married and having just bought his first house, was in a 'happy place'. 'The references he was coming up with I can't pretend to know half of them,' said Wire. 'At the time he was reading five books a week. I was still stuck on Fred Truman's autobiography. I just wasn't on my game so much.' As usual, Edwards had distributed his writing to Moore and Bradfield so that they could work on the music before the sessions began. They were surprised and confused by some of the writing put before them. 'I remember getting the lyrics to "Yes",' said Bradfield, 'and thinking, "You crazy fucker, how do you expect me to write music to this?"' The singer had to work out ways of getting inside Edwards' head. Some of the words were autobiographical and some were written as Edwards seeing things through someone else's eyes, making it a step more difficult.

Before getting really stuck into the new album the band played a one-off benefit show at London's Clapham Grand for Cancer Research in memory of Philip Hall. The Pogues provided the support, as they were long-time friends of the Halls. The show was obviously an emotional one, coming just three months after their manager's death, and this seemed to energise the band. Richey Edwards gave it his all, flailing boisterously around his side of the stage, jumping up on the drum riser, his single earring flapping wildly about. When Suede's Bernard Butler joined the band for three songs, the presence of an extremely gifted young guitarist only highlighted the deficiencies in Richey Edwards' own playing. But the show was considered a huge success in that it raised £20,000 for Cancer Research.

•

Soundspace studios were located in Cardiff's red light district, just half a mile from Richey Edwards' flat. Having turned down the opportunity to record in Barbados, they chose the £50-a-day studio that they had previously used for demos and 'The Theme from M\*A\*S\*H'. James Dean Bradfield described the thinking as being 'method recording', as opposed to 'method acting', in the hope that the atmosphere of the very basic studio and its seedy location would transfer into the music they were recording there. There were no visits from the record company or management. The band was taking back control of their own destiny and self-producing the sessions. No one was pressurising them into doing anything they didn't want to do, and the studios were so bare that there were few distractions. They could slip in and out of the studio with parkas pulled up in the driving rain, which seemed to stay for the duration. Richey wanted to rewrite the Ten Commandments in relation to the dirty businessmen and prostitutes he saw going about their daily routines. How hypocritical would this turn out to be in light of events later in the year? For three of the band, the sessions were almost a nine-to-five routine: Sean Moore and Nicky Wire would go home to their women after being dropped off by Richey at the station. Edwards saw the happiness that his bandmates and the Halls had enjoyed by being in stable relationships, and seemed to equate that with the only way to be a happy, fulfilled adult. He told Terri Hall that he'd be married by the end of the year and that he would then be happy. She pointed out that he didn't even have a girlfriend yet, let alone a fiancée.

After the others had gone home, James Dean Bradfield spent additional hours in the studio with engineer Alex Silva. The atmosphere around the actual studios, the oppressive nature of the songs,[28] and things happening outside the band made the experience a potentially draining and difficult one. The first day of recording was 14 February – Valentine's Day – and after completing a new song about a young girl wasting away – '4st 7lb' – James Dean Bradfield bumped into his ex-girlfriend (she'd recently dumped him). He'd also found out that his mother had cancer. 'We started writing it last summer [1993] and some of the early songs were written quite a while ago,' said Richey Edwards after the sessions were completed. 'I think it was a difficult time for everybody really. There was lots of things happening outside the band, personally. But I think it's our most complete album, by a long way.'

The music that was going to influence the band's thinking for the new record was different to what it had been in the previous few years. They went back to the music of their youth and spent time listening to the post-punk of Wire, Magazine, The Skids, PiL, Gang Of Four, and – most importantly for Richey Edwards – Joy Division. Edwards had also been listening to a lot of Nirvana, including their most recent album, *In Utero*.

On some days Richey would walk into the studios at around lunchtime, often having already started drinking. He would lie down for a sleep before wandering off for a walk in the afternoon. Having passed the lyrics over to his bandmates, he once again had little input into the rest of the process. He made himself feel a little more involved by driving some of the others around, a throwback to the days before he joined the band. Sometimes, when Wire and Moore had departed, he would head out into Cardiff for the night with Bradfield. '[We'd] have a really good drink and stuff, go to the dodgy disco, and we'd have a good laugh,' says the singer. 'A bit of pullage, all that kind of stuff. Try and get girls. Really ordinary things.'

At the time of recording the album, which was to be called *The Holy Bible*, the Manics were a long way from the high targets that they'd initially set out with. With singles charting lower than they had hoped and a growing backlash against some of the band's more outrageous statements, any failure with the next album might condemn them to being seen as little more than a cult band. How were they ever going to sell sixteen million albums with Britpop about to wash away everything in its path?

'I think we did it badly in that we alienated a massive record-buying public before we even had a record in the fucking shops,'

Climbing trees in the 1970s; Richey Edwards' childhood would hold his favourite memories (*Wales News and Pictures*)

Richey saw his 2:1 degree as being his first academic 'failure' (*Wales News and Pictures*)

Richey, in his Bunnymen phase, tries to get Snoopy to focus on the camera (*Wales News and Pictures*)

The look with which the Manics
burst into the spotlight: white
jeans and stencilled slogans
(*Retna*)

Never one to be afraid of going
against the grain of fashion, here
Richey sports the Val Doonican
look in 1994 (*Tom Sheehan*)

Posing in the Parisian catacombs in 1994 (*Tom Sheehan*)

Making a statement '4REAL' in
Norwich, May 1991 (*Ed Sirrs Retna*)

The Glamour Twins show off
love-bites and slogans; Richey
forgot he was looking in a mirror
when he carved 'HIV' into his chest
(*Kevin Cummins*)

Backstage in the early 1990s
(*Ed Sirrs Retna*)

Richey, plastered with
Marilyn, carried his own cross
(*Kevin Cummins*)

Ready to conquer the world in white jeans and leopard print (*Retna*)

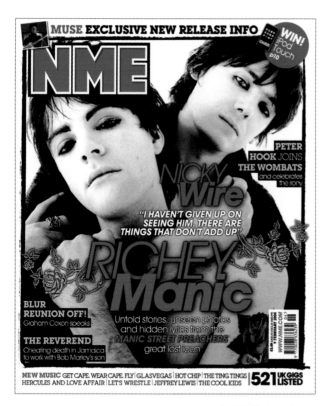

Cover stars again
(*NME/IPC+ Syndication*)

Though his guitar playing
was questionable, Richey
always *looked* like he
could play (*Retna*)

Richey wearing his war paint on
stage, Glastonbury, June 1994
(*Getty*)

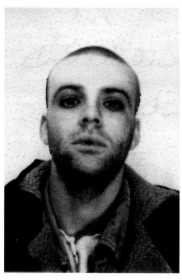

Shaven-headed and looking
as he did when he walked
out in February 1995

admitted Richey Edwards. 'There's a certain type of indie fan who was going, "I'm not buying their records, they're cunts." We can really understand that.' They were also quick to disown their previous album. 'The others mightn't necessarily agree,' said Bradfield, 'but I thought a lot of *Gold Against the Soul* was shit. We were under enormous pressure – both internally and externally – to produce a big hit album and allowed ourselves to become self-indulgent. Most of the songs were based round the theme of lost innocence and as that's precisely what we were experiencing at the time, we tended to look inwards rather than outwards.

'I don't agree that we turned into Guns N' Roses but we were listening to too much classic rock and those influences didn't sit comfortably with what we'd done before. *The Holy Bible* took four weeks as opposed to six months to record and the stuff that we were playing on the studio hi-fi was The Clash and Joy Division. That's more where we're coming from.'

As the sessions drew to a close and mixing began, the band set up meetings with journalists and photographers. James Dean Bradfield was really pleased with what they'd achieved, and thought that, 'If this is our last album it's a fucking brilliant album to finish on.'

While the band were partaking in a photo session on London's Fulham Road, Richey Edwards was filling in a questionnaire for *DV8* magazine. 'Self-mutilation is a very different issue to suicide,' he wrote. 'It is a controlled pain personal to you, allowing you to live/exist to some degree.' When one question asked what he would say to the next inhabitants of the world he replied, 'I'd cut off my cock, nail it to the wall with a message. "If you can live without this you might do a better job than humanity."'

The mixing of the *Holy Bible* tapes took place at the Britannia Row Studios in Islington, where, in 1980, Joy Division had recorded *Closer*, an album that had been part of the sonic backdrop to the Manics' recordings that spring. After the *Closer* sessions, Curtis was suffering epilepsy seizures and a lack of sleep. These problems were affecting his on-stage performance and he made a drug-overdose suicide attempt on 7 April 1980. Several Joy Division shows were cancelled while Curtis recovered before a planned trip to the United States that May. Curtis pretended to be looking forward to the trip, but the day before he was due to leave he returned home to Macclesfield. On 18 May, he hanged himself.

While Richey was sitting in on the *Holy Bible* mixing sessions at Britannia he heard the news that another of his musical heroes, Kurt Cobain, had killed himself in Seattle. When asked about it for the *NME*, Nicky Wire replied, 'I find the idea of him taking his own life frighteningly powerful. I've always been a sucker for that.' The band would cover Nirvana's 'Pennyroyal Tea' at festivals that summer. For Richey Edwards, it was the latest in a list of depressing events. After the death of Philip Hall, he'd also heard that an old university friend, Nigel, had committed suicide. Now, it was Cobain. The previous year he'd been upset at the death of actor River Phoenix and had told a story about hearing the news on the car radio. Apparently he'd been so shocked and upset that he'd almost crashed his car into a ditch.

With these problems lingering in the background, Richey began exhibiting ever more unusual behaviour. As a dedicated dog lover, his comments about animal testing were surprising to say the least. The sensational headline of 'I Don't Care If Chemists Slaughter 10,000 Beagles!' greeted the readers of *Metal Hammer*. 'I've never really understood our fans, to be perfectly honest,' he ranted. 'Even the ones that have been seeing us at our earliest gigs. They've got very strange views. They go on about vivisection and fox hunting and I don't give a fuck about that! I'm quite happy for every beagle in the land to be killed. Man is the dominant animal, we are part of nature just like everything else, and if it's [not] for something as petty as eyeliner or hairspray then that sacrifice is worth it.' With his beloved dog Snoopy now suffering through signs of extreme old age, these were strange comments indeed.

Around this time he'd become friendly with the journalist Emma Forrest. 'The reason he liked hanging out with me was because I was young and he thought of me as non-sexual,' says Forrest. 'But I was starting to feel sexual, so to be around this beautiful man who I know had absolutely no interest in me was just so tortuous.

I did stay up all night talking to him, or slept at his hotel room, but again these were entirely non-sexual things. I was learning from the wise master, how to be a teenager – how to be miserable and self-loathing, how to be totally selfish and self-obsessed.

'I remember seeing all these fresh cuts all over his arms. He was always so flip about them, almost boastful. And like a retarded teenager, I said, "Wow, those are so cool!" And he was so angry. That night, he was so drunk that I think I saw a level of honesty I never saw before or after. He said, "That is not cool. It's pathetic." Actually, after that, we never had any profound interaction. Maybe it's because I'd seen behind the curtain.'

Before the night described above, Forrest and Edwards were invited by Julie Burchill to a dinner with American writer Douglas Coupland. Edwards arrived at Burchill's house wearing a pink T-shirt with 'Fairy' written across the chest. Edwards asked Coupland who his favourite writer was. When he got the answer, 'Joan Didion', he was upset because he didn't know who she was. When the party moved to the Groucho Club, Coupland asked Richey, 'So what do you do then? Are you part of Generation X?' Richey was reported to have shunned the question and made a show of turning his chair around so that his back faced the Canadian. He later told Nicky Wire that he thought Coupland 'was a complete fuckwit. I hated him. I thought he was empty and fucking thick.' I don't think he told Wire that he'd never heard of Coupland's favourite writer, though.

•

Reserved, monarchist Thailand was not a place you might expect to embrace the Manic Street Preachers, but that's exactly what it did. *Gold Against the Soul* had shifted fifty thousand units, earning the Manics a platinum disc, and they were eagerly awaited there in the spring of 1994. With *The Holy Bible* completed and ready for distribution, the band flew out in late April for a pair of shows at the MBK Hall in Bangkok. Tagging along for the trip were several journalists and photographers. With the press on hand, you just knew something was going to happen. And it did. Several times.

The band members were greeted like returning heroes. Sony

had set up a meet-the-fans autograph session under a banner that read 'From Despair To Bangkok'. Richey Edwards was met by women bearing garlands of flowers that were then placed around his neck.

The band were warned that any anti-monarchist rhetoric wouldn't be tolerated and could even lead to execution. They were also told not to play 'Repeat' at any of their shows because of the line 'Fuck Queen and country'. Around three thousand fans had gathered to get the band's signatures on CD sleeves, posters and glossy A4 photos of Richey's infamous '4REAL' image. Other fans wanted Richey to sign '4REAL' on their own arms in marker pen. One fan spoke to a British reporter and had a stark message for Steve Lamacq. 'We understand why Richey did what he did,' they said. 'We have a culture of self-mutilation in this country. If Steve Lamacq ever comes here, we will . . . kill him.'

During the first show the band did, of course, play 'Repeat'. It was like The Beatles at Shea Stadium: young girls were crying and screaming and pulling their hair. The hall rocked so much that officials were worried the floor would give way and asked the band to play more quietly for the second night.

Girls had been hanging around the band's hotel since they arrived, with Richey being the favourite target. As well as asking him to pose for photos and sign autographs he was bestowed with presents including an oversized stuffed 'Snoopy', which he carried around on the trip for a while. Before the second show, a female fan approached Edwards and presented him with a box that contained a set of ceremonial knives. She said they were for Richey to cut himself with on stage that night and she requested that he look right at her while he did it. Edwards didn't like the idea of someone else calling the shots and cutting himself on stage while everyone looked on. He did like the idea of doing it in private, however. Part way through the set he got his chance as James Dean Bradfield performed a solo acoustic section of the show and the others retired to the dressing room for a few minutes.

Photographer Kevin Cummins was backstage at the time. 'He'd

left them in the dressing room,' says Cummins. 'He said it was tacky and he wouldn't do it. Towards the end of the gig, when James was alone on stage singing 'Raindrops Keep Falling on My Head', I went backstage to get some shots of the band slumped around in the dressing room. Richey was standing there with blood dripping down his chest. The cuts were pretty superficial. I took him in the bathroom and took some photos with him looking in the mirror. When I asked him why he'd done it he simply said, "Because they asked me to."' In the photos, Sean Moore can be seen just sitting there next to Richey as though having a band member cut himself open was the most normal thing in the world: an everyday occurrence in the world of the Manics. The others returned to join Bradfield on stage with Nicky Wire now wearing a floral dress that was quickly ripped to pieces by the fans. Richey returned bare-chested with a slew of horizontal lines dripping blood down his torso.

With the press pack in full attendance the band used one of their nights off to hike the tourist trail around the notorious red light districts, except for Nicky Wire who was homesick and unhappy with the local food. He returned to his room for an early night. The mini-van used to transport the rest of the band loaded up and headed for Pat Pong, famous for pole-dancing, stripping, massaging and fucking, not to mention its huge AIDS risks. After watching a selection of teenage girls pole-dancing, Richey Edwards said he was bored with it all and went off alone for a walk. When he resurfaced, hours later, he had a tale to tell. He'd wandered streets that were exactly as they had been portrayed in *The Deer Hunter*; a mass of humanity swirling around neon light and clubs, women at every doorway touting for business. Richey had been approached by a young girl and followed her inside. For seventy bahts she would undress you and offer massage; for more, she'd undress; for more still, a hand job; for even more, she would have sex. 'I'm not a very sexual person,' Edwards said. 'I don't need the physical closeness of a relationship. And I'm afraid of the pain that goes with it, to be honest. I think it's more of an animalistic urge. Every man masturbates, it's something you just do, two or three times a day. It's not the same as lust. Every time I've slept with a groupie, I've always felt dirty afterwards. It's very functional. I know for a fact that I could go downstairs now and come back up and fuck somebody. I don't like doing that, so if I go and pay two thousand bahts at a massage parlour and have a bath and get jerked off, to me it's preferable. For me, everything is very carefully thought out. This is the way I choose to live my life. I'd never been with a prostitute before and I've never had a girlfriend so I wasn't being unfaithful to a memory. It was something I wanted to experience to see whether it would make me happy, and it didn't really. I couldn't really expend any emotion on it. It just helped pass a few hours.'

If nothing else, the Thailand trip served to highlight some of the issues that Edwards was struggling with. Later, his band mates would pick out Bangkok as a turning point and a sign that things were getting worse. His self-harming was once again out in the open. 'When I cut myself I feel so much better,' he said. 'All the little things that might have been annoying me suddenly seem so trivial because I'm concentrating on the pain. I'm not a person who can scream and shout so this is my only outlet. It's all done very logically.' His inability to forge relationships with women was now all over the press in light of his public use of prostitutes and his interviews relating to the subject, plus his drinking was under the spotlight.

Early in the year, Richey had talked quite openly to *Melody Maker* about his drinking but stopped short of saying that he was an alcoholic. '[An alcoholic is] someone who wakes up and needs a drink straight away,' he said. 'My need is more functional. By about midday, I need a drink to stabilise me, but I've got to drive the group to rehearsal, so I can't have that drink. But on tour, I drink all day, just so I don't have to think about going onstage. I get paranoid about not being able to sleep and if by about eight o'clock at night I haven't had a drink, I get massive panic attacks and I'll be awake all night, and that's my biggest nightmare. I know that until about one in the afternoon I'm going to be shaky and have cold sweats. By six o'clock I feel good, but by eight it starts coming around again. I can't stomach the thought of not sleeping. That's why I drink. It's a very simple choice.' By May, it was getting more serious. 'Nicky and Sean are still true to the way we were, true to the spirit of the Manics,' admitted James Dean Bradfield to the *NME*. 'Whereas Richey and I are tending to lose the plot a bit.'

Carl Bevan of Welsh band the 6oft Dolls knew Richey and had witnessed his excessive self-perpetuating cycle of drink and depression. 'Richey was into some serious alcohol abuse, which seemed to be symptomatic of something – which I can say, knowing piss artists and possibly being one myself,' he said. 'He liked nothing better then to get absolutely trashed. You'd see him in the Murringer or Le Pub, drinking a lot of vodka. His head was in his hands, or in an ashtray, or something.' Around this time the heavy drinking caused him to stop his daily exercise regime, but still being obsessed with having a flat stomach he decided the best way to keep one without exercise was to stop eating. By now Richey was not even interested in his beloved Sega Megadrive. The band decided it was time for his third trip to a health farm. 'Thailand was the first time that I felt something was going wrong,' said Nicky Wire. 'And then we went to Portugal and things were going awry. It's not as if it was a matter of time, but I did feel something was gonna happen.'

At the end of May the band released 'Faster', the first new track to initiate a summer build-up to *The Holy Bible*, which was due for release at the end of August. The song contained some of Richey Edwards' most quoted and analysed lyrics, but it opened with someone else's words – a sample of John Hurt from the film *1984*. 'I hate purity. Hate goodness. I don't want virtue to exist anywhere. I want everyone corrupt.' The first lines of the song are Richey Edwards attempting to deal with being misunderstood and dissected in the press: he's an architect, he writes the songs and constructs the manifestos, but his self-harming makes him a butcher; he's a pioneer at the cutting edge of lyric writing but his lack of guitar skills make him seem like a primitive; he sees his actions as chasing purity but the very same actions get him accused of perversion.

The rest of the song is Edwards' condescending look down from his self-appointed intellectual perch. 'I am stronger than Mensa, Miller and Mailer / I spat out Plath and Pinter,' he claims, adding the chilling, 'I believe in nothing but it is my nothing'. Edwards claimed he was inspired by Yukio Mishima when writing the song. Psychologists sometimes say that the claim of being of superior intelligence to an impressive list of people is indicative of an impending collapse.

In early June, the band appeared on *Top of the Pops* to play 'Faster'. A caption on the screen revealed that this was the band's twelfth Top 40 hit and it was introduced by Vic Reeves and Bob Mortimer. As the camera zoomed in across the studio, the viewers were greeted by two bowls of real fire on stands either side of the band. This was the first major opportunity for the band to reveal their new aesthetic look. Richey Edwards was wearing a sailor's uniform, while the stage was covered in army netting and bathed in green light. Most striking, though, was James Dean Bradfield, who stood centre-stage, screaming live lyrics into the microphone, while the others mimed. He was wearing a black balaclava with 'James' written across the forehead. This single item of clothing, with its obvious IRA connotations, brought in more than 25,000 complaints to the BBC.

Bradfield's thinking behind the mask was, in fact, nothing to do with terrorism. He was undergoing the very personal strain of singing someone else's words and felt he needed a persona to hide behind as he inhabited the writer's brain. While actors wore face-paint, he chose a balaclava. The rest of the band's military attire had been built up over the preceding months. Sean Moore had chosen a United Nations blue beret, harking back to The Clash's *Sandinista* look. The 1994 military uniforms updated the band's 1990–91 era uniform of stencilled shirts and white jeans. 'The uniforms represent the control and discipline that we are trying to get back,' said Nicky Wire about the two traits that Richey Edwards thought were of the utmost importance. Edwards himself added a Soviet war veteran's medal to his own outfit, saying that the failure of communism reminded him of the band's own initial 'failure'. Another TV appearance was a short set for Channel 4's *Naked City* music programme. It was filmed the day after Richey Edwards had heard about the suicide of his university friend, Nigel. He spent several hours crying down the phone to Hall Or Nothing's Gillian Porter and then had to put on a brave face to go and record the show the next day. But as the band ran through half a dozen songs live in the studio, Edwards was a ghost, lurking in the amplifier shadows and fading into the dry ice.

After the bleak madness of Thailand the band's next shows were in Braga, Portugal, a place that had distinctly unhappy memories for all concerned, and things weren't about to get any better. During their first visit they'd heard the news that Philip Hall had died. This time, they had to deal with Richey Edwards suffering from uncontrollable bursts of involuntary crying. 'We had to put him to bed one night 'cos he just burst out crying in the car,' recalled Nicky Wire. 'And then he phoned me up at about half-three in the morning and – you know those terrible commercial presentations you get? Some American twat showing you how to flatten your stomach or something? – and we were watching that together, and it seemed so bleak and nondescript. We didn't have a row or anything, but he kept yapping and I was really tired. The next morning, he comes up to me and says, "Here you are, Wire", and he gave me a fucking Mars bar.'

Back in the UK, the Manics called in at Roadmenders in Northampton to play a warm-up show before their appearance at the Glastonbury Festival on 24 June. This was the first of a series of festival dates they had booked across the summer, culminating with the Reading Festival at the end of August. Glastonbury 1994 is now seen as the breaking point for Britpop to smash its way into the mainstream and go ballistic. Never again would Oasis, Blur, Pulp and Radiohead be able to play on the same stage on the same day. Oasis were some way down the bill and Blur's Graham Coxon got into the military spirit by wearing army gear and an American paratrooper helmet. The Manics were booked for the *NME* stage. James Dean Bradfield wore his balaclava and a sailor suit, while Richey Edwards looked extremely thin in camouflage trousers and green T-shirt. He thrashed and hacked away at his guitar on the smaller stage in darkness, the best way to see a band at a festival. 'I really enjoyed Glastonbury,' said Richey. 'I did actually enjoy the gig. More than everybody else in the band, really. I don't really enjoy many concerts. And then it was back to Wales . . . '

# X

## HELL IS IN HELLO
### *July to August 1994*

*Wire, briar, limber-lock,*
*Three geese in a flock,*
*One flew east, one flew west*
*One flew over the cuckoo's nest.*

*One Flew Over the Cuckoo's Nest,* written in the late 1950s by mental institution orderly Ken Kesey, told the story of Randle Patrick McMurphy, a man who faked mental illness to try and get an easier time of serving his prison sentence for battery. His free-spirited ways resulted in many confrontations with the female nurse who ran his ward, but he was determined to force his fellow, heavily drugged, patients to live their lives and have some fun. His heroic attempts struck a chord with the Manics, who wrote one of their earliest songs, 'R P McMurphy', about him.

The aftermath of an illicit party that McMurphy organised on the ward leads to the suicide of one of the young patients, Billy. McMurphy blames the nurse and attacks her, damaging her vocal chords and essentially silencing her voice of authority, but he is taken away and lobotomised. When he is returned to the ward his friend the Chief sees that McMurphy has been turned into a vegetable and smothers him with a pillow before making his own escape. McMurphy and Billy are dead, but the Chief flies the nest. The screen adaptation of Kesey's book was one of Richey Edwards' favourite films.

•

A competition in the *NME*'s 11 June 1994 issue offered readers the chance to 'WIN MANICS' LATEST CUT!'. The details below added: 'Signed by the band, and who knows, perhaps even bled upon in Richey's case.'

•

At the end of the 1969 movie *Paint Your Wagon*, Lee Marvin's character Ben Rumson is heading out on the road from No Name City, the gold rush town which has dried up. This being a musical, he breaks into song. 'Wand'rin Star' provided Marvin with an unlikely deep-voiced novelty hit around the world, topping the charts in the UK and keeping The Beatles' 'Let it Be' at number two. Marvin's delivery of the song wasn't the only quirky thing about it. The lyric, outwardly a simple lament from a drifter moving along, contains some interesting couplets. In the summer of 1994, Richey Edwards caught bit of a show on early morning TV. 'Do I know where hell is, hell is in hell-o,' sang Marvin. 'Heaven is goodbye forever, it's time for me to go.' Edwards was struck by what he'd heard; in fact, he couldn't stop thinking about it. '[It] was just a tiny little thing on *The Big Breakfast* from Lee Marvin singing that stupid song, "I Was Born Under a Wandering Star" [sic]. There's a line in that, "Hell is in hello", and for two days, I couldn't do fucking anything. What's it mean, "Hell is in hello"? What are they trying to say? What is the point in that? Just little things. And then I realised that something was not quite right.'

It was only with hindsight that Edwards could convince himself that he didn't have to spend the rest of his days searching for the meaning and that it was just a line in a song. He could accept that it was just a line but couldn't take his mind off the subject, everything else just faded into the background. That wasn't the only thing that had him mentally paralysed. 'I couldn't understand *Prisoner in Cell Block H*,' he said. 'It was doing my head in. And then I realised that I'm not stupid. I had to convince myself that I wasn't stupid. It was just a silly little thing. The little things, you see, are the worry, that put me in a mood that I can't really control. Nothing else happens in my mind, I just get swamped by one idea. I can just see one little thing on TV and that'll be it. It can be anything, and then I'll just stop functioning. I think, what does it mean? I'm intelligent, why can't I understand that? Just a line in a film or a book, and I've lost it.' This was the frame of mind he found himself in when he returned from the Glastonbury festival.

One balmy night in early July, Richey called Nicky Wire, as he was prone to do. He didn't really make much sense but he rambled on for a while. It was like many of the other late-night calls he'd received, but, after he hung up, Wire was left with the nagging feeling that this time something really wasn't right. The next morning Wire called Richey's flat to make sure that things were OK. When he failed to get an answer, his suspicions rose. He called Edwards' parents house in Blackwood to see if Richey was there, but they hadn't seen or heard from him for a few days. Richey's parents decided to drive down to Cardiff and check things out.

They pulled into the central car park and went up the three flights of stairs. When they let themselves into the apartment they were shocked at what they found. The usually spotlessly clean flat was in disarray. It was soon clear that things were wrong and that Richey had been on a binge of drinking and self-harm. Drunk and bleeding from a heavy session of self-cutting, he was admitted to hospital right away. The music press was soon filled with speculation. *Melody Maker* later printed that 'Richey's spell in hospital began, one lurid rumour goes, after a suicide attempt. The myth goes like this: Richey tries the old slit wrists/hot bath method, and, surprised to wake up the next morning and find himself alive, phones up his mother to say, "I've done something a bit stupid . . . I think you'd better call an ambulance."' Whether any of this is true was never confirmed; in fact, most things that summer were denied. Despite these denials, later police files did reveal that Edwards had made at least one suicide attempt, and this was most likely it. Richey did later say that, 'In terms of the "S" word [suicide], that does not enter my mind. And it never has done, in terms of an attempt. Because I am stronger than that.' So maybe this was an attempt or maybe it was a mistaken judgement about what his body could actually take in terms of alcohol and self-harm.

Many things about Richey's last known months would later be judged alongside the songs on *The Holy Bible*. In this case, people looked back in relation to the song 'Die in the Summertime', with its harrowing lines such as 'Scratch my leg with a rusty nail / Sadly it heals.'

'I did feel that we were taking it so far with the record, and some of the lyrics were so self-fulfilling for Richey,' said Nicky Wire. 'Like "Die in the Summertime", I'm sure he felt that, "People are gonna say I'm a fake if I don't do something about it."'

'I wasn't in a very good frame of mind,' Edwards explained several months later. 'My mind wasn't functioning very well, and my mind was stronger than my body. My mind subjected my body to things that it couldn't cope with. Which meant I was ill. For the first time, I was a bit scared, because I always thought I could handle it. I've read lots of books about tolerance of pain, and pain thresholds. The euphoric agony, basically, is a sensation which your mind blocks off. You control yourself. It's all about control. About proving a point to yourself, which I did very easily, but then I realised that I couldn't do anything.'

'It came to a point where his self-abuse had reached a peak, in a lot of ways – his drinking, he'd virtually become anorexic, his mutilation,' said Nicky Wire. 'Everybody just got really scared when we saw him. We're in a position where we don't know what to do.' The only thing they could do was get help. Everyone agreed – the band, Hall Or Nothing, Richey's parents, and, luckily, Richey himself – that he needed to be admitted to hospital.

By Richey's own thinking, he had been OK, but things slowly and gradually built up until he was out of control. The self-harming had always been his badge of self-control: when he cut himself he was showing himself and the world that he was dealing with things in his own way, and that he could handle the pain and control his body. When that mechanism for self-control broke down, so did everything else in his mind. A descending spiral into chaos quickly followed.

'There were contributing factors to his decline,' said Martin Hall. 'But now Richey says he would probably have ended up the same way regardless. The thing is, he doesn't see anything wrong in cutting himself. It makes him feel better. It's his way of releasing pain and his argument is, it doesn't harm anyone else. He was at the point, though, where no one – not even himself – knew how far he might go. If he had carried on without any help he might have ended up killing himself.'

'[Richey] has a very acute perception of things, and you can't lose that perception,' added James Dean Bradfield. 'It's just a matter of how you channel it. And this is it. It sounds insultingly flippant to say, "Oh these things happen" or something, but, basically, what is is. We all saw Richey's problems getting to a stage where things were gonna get very nasty, and now he's going to see a psychiatrist and try to nip that in the bud. That's the true story. Those are the facts.'

Edwards was found a place at Whitchurch Hospital, the local NHS psychiatric unit. With an immaculate lawn in front of it, the hospital actually looked more like a stately home. Edwards voluntarily checked in. Nicky Wire visited every day, and Sean Moore and James Dean Bradfield also made visits. All were shocked at the state in which they found Edwards. He was dressed in pyjamas and wandering around aimlessly, 'drugged out of his skull', according to Wire. 'When they took him into the hospital, they said he was on the verge of anorexia,' said Wire. 'Anorexia is the ultimate act of self-control, total withdrawal, no one can get to you, a kind of suicide where you don't have to die.'

Sean Moore commented that Edwards was never seen once by a psychiatrist during his stay there; they seemed happy just to keep him under control by medication. Moore was sure that Edwards would get no better in Whitchurch and would have to leave sooner rather than later. Edwards had gone beyond the stage of being able to sit down with his friends to talk things through. He needed serious help and plans were soon made to move him somewhere else. 'NHS hospitals are people banging off the walls in long corridors,' reported Edwards. 'Long, endless corridors. In communal wards, nobody sleeps. They can give you as many drugs as they want, but the noises in there are pretty horrendous. Then the next day, you wake up, have your drugs and sit in a big communal room, and you don't hardly see any fucker. And then you just, if you're like me, try to keep out of everybody's way. Know your place. Don't get in anybody's shadow. When I got taken to hospital, they didn't know who the fuck I was, y'know? I'm not in Take That. I'm not even in The Stone Roses. I'm in a moderately successful British band. I wasn't there in my Manic Street Preachers T-shirt. They didn't have a clue.'

There were rumours that Richey was still a danger to himself while in Whitchurch. He might have attempted suicide, or at least further self-harm, but these stories were never proved either way. Richey almost seemed to say something about this when discussing the ability to do what one wants to one's own body. 'The best thing is knowing that no one can do fucking anything about it,' he said. 'When I was in Whitchurch [long pause] People can't actually hold you down and force food into your mouth. They just can't do it. And someone can't be near you twenty-four hours a day to stop you doing something to your body. And ultimately they've got no right to anyway, because it is *your* body.'

Initially, the band agreed not to talk to Richey about business matters. 'To be honest, we were all quite numb to any sort of discussion about the group's future because we were too concerned about Richey,' explained James Dean Bradfield. But after a few days, Richey brought up this subject himself. During one visit, Edwards told Wire and Bradfield that he'd like to take a step back. He would continue to write lyrics and work on the artwork but would refrain from being a touring member of the band. The visitors agreed and said they'd go along with anything he wanted to do. 'I'd seen them down to the front door and when they'd gone, I was really upset,' Edwards explained later. 'I couldn't think what I was going to do. Because it's not enough for me just to do the words. I kind of think I'd be cheating on them, because the touring part is the worst bit, the bit that no band really enjoys. It's the thing that makes it feel like a job, because you know what you'll be doing in three months' time at two o'clock in the afternoon. I felt bad thinking, well, I'll just stay on my own in the flat and just write words. That's not enough.' That evening he phoned Nicky Wire in tears; he had to go back on what he'd said he wanted. He had to be fully involved in the band. It was his life. If he didn't have that, he'd have nothing. He promised to practise hard with his guitar playing and be ready for the planned autumn tour starting in September.

After eight days at Whitchurch, there was no visible improvement in Richey's condition; if anything, he seemed worse because of the medication. 'I didn't know what the fuck was going on,' he said. 'James will tell you, I couldn't even talk. I was just stuttering. I was taking medication, Librium and stuff. Though it calmed me down, because I could get to sleep at night.' It was decided that in view of his static condition, Edwards would be moved to the private Priory clinic at Roehampton.

The main hospital at the Priory consists of a general psychiatry unit, which deals with all types of mental illness. Separate to this are the Addictions Unit and the Eating Disorders Unit. The usual admission route is via a GP, unless the patient is known to the hospital from previous visits, but the GP referral route can be bypassed, particularly by famous patients who can simply turn up, pay their deposit and then be assessed by the doctor on call.

The Priory was and is the celebrity clinic of choice in the UK. It's a typical rock cliché. Rock star gets hooked on drugs and/or booze, embarks on a downward spiral, checks into rehab, comes out and starts the cycle all over again. Today, it is almost expected. Celebrity magazines seem to live on the stories of rehab and relapse. Do the clinics ever actually work? 'If a person is forced into rehab, it is almost certain not to work,' says addiction therapist Shelley Assiter, who has worked with many rock stars. 'It has to come from them. They have to want to stop being slaves to drugs. Some treatment centres make addicts share two or three to a room and undergo intensive one-to-one and group sessions,' says Assiter. 'The Priory does some good work, but it is so luxurious that people are basically imprisoned in a five-star hotel. It's no surprise that they leave and then relapse.' Edwards didn't volunteer to be admitted there, but he still had enough about him to agree to treatment.

One of the Priory's main weapons in addiction treatment is the well-publicised 'Twelve-step Programme',[29] which is also widely used by Alcoholics Anonymous, an organisation that Richey Edwards signed up to while in hospital. In the Priory Addictions

Unit, there is a set treatment period after the completion of which – if the patient remained abstinent – they would be discharged and enter into an outpatients programme. Patients are encouraged to start and complete the programme together in groups.

When Richey was put on this programme in the Priory, it had already been in use for around forty years. He got through step one well enough (admitting that he had a problem and needed help), but steps two (admitting that a greater power should control him) and three (turning over his life to a god of his understanding) were problematic. Step two required that any intellectual self-sufficiency be jettisoned in favour of obeying a higher power, which meant that Edwards would have to surrender a core feature of his very being. His intellect had been his greatest weapon since his school days; how could he be expected to just drop that overnight? He had been against organised religion since he'd stopped attending Methodist services at the age of thirteen, so handing himself over to a god was also difficult. 'Step three is hard,' Richey told the *NME*'s Stuart Bailie. 'When you have to reconcile yourself to a god of your understanding. Step one is fairly easy, to admit. Well, it's easy to *admit*, it's hard to accept in your own mind. Because I do feel my mind's quite strong. Obviously not as strong as it could be, but step three was hard. It's gonna take a long time for me to figure out.' Edwards explained that although some people take family members or pets as the 'god of their understanding' he was having a difficult time figuring out who or what to concentrate on. 'The closest I can get to it is nature, probably, but then nature is very cruel,' he said. 'It's a question of working it all out, which is why I did history, to try and work out the central point. A god of your own understanding, mine's not gonna be my dead grandmother or my pet cat, and it's not gonna be the Big Man upstairs. And I've got to understand what nature means. It's just a question of working it all out, and I've got a lot of time on my hands, so I can think about it.' Despite this apparent rejection of the Big Man upstairs, Edwards would be carrying around notes of Bible passages later in the year, quoting them to the others on tour, and also had tattoos with religious themes added to his arms.

The fourth step could actually be described as exacerbating some of the problems that Richey was wrestling with. Making 'searching and fearless' moral inventories of himself was exactly the kind of self-critical over-thinking that had contributed to his depression in the first place. When the rest of the band visited, they noticed a change in Richey and they didn't think it was necessarily for the better. 'We all think that the Priory filled him up with a lot of shit,' said James Dean Bradfield. 'All the things the Priory stood for, in one way or another, Richey had ridiculed viciously in the past. Deep down, he knew it was crap.'

'The Priory ripped out the man and left a shell,' added Nicky Wire. 'They say they've got a cure in places like that, but all they do is completely change the person you are. I don't think that's a cure. And you could see him struggling with this, wondering if this was the only way. They loved him in there, because he's so intelligent and sharp-witted, and he got into it, played along with them. But they ripped the soul out of him. The person I knew was slowly ebbing away.' He did have some strands of humour left, however. In a possibly apocryphal story, Eric Clapton was working as a volunteer and popped in to see Richey at the Priory. Clapton apparently said that on his next visit he'd bring along his guitar. Richey Edwards is said to have told James Dean Bradfield, 'That's just what I need. I'm going to be confronted by God, and God's going to realise that I can't play guitar.' He also said that maybe he should put a cake on his head or talk to an imaginary giraffe to convince 'them' that he was mad. Furthermore, he was disappointed that his liver test results indicated that he didn't drink as much as he'd claimed.

Edwards was now a member of Alcoholics Anonymous, was being prescribed Prozac and was smoking around sixty a day. His weight was becoming a problem again, but the band offered some good-natured mockery and he took it in good humour. Gillian Porter from Hall Or Nothing smuggled him in some coffee and they sat around talking about various bands. Sean Moore took in a Nirvana songbook and sat patiently with him, showing him the way through a couple of songs.

166 · A VERSION OF REASON

'Richey never had as many setbacks as a kid as me, he's more acutely intelligent than me, he's more beautiful than me – and yet he has more problems,' said James Dean Bradfield. 'Problems that I'd just snip off with fucking scissors in two seconds flat really get to Richey.'

In its 6 August 1994 issue, the *Melody Maker* ran a story under the heading 'Manic Depression' and reported that Edwards was suffering from 'nervous exhaustion'. Outwardly, Hall Or Nothing were downplaying the issue. A spokeswoman was quoted as saying that he'd 'just had enough'. The official line was that he'd be in for at least a few weeks, he was 'a bit exhausted' and needed to rest. Later, it was hinted that things were actually pretty bad. On 8 August, a statement was issued to the effect that Edwards was 'very ill' and that things had 'developed to a point where the band, but more importantly Richey, decided that he needs to seek psychiatric help to deal with what is basically a sickness'.

Band business continued, if not as normal, then with at least a smidgeon of normality. James Dean Bradfield and Nicky Wire popped into the MTV studios for *MTV's Most Wanted*, performing poignant acoustic renditions of 'She is Suffering' and '4st 7lb'. Filmed in noir-ish black and white, '4st 7lb', especially, was even more harrowing in this stripped-down setting.

In August, 'Revol' became the band's next single. The promotional video, directed by Chris D'Adda and given a cinematic feel, was obviously filmed before Edwards' hospitalisation. He appears with the others in his military uniform while they play the song in an airplane hangar. 'Revol', with its initially baffling lyrical content, hovered around the low twenties in the charts while Wet Wet Wet topped them with a dire rendition of the Troggs' 'Love is All Around'. Sony paid for a big advertising campaign to promote 'Revol', taking out full-page adverts to print the song's lyrics, and producing other ads that read:

THE WHITE LIBERAL
IS THE VD
OF THE REVOLUTION

In between visits to Richey, the Manics had kept a handful of festival engagements that they'd been booked for. Part of the reason was that they wanted to honour what they'd promised; another reason, which became more apparent as the summer wore on, was that they needed the money to pay Richey's bill for the Priory, which would amount to about £20,000. The first of these festivals was Glasgow's T In The Park on 30 July. Bringing in a replacement for Edwards was out of the question, so the three remaining Manics played on without additional help. On the day, fans were simply told that Edwards was ill. 'We haven't turned into one of these power trios like the fucking Jam or anyone like that,' Wire said from the stage. Privately, he said that he felt the appearance had been a 'massive spiritual betrayal'. Shows in Germany and Holland followed.

'I've never been late for anything,' said Edwards. 'I've never missed a flight, I'm not indisciplined. I'm not a member of Happy Mondays or Primal Scream or whatever. I'm always on time. I haven't got many things to cling to, but I cling to that. That's what pissed me off about missing Reading and the German gigs, I had nobody else to blame. It was my fault, and I accept it was my fault.' There had previously been talk of Richey possibly being fit enough to return for Reading Festival at the end of August, but as the month progressed this became more unlikely. 'I think he feels deep down it would have come to this whether he'd been a teacher or a bank clerk or anything, but I personally think being in a band has accelerated it,' said Bradfield to the *NME* that summer. Bradfield felt like his visits to see Edwards made him a psychiatrist for half an hour. He also felt that if Edwards were not well enough to retake his place in the band, then they'd cancel the autumn tour.

The Manics that took to the Reading Festival stage were an angry, pissed-off trio. Not only had Richey failed to improve sufficiently enough to play but the day would have been Philip Hall's thirty-fifth birthday. The headliners that year were Cypress Hill, Primal Scream, and the Red Hot Chili Peppers. Britpop was still gathering steam with Pulp, Elastica, Gene and Echobelly appearing lower down the bill. Courtney Love's band Hole played in tribute to Kurt Cobain and Hole bassist Kristin Pfaff, who had both died that year.

Before the Manics played their set, they were interviewed in their caravan backstage. Getting the obvious question out of the way first, Nicky Wire's update on Edwards' condition was 'Since he reached the zenith of shitness he's improved.' James Dean Bradfield explained that they hadn't seen such serious problems approaching, and that they had had to take a sharp intake of breath. In a separate interview, Sean Moore said that they had reached the point where they had nothing left to lose at Reading: '[I] thought we'd go out in our own little blaze of glory.'

The band took to the stage as the hazy glow of the setting sun was just breaking through the day's clouds. A gentle breeze blew across the combat netting. James Dean Bradfield was wearing camouflaged waterproofs while using one of Richey's guitars on some songs. The panda-eyed Wire wore desert-camouflage khakis and the massive stage seemed even bigger with only the three of them on it. At the rear, Sean Moore in his backwards baseball cap looked like he was sat up in the cockpit of a tank rumbling into the festival masses laid out before them. As the final words of 'From Despair to Where' were screamed into the gathering gloom, those present didn't realise that these lyrics would provide the headlines most frequently used in relation to the band over the next eighteen months. Stuart Bailie, reporting for the *NME*, wrote, 'you watched, dismayed, when the Manics played as a three piece at Reading, fans and colleagues around you weeping at the tragic significance of it all. And of course, you heard many terrible rumours.'

In early September, Richey finally checked himself out of the Priory – against medical advice. At the time, Dr Desmond Kelly was head of the Priory. He believed in 'divine providence'; Richey had been encouraged to partake in drama, had been told to keep a log and read *Believing in Myself*.[30] Edwards took his reading responsibilities seriously but his talking about them made the others feel uncomfortable. He also started reading the Bible again, and would quote sections of Ecclesiastes and Leviticus. 'A lot of letters I've got have said, "Oh, it's natural, it always happens to poets." Which is fucking bullshit. When you're in the places I've been in, the first place especially, it's just any job, any occupation.

Housewife, bricklayer, plumber, somebody who works for South Wales Electricity Board, whatever. It doesn't pick or choose people who pick up a pen. When you write something down, it's not like, here we go. It's something nobody really knows anything about, apart from that some things work and some things don't, to stabilise you again. It's very romantic to think, "I'm a tortured writer", but mental institutions are not full of people in bands. They're full of people with so-called normal jobs."

'People coming out of rehab are highly vulnerable and need a strong support network,' says Shelley Assiter. 'It is very dangerous for a musician to go straight back on tour because they are returning to their old lifestyle, and I would say ninety-nine per cent of them will then relapse.' Richey Edwards left the Priory with one aim on his mind: to be well enough to join the rest of the band on their autumn tour.

# XI

# THE BIBLE

*September 1994*

Richey Edwards was still a patient at the Priory when *The Holy Bible* was released on 30 August 1994. With that wonderful thing people call hindsight, the album has been held up as Edwards' requiem, his suicide note, his long goodbye. But although he wrote a lot of the words, about 25 per cent of the lyrics were Nicky Wire's and all of the music was Sean Moore and James Dean Bradfield's. That said, it's still very difficult to have any sense of objectivity about this album and to evaluate it without thinking about Edwards' legacy.

Both Richey Edwards and Nicky Wire provided track-by-track commentaries on *The Holy Bible*, with Wire's entering the public domain with a full page in the 27 August issue of *Melody Maker*. The bassist's comments were longer and a little less cryptic than Edwards', but both were fascinating – if slightly disturbing. Not content with that, two-page adverts featuring the entire album's lyrics were placed in the music press. With Edwards' mental and emotional state becoming tabloid fodder and the news that he'd written most of the lyrics, the questions about the songs' autobiographical nature were quick in coming. Equating the singer (or in this case, the lyricist) with the song can be a dangerous game. Having previously written about Beck and Michael Stipe, I quickly learned that fact and fiction merge like a nasty motorway slip-road. The blurred lines between Edwards' reality and everyone else's were difficult to identify, but it's fair to say that many of the songs were taken from his own experiences, if not being directly autobiographical. He'd never plummeted to 4 stones, 7 pounds in weight, but he could relate to that.

172 • A VERSION OF REASON

As with *Gold Against the Soul*, the sound of *The Holy Bible* was markedly different to that of the album that came before it. While the overt metal and glam of *Generation Terrorists* had been replaced by the classic rock sounds of *Gold Against the Soul*, this time they had been swept aside for a grungy rock, influenced not only by current trends but also by the source material that had influenced the likes of Vedder and Cobain. James Dean Bradfield's revisiting of Wire, Magazine and Joy Division is evident from the first couple of songs, even if the language is a bit stronger.

'For sale? Dumb cunt's same dumb questions,' James Dean Bradfield sang to open 'Yes'. Before that, a snippet of dialogue about everything being for sale had been added by Richey Edwards from a Channel 4 documentary he'd seen about prostitution, called *Pimps, Pros, Hookers and their Johns*. Musically, this is styled as a solid rock song with metal-like guitar parts, and is quite uplifting if you don't listen to the words! Lyrically, Edwards is talking about his life of the last couple of years. His view had long been that life revolved around doing something you didn't want to in order to get things that you didn't really need – and so the cycle continued, and then you died. He mentions purgatory in the song – something that would linger with him after leaving the Priory and a word he would literally tattoo on himself later in the year. 'We feel that we've prostituted ourselves over the last three or four years,' said Nicky Wire, 'and we think it's the same in every walk of life. You do get to a position when you're in a band where you can virtually do anything you want, in any kind of sick, low form. It's not something we've particularly indulged in, but it is a nasty by-product of being in a group.'

'He's a boy, you want a girl so tear off his cock,' said the song. Edwards could barely conceal his contempt for the power that celebrity could bring, harking back to his experience at Cardiff's Metros club with Stephen Gatehouse. 'Ifwhiteamericatoldthetruthforonedayit'sworldwouldfallapart' was the band's first overtly political song for a while and was a title taken from a Lenny Bruce quote. 'It compares British imperialism to American consumerism,' explained Nicky Wire. 'It's just trying to explain the confusion I think most people feel about how the most empty culture in the world can dominate in such a total sense.'

So two tracks in and they'd covered prostitution and American politics, but then the real heart of the album began to be revealed with 'Of Walking Abortion'. The title came from Valerie Solanis' description of men. The uncredited spoken-word introduction was key: 'I knew that someday I was gonna die. And I knew before I died two things would happen to me. That, number one, I would regret my entire life. And, number two, I would want to live my life over again.'

The problem as Edwards saw it was that we'd learned nothing from the past. That dictators such as Mussolini, Hitler and Horthy had been allowed to ascend was not an accident but was somebody's fault. There was spilled blood that stains everyone, he wrote, and when the question of who is at fault was asked, the answer is loud and clear – 'You fucking are!'

Not many people in rock were writing about sex and desire in terms of suffering. The 'She' of 'She is Suffering' is 'desire'. What sounds like a gentle song is actually Richey Edwards' outpouring of pain and has deeply sinister undertones. Edwards writes that 'She' is scarred into a man's soul, that it's 'Nature's lukewarm pleasure.' The nature of beauty had also been a tortured question that Mishima had addressed in the 1960s. 'It's kind of like the Buddhist thing where you can only reach eternal peace by shedding every desire in your body,' said Nicky Wire. 'I think the last line, "Nature's lukewarm pleasure", is Richey's view on sex. I can't really explain it, but that's the way he sees it.'

'In other Bibles and Holy Books no truth is possible until you empty yourself of desire,' added Edwards. James Dean Bradfield would perform stirring acoustic versions of this song while promoting the album.

'Archives of Pain' opened with another spoken-word piece, this time a recording of a mother of one of the Yorkshire Ripper's victims. This is a pro-death-penalty song, which might have come as a surprise to some fans, especially since both Wire and Edwards contributed to the words. Richey Edwards can often be analysed as having a victim persona, but here he hits back: 'Pain not penance, forget martyrs, remember victims.' A list of killers is read out with the blunt message, 'Execution needed'.

Wire and Edwards worried a lot about the song and worked on it endlessly because of the tricky subject matter. 'It was written as a reaction to the glorification of serial killers,' says Wire. 'In *Silence of the Lambs*, Hannibal Lecter is made into a hero in the last scene of the film – people feel sorry for them.

'There's a book by Michel Foucault with a chapter called "Archives of Pain". Richey and I did that book at university, and it had quite an influence on us. It talks about the punishment matching the crime. But the song isn't a right-wing statement, it's just against this fascination with people who kill.' Meanwhile, Edwards' explanation of the song was more succinct: 'Bentham's "Panopticon" – visibility is a trap. Foucault – Savagery is necessary.'[31]

'It appeals to me, but you shouldn't only bring back capital punishment,' Edwards said several months later. 'It should be compulsory that your body be kept, have oil poured over it and be torn apart with horses and chains. It should be on TV, and four- or five-year-olds should be made to watch it. It's the only way. If you tell a child, "That's wrong", he doesn't really learn. But if you show a body being ripped to shreds, after *Blue Peter*, he's gonna know.'

'Revol' is a fascinating and possibly confounding song. James Dean Bradfield has commented that he would have to know what a song is about before he could sing it, although he and Nicky Wire have said they don't know what 'Revol' is about. Musically it's one of the heavier efforts on the album and the lyric is fast and dizzying. Taken at face value, the song seems to be a list of political leaders coupled with strange comments on the failure of personal relationships, but that would be all too simple wouldn't it? 'Some of it's beyond my head,' said Nicky Wire. 'He's saying that all of these revolutionary leaders were failures in relationships – probably because all his relationships have failed!'

It was common knowledge that Richey Edwards weighed little more than six stones when he was first admitted to hospital in 1994 and that he'd been down to about that weight during his university finals. This offered him direct insights into the workings of eating disorders. Although the numbers are slightly different and the words are sung from a woman's perspective, '4st 7lb' is another closely autobiographical lyric. Like self-cutting, this was another expression of self-control, but was thought to be the weight at which an adult body would give up and die.[32] 'I wanna be so skinny that I rot from view / I want to walk in the snow / And not leave a footprint' are pretty harrowing words by any measure. 'I'm not sure what the textbook definition of anorexia is,' said James Dean Bradfield, 'but you don't expect a twenty-five-year-old man who's five foot seven to weigh six-and-a-half stone. Anorexia is the ultimate negative vanity. It's a schizophrenic disease whereby you don't know whether to love or hate yourself, which is Richey down to a tee.'

'Mausoleum' and 'The Intense Humming of Evil' were, in the words of Richey Edwards, 'brother/sister' songs, both addressing the Holocaust and both inspired by the previous year's visits to Hiroshima's Peace Museum and the concentration camps at Dachau and Belsen. The visits had deeply affected all of the band, but as usual Edwards felt it more deeply than most. The humming of evil was the 'humming silence' that they heard at Dachau. The scratchy post-punk almost constantly playing on the band's stereos while recording the album included the two Joy Division albums. 'Mausoleum' opens like a long-lost Joy Division song before exploding in anguish. Likewise, 'The Intense Humming of Evil' opens with a long industrial grind that recalled some of Joy Division's experimental percussion.

The previously released 'Faster' follows 'Mausoleum', and then comes another respite – musically, at least – with 'This is Yesterday'. Its mellow guitar and rhythm parts belie the intense melancholy of the lyric. One American review claimed that 'The lyric describes nervous breakdown from the point of view of the sufferer', but it was the twisted-around view of someone longing for the simpler world of childhood.

Once the echoes of 'This is Yesterday' fade into oblivion, we get another song about looking back – 'Die in the Summertime' – but this time it's musically threatening and lyrically harrowing. While Edwards claimed that the song was about fondly remembering youth from the point of a pensioner, it also fits well with Edwards' feelings. He's looking back at childhood pictures, happy that the lines of age are yet to appear and content with infant pastimes.

'There's lots of disturbing images,' says Wire. '"Scratch my leg with a rusty nail / Sadly it heals . . . / A tiny animal curled into a quarter circle". It was one of the first songs we wrote for the album, and I found it pretty disturbing when Richey first showed it to me. Now, of course, it's even more so, and I think this and "4st 7lb" are pretty obviously about Richey's state of mind, which I didn't quite realise at the time. Even if you're quite close to someone, you always try to deny thoughts like that.'

After the concentrated personal outpourings across the album, 'P.C.P.' was perhaps a strange choice to close proceedings. The title is a play on words – Politically Correct, Police Constable, Portuguese Communist Party – but it is essentially a song about censorship and freedom of speech. Edwards felt strongly that *anything* should be allowed on TV, and that no one had the right to decide what was 'good' or 'bad' taste. 'Obviously, "PC" as an idea is inherently good,' said Nicky Wire. 'So is socialism and so is communism, and they ended up being abused. A lot of PC followers take up the idea of being liberal, but end up being quite the opposite.'

Richey Edwards had taken control of the album cover before his hospitalisation. Again he'd scoured art galleries looking for an image that he felt fitted his lyrical vision. At the Saatchi Gallery, he saw a striking piece by 24-year-old Jenny Saville – *Strategy (South Face/Front Face/North Face)*. It showed an obese woman in her underwear from either side and from the front. Edwards thought it would be perfect for the album cover, but the gallery wanted £30,000 for the picture. Unperturbed, he tracked down the artist and spent half an hour talking to her about his vision of the album and talking her through it, track-by-track. At the end of the phone call, she said he could use it for free.

By this time, the Manics' stock had fallen to the extent that when

I looked back for the Q magazine review, I had to skip back and forward between a few copies before locating it. The review wasn't even listed on the contents page, although Status Quo, June Tabor and Edie Brickell were! Eventually I found it – a couple of inches tucked away on about page fifteen of the review section – but at least Tom Doyle had liked the album. He gave it '4/5', adding 'The Holy Bible proves the Manics to be a band who can subtly reinvent themselves at every turn.' This enthusiasm spread across the critical spectrum: 'the Manics' finest attempt to put militancy into music,' said Vox ('8/10'). Simon Williams, writing in the NME, said, 'it isn't elegant, but it is bloody effective' ('9/10').

The critical praise received by The Holy Bible was not translating into big sales, but many reviews cut straight to the point and linked the lyrics to Richey's personal troubles. Its current status as something of a lost classic is no doubt partly because of what happened to Edwards. In retrospect, some critics' observations were unnervingly accurate. In Melody Maker, Simon Price called it 'the sound of a group in extremis. At crisis point. Hurtling towards a private Armageddon. It's Richey's album.' Roy Wilkinson, in Select, said it 'might be a little too close to home', but Craig Fitzsimmons, writing for Hot Press, went further still. 'The Holy Bible is a profane, mean, angry-as-hell powerhouse of an LP,' he wrote. 'They're literate as hell and they're angry about something. It's recommended, except for those contemplating suicide.'

**I**n Anton Corbjin's film about Joy Division, *Control*, he took extracts from several letters that Ian Curtis wrote to his Belgian girlfriend, Anike, and distilled them into a single harrowing correspondence. Towards the end of the film, shortly before his suicide, Curtis is seen writing the letter in his typical capital-letters-only script. 'I saw *Apocalypse Now* at the cinema, I couldn't take my eyes away from the screen,' he wrote. 'On the record there's Marlon Brando reading *The Hollow Men*, the struggle between man's conscience and his heart until things go too far, get out of hand, and can never be repaired. Is everything so worthless in the end? Is there any more? What lies beyond? What is left to carry on?'

Richey Edwards often wrote in a similar style: his manifestos sent out to fans were usually in capitals only. Ian Curtis was probably Richey Edwards' biggest musical hero. *Apocalypse Now* was probably Richey Edwards' favourite film – it's fair to say that he was obsessed with it. The Manics, circa 1994, with their military costumes, warfare face paint and army-camp netting, was straight out of the film. 'When someone phones you up at five a.m. five times a week asking if General Kurtz is telling the truth in *Apocalypse Now* then you know something's gone wrong,' said Nicky Wire about his bandmate's fixation.

At the start of the film Martin Sheen's character smashes up his hotel room, cutting and smashing himself into a bloody mess. Sheen is sent further up the river into the jungle to track and kill the notorious General Kurtz, played by Marlon Brando.

The further Sheen went, the more suffocating madness he found, until Brando himself was confronted, hidden in the shadows of his temple-like encampment. This was *Heart of Darkness* for the Vietnam generation.

During the autumn leg of the Manics' 1994 tour, Richey Edwards found and purchased the exact same make and model of camera used by the photojournalist played by Dennis Hopper in the film. Edwards toured Europe with it hanging around his neck. No one confirmed whether or not he ever used it to take photos. While in his Dennis Hopper phase he also had more tattoos added to his arms, one of which simply read 'I'll surf this beach' – a line from Robert Duvall's maverick character in the film. The links to *Apocalypse Now* didn't end there: in Richey Edwards' last ever photo shoot, which he allowed to take place inside his Cardiff flat, he posed in front of a large, framed poster for the film.

# XII

# A MAN WHO WOULD MUTILATE HIMSELF

*October to November 1994*

Against medical advice, Richey Edwards had checked himself out of the Priory in early September. The band agreed that it would be better for him to come on tour with them so they could keep a close eye on him and so he wouldn't feel dislocated from his only meaningful purpose in life. What soon became apparent was that he'd changed. He had managed to stop drinking, but he was smoking to excess. He would also talk about religious texts and carry Bible quotations around in his notebook, talking about them to anyone who would listen.

He might not have been 'born again', but it was clear that some religious event had happened to him. Despite saying he was going to use nature, not God, as part of the twelve-step process, he increasingly seemed to be using religion. Had he really found God in the Priory without wanting to admit it? He was also following a new motto each day, he would pray before each gig, he wrote 'Love' on his knuckles, and he said he wished he'd written Prince's 'The Cross'. He would soon add further tattoos with religious overtones as well.

'It's something that interests me,' said Edwards, when asked about religion. 'You've only got to look at our name, we've got Preachers in our name, I was made to go to chapel till I was thirteen, on our first album you've got "Crucifix Kiss", a cross on the cover, a quote from Nietzsche about Christianity, so it goes deeper.'

'I don't necessarily understand the contradictions myself,' Edwards tried to explain to *Melody Maker*. 'In Ecclesiastes there's a line, "All is vanity", and I do really believe that. I think everybody's first love is themselves. Some more than others. Some can divide themselves, and give something of themselves to another person. Which I've never been able to do, because I've never trusted another person enough to do that. I don't feel strong enough that I could cope with the rejection if they left me. A lot of people don't cope with it, if something like that happens. I would not allow myself to be used like that.'

By the middle of the month it was still unclear whether Richey would be touring or even if the tour was going to happen, in light of comments that the others wouldn't do it without him. Publicly the PR machine said there was nothing to say, but everyone around Edwards knew he was still on the edge of needing hospitalisation.

The band moved into Blue Stone Studios to rehearse for the upcoming concert dates. Set in the Pembrokeshire countryside, this converted farm was a perfect retreat. Richey was trying hard to learn how to play the new songs and although he was cutting himself, he was eating fairly well. Later, the band allowed journalists and photographers to visit the farm for interviews about the album and tour – and, of course, the health of their rhythm guitarist. *NME* sent writer Stuart Bailie and photographer Kevin Cummins to meet the band. Bailie was perhaps fearing the worst in Edwards, who he'd known for a few years. 'The cheeks are sunken,' he wrote, 'the gaze is maybe more abstracted than you remember, but Richey, freshly released from hospital, looks alright.'

Edwards explained to Bailie that he was no longer to be called 'Richey' but was now to be known as 'Richard'. 'That's my name,' he said. 'It's always been my name, ever since the day I was born.' Was it symbolic of some personality change? 'No, nothing like that. The band have never called me Richey anyway. They've always called me Android, or something like that.'

Edwards drove the entourage out to a nearby beach for a photo session with Kevin Cummins (for the 1 October 1994 issue of *NME*), and then back to the farm. After some cajoling, he agreed to pose for more photos alone and the shots of him at the farm hugging a statue have become almost legendary. 'It was bloody cold that day,' recalls Kevin Cummins. 'Richey was pretty withdrawn by then. James only really wanted me to shoot band shots but I talked them into doing some pairs. Then when we got back to the recording studio I saw the statue. I was only going to use it with Richey standing slightly behind it but he clung onto it and transported himself somewhere else. It was a very harrowing picture to take and I doubt that he was even aware I was shooting it by the end.'

For his interview, Edwards and Bradfield sat in Edwards' room while Bailie asked the questions that had been on everybody's lips. Edwards admitted that he had locked himself away in Cardiff for two days before being hospitalised. He also explained why he'd stopped eating. 'You could say that I had an eating problem. Because if I ate too much, and I was drinking, I got all puffed up and blotchy. And I'm too vain to be like that. I am a vain person. I couldn't handle looking like that, I couldn't look in the mirror. All is vanity.'

The first leg of the tour was intensive. The band flew to Paris, then performed ten shows in eleven nights. It was a test – one that tentatively Richey Edwards managed to pass. He kept himself to himself, he wasn't drinking, and was pretty much left to his own devices while the band kept an eye on him from a distance. 'The first day, I was really, really nervous. I was so on edge,' said James Dean Bradfield. 'I kept thinking, "If you cut yourself up now, son, everything will be wasted." He has wanted to cut himself on this tour already, but hasn't. And that's a first.

'We have to watch how we govern ourselves now. Without being corny, Richey and I were, if not quite birding and boozing buddies, something like that. We'd go out or stay up after the gigs. We can't do that now. I wouldn't want it for him. As far as his agenda is concerned, it's just not on the agenda. We don't want to be unfeeling dickheads.' The band, as ever, were sensitive to Edwards' plight, but not exactly sure how they could help. Edwards'

Prozac ingestion helped to smooth out his highs and lows, but he was left with a feeling of semi-numbness. The filing down of the rough edges had left a different man to the one that had started the summer: a different man to the one that the band knew and loved. It was like having an alien in their midst − although they all loved him, it unsettled everyone.

'She is Suffering' was released as a single in early October. James Dean Bradfield flew over to Ireland for promotional interviews and a solo TV performance. Sitting behind a desk with the Irish presenter in a neat white shirt, the opening banter was pretty banal − questions about how he liked Ireland − before the presenter casually tossed in, 'Oh, by the way I was just reading about Richey Edwards. What's the situation now with him?' Bradfield was slightly taken back, although he was no doubt used to being quizzed like this. 'Oh, he's alright,' he stalled. 'All his vital signs are flashing, he's fine, he's breathing.' Difficult smiles followed, and then Bradfield gave a solo acoustic performance of 'She is Suffering'. The video for the single showed Edwards filmed earlier in the year, playing with the band in a room filled with gothic candles on elaborate stands. As lightning flashes, Edwards tilts his head back and looks to the heavens.

'I was worried that, because Richey's undergoing treatment, he'd turn into Peter Gabriel, lyrically,' said James Dean Bradfield. 'He's living on a different proverb a day at the moment and I didn't want our songs to turn into psychobabble. But he's kept his own voice, which is admirable. It hasn't weakened us. But I'm not prepared to say, hey, it's made us stronger.'

The UK dates began on 5 October in Glasgow. 'It's a well known fact that anorexics try to cover up their condition with baggy clothes all the time,' says Nicky Wire. 'And on the first day of the British tour, Richey walks in and he's wearing the tightest pair of girls' leggings that I've ever seen in my life. He still wanted the rest of the world to know that he was completely fucked up. Everyone knew already. I said, "Why are you doing that? You haven't got to prove that you are whatever you are."'

The band played thirteen shows in sixteen nights and then moved on to Ireland with support coming from the female-fronted bands, Sleeper and Dub War. Edwards was the thinnest he'd been since the Manics had achieved fame. He dyed his hair ginger and had it cut into a fringe/wedge. As well as wearing skin-tight leggings, he walked around in a skinny-rib T-shirt that displayed the slogan, 'THEY FUCK YOU UP, YOUR MUM AND DAD'. With his emaciated looks, very public personal problems and history of a private cult of fans, it could have been expected that he'd draw more extreme fan worship than ever before. More people were appearing at the band's shows and hotels, in ever more extreme make-up. Fans were reported to have broken into his hotel room, drunk from his used coffee cups, stolen his partially used bars of soap, and rolled around in the bed he'd slept in.

*Mojo*'s Keith Cameron was at the Norwich show on 7 October. The autumn gigs saw the band use a Martin Hall idea and make their entrance to the theme music from the TV series *The World at War*, but on this occasion the CD skipped and a German 'oom-pah' band started up just as the band was about to walk on, totally ruining the atmosphere and tension that had built up. Cameron reported that the band went ballistic and Richey just stubbed a cigarette out on his arm. On stage, Edwards' return was noticeable to those who had heard the summer shows without him. The guitar sound had more solidity and the *Bible* songs were more threatening for it.

After playing Manchester on the thirteenth the band had an off-day before a show in Sheffield on the fifteenth. Richey Edwards used his free time to get some more tattoos in Sheffield. These tattoos seemed to shed light on his spiritual awakening in the Priory: one of the new additions was a ring of vines and roses, inside which were smaller circles. The words around the next smaller circle read 'Hemisphere of Land' at the top and 'Hemisphere of Water' at the bottom. At the twelve o'clock position it read 'Jerusalem' and under a line below that was the word 'Hell'. At the bottom of the inner circle was a triangle with the legend, 'Mount Purgatory'. This all comes from Dante's 'Inferno' in the *Divine Comedy*, a massive work of twelfth-century Italian literature. In his 'Inferno', Dante divided the world into two hemispheres: one of water and one of land. Jerusalem was the centre of the world and below was the inferno, like a giant cone, at the point of which was Hell at the middle of the planet. If you were to pass through Hell and out the other side you would reach Mount Purgatory in the hemisphere of water. The *Divine Comedy* suggests that no man can live a 'right' life and must pass through Hell before eventually getting to Heaven. This would be done by ascending Mount Purgatory, made up of seven steps, with each one representing one of the seven deadly sins.

The second tattoo was equally heavy in terms of its subject matter. Another circular design, it included the words 'Caina', 'Antendra', 'Ptolomae' and 'Judecca'. Again, this concept comes from the 'Inferno' – this time, from the Ninth Circle of the Inferno: the one closest to Hell and Satan himself. The Ninth Circle contains four types of treachery and the souls captured here are cased in varying amounts of ice. Some have only their faces above the ice, some have tears frozen to their faces, some are covered completely. The rest of this second tattoo read, 'Traitors to their lovers, traitors to their guests, traitors to their country, traitors to their kindred'. These words tie in directly with 'Caina', 'Antendra', 'Ptolomae' and 'Judecca' – the four types of traitors captured in each of the four regions.

These new tattoos held worrying signs: Richey had felt the need to map out on his arm the journey through Hell and the reminders of the Ninth Circle's areas of treachery. He'd labelled himself as a traitor. It looked as if he was expecting to have to pass through Hell before reaching his own salvation.

•

In November, the tour headed back to mainland Europe with Suede. Playing just a couple of shows in each country before moving on meant that it was a hectic schedule. The pressure was bound to come to a head. 'It was possibly the worst time I've ever experienced in my life,' said Nicky Wire. '[Richey] was on the verge of madness. And James just didn't stop drinking.' So much so that one night when Wire had had enough and told Bradfield that he was quitting the band, the singer couldn't even remember having the conversation the next day. After each show,

Bradfield would go off drinking and partying away from the rest of the band – partly because he didn't want to get drunk in front of Edwards. They would rarely see him again until the sound-check for the following night's show. Nicky Wire was feeling homesick, had lost some of his luggage and had to fly home at one point for some medical treatment. When he got back to the tour, Richey Edwards had taken another turn for the worse. He'd read an interview with Dub War in which they'd discussed the earlier dates with the Manics and they'd made a couple of negative comments about Edwards. One statement was that he wasn't drinking as much as had been previously reported in the press – well, he was now a member of Alcoholics Anonymous – and another said that he and Nicky Wire walked around Blackwood as though they were big stars. Neither comment was particularly nasty, but for Edwards it was another body-blow. His fragile mental state was struggling to cope with even the smallest upset. Richey was also driving Wire crazy with his constant smoking in their shared hotel room. Edwards' day-to-day existence was limited to hotel rooms, tour bus and concert venues. He never wanted to try and explore the towns and cities they played in, saying that one day was not enough to understand anywhere. He and Wire would stay in a hotel Ibis each night. 'The only nice thing was waking up together and having breakfast together, with a bit of French bread and apricot jam,' says Wire. 'That was the only smidgeon of normality during the whole tour.' It was rare to see Edwards without a cigarette and a cup of coffee in his hands at any time of the day. Everyone in the band had their own problems and everyone seemed to be dealing with them by keeping themselves to themselves, each in their own little world.

Writer Simon Price joined the band for a couple of the French dates in Lyon and Paris. On the bus, Edwards was usually wrapped in a blanket – either watching videos or playing Sega games. One night Price was warned by James Dean Bradfield not to go on the tour bus as Richey was 'teetering'. Price asked if Richey had gone to bed, and Sean Moore replied, 'Richey doesn't go to bed. He goes to *the abyss*.' In Paris, the band agreed to do a group photo session with Tom Sheehan at the Montparnasse Cemetery. Edwards was wearing the over-sized boiler suit that he'd been wearing on stage. On the back he'd scrawled, 'Once, I remember well, my life was a feast where all hearts opened and all wines flowed. Alas the gospel has gone by! Suppose damnation were eternal! Then a man who would mutilate himself is well damned, isn't he?' Then they headed into the Catacombs. Edwards was initially taken aback by the sight of hundreds upon hundreds of bones and skulls. He told Sheehan that he could take his picture as long as he didn't have to touch the bones, but by the end of the session he was rubbing his face across the wall of skeletons and even kissing them, smiling as he did so.

From France they moved north for a show in Amsterdam. The show wasn't the best they'd ever played, but afterwards Richey Edwards seemed to be in a good mood. Throughout the tour Nicky Wire had had a routine of asking Edwards to lift his shirt up each night before bed so that Wire could check if Edwards had been slashing himself. This night he had been: there was a vertical slash down the centre of his chest. The sight of the blood depressed and angered Wire, who sat down and talked to his friend for hours, but all he could get in response was, 'I feel alright now'. Unfortunately, Edwards wasn't alright: he was far from it. He'd been reading about Def Leppard guitarist Steve Clark who had suffered such bad stage fright that he'd smashed his hand so that he wouldn't have to go on stage. Richey Edwards slipped away to the shops and returned to the tour bus with a meat cleaver. It was thought that he was considering chopping off some of his fingers so that he wouldn't have to play. The band and crew talked him out of it and got rid of the weapon. There were other unreported problems, too. At the end of the tour, an unnamed member of the road-crew quit because being required to kick down a toilet door and retrieve Edward's body was not part of his job description. 'In retrospect I think it was the wrong decision,' said Sean Moore. 'Touring, especially on that European tour with Suede, proved to be very detrimental to his health and personality.' He was right: the damage that had been done was probably deeper than anyone imagined.

**T**he **American Psychiatric Association** describes depression as 'a disorder of mood, characterized by sadness and loss of interest in usually satisfying activities, a negative view of self, hopelessness, passivity, indecisiveness, suicidal intentions, loss of appetite, weight loss, sleep disturbances, and other physical symptoms.' Most of these characteristics were exhibited by Richey Edwards prior to 1995. They were also shown by Sylvia Plath. Plath, like many others, would only gain widespread fame and recognition after her death. Mainly known as a confessional poet, she broke through to prominence as a novelist. She had a history of suicide attempts and mental breakdowns, some of which she wrote about in *The Bell Jar* (initially under an assumed name), which was based on her work experience from college at *Mademoiselle* magazine in New York. She was committed to a mental hospital and underwent electroshock therapy. She married and had two children, but the short marriage broke up when her husband had an affair and she was left in London trying to earn enough from various writing assignments to survive.

Despite having two young children to mother, she seemed inept at the basics of life, always needing help.[33] She was also known to turn her frustrations in on herself and once she'd sliced off the top of her own thumb. She wrote about this incident in *Cut*.

At Christmas 1962, she was left caring for the children in a London flat: it was a miserable time. All three of them fell ill, and she had no central heating while the country was gripped by an icy winter. But, during January, she seemed to snap out of it, even managing to attend a party. During these final weeks, she embarked on a flurry of writing and she had a stack of poems finished by the middle of February.

On Sunday, 11 February 1963, she carefully left some bread and milk for her children's breakfast even though she would have known they were too young to feed themselves. Plath opened the children's bedroom window and sealed the kitchen door with towels and tape, then she turned on the gas oven, left a note on the pram and put her head in the oven. She was thirty-one years old.

It is now considered that a good portion of Plath's work was an elongated suicide note stretching over many years. 'That such a final, tragic, and awful thing as suicide can exist in the midst of remarkable beauty is one of the vastly contradictory and paradoxical aspects of life and art,' says Kay Redfield Jamison in the book *Touched with Fire: Manic-Depressive Illness and the Artistic Temperament.* 'Recent research strongly suggests that, compared with the general population, writers and artists show a vastly disproportionate rate of manic-depressive illness.'

# XIII

## FEVER AND EXHAUSTION
*December 1994*

Hamburg, Germany, 2 December 1994. Hamburg, the city of The Beatles' early Star Club debauchery, a city where the Fab Four had surpassed the Manics' excesses thirty years earlier. But now the touring was pushing the Manics to emotional limits they'd never reached before, especially Richey Edwards. After the show at the Markthalle, they returned to their hotel. Early the next morning Nicky Wire awoke and found that Richey was gone from his room. He immediately headed down to the lobby.

'Where's Richey?'

'I think he went outside.'

At these words, Wire left the hotel to look for Edwards. He soon spied him standing outside, facing the wall of the hotel. As Wire approached he saw that Edwards was rocking slightly back and forth, in his pyjamas. He also noticed that there was blood running down the wall, and down Edwards, from a cut on his face. 'I want to go home,' said Edwards, and before Wire could stop him he rammed his head against the wall again. 'I want to go home,' he repeated. 'I want to go home.' Gently, Wire pulled Edwards away from the wall and managed to get him back inside the hotel. At that moment the European tour was effectively over.

The final dates of the European tour were cancelled, leaving almost three weeks of down time before the three high-profile shows planned for London. Cancelling these gigs was not really an option. Whether or not Richey would be able to play them was another matter as the Manics tour operation headed for home.

Richey Edwards' drinking seems to have made something of a comeback during the autumn. John Robb saw him in London. 'I interviewed Richey and Nicky shortly before Richey disappeared; it was in that hotel in London that he was last seen in [the Embassy],' says Robb. 'They were both sleeping in the same room but the vibe had changed and Richey was telling me he had to drink a bottle of vodka every night to fall asleep, which seemed a bit dramatic but not in a way you would think, "He's really on the skids." He was talking more darkly than a couple of years before but not in a way that you could tell what was about to happen. He had a bottle of vodka by his bed. He was saying things like, "I'm an alcoholic now", which I thought was quite strange because most people who are alcoholic don't realise they are.'

The Astoria on London's Charing Cross Road was the venue of choice when the Manics decided to play three massively anticipated shows on December 19, 20 and 21. It was hoped that these concerts would provide a triumphant end to what had been a terribly traumatic year. Richey Edwards' problems at the end of the European leg of the tour cast a shadow over what might happen in London. Perhaps the elongated break leading up to these shows would be sufficient to get Edwards into a state that he was stable enough to get through them.

The first two shows were being filmed by video-maker Tony van den Ende, who was also filming them in close-up during sound-checks at the venue in the afternoon. This footage would then be added to the film of the gig itself.

There was something about these three shows – no one quite knew what it was – but something was lingering just outside any conscious perceptions. During the concerts, a technical problem with feedback from the monitors meant they were all suffering from nose bleeds (much to Richey's glee), partly because the shows were so very damn loud. Afterwards they said that everyone felt that it was a 'moment' in their career, and Richey was peaking in his weirdness. During a break in the afternoon's filming, Tony van den Ende and Nicky Wire were chatting while sat on the drum riser and Wire was in a good mood, but then he glanced at his watch and that changed. 'Get a fucking move on!' he snapped and everything was hurried up again. Van den Ende later found out that this was because they absolutely had to finish by five thirty so that Richey could eat at an exact time. Nothing could be done that might upset the schedule.

During the actual shows the Manics were almost unrecognisable from the band that had struggled across Europe. The first two nights had eight or nine *Bible* songs in the set-list, a sprinkling of older singles, and James Dean Bradfield donning a Santa hat for solo renditions of 'Raindrops Keep Falling on My Head' and 'Bright Eyes'. Both nights ended with 'Motown Junk' and 'You Love Us'. The shows were adrenalin-fuelled, tight and – despite a lot of the material – joyous.

Richey would write out a quote on the evening's set-list and add a few doodles. On the last night he had written out a quote by J. G. Ballard, which began 'I believe in alcoholism, venereal disease, fever and exhaustion'. On this night, Richey was keeping back from his microphone. People commented that they could actually hear his guitar playing in the mix, and that it wasn't too bad. 'Faster', 'Yes' and 'She is Suffering' opened the show with a *Bible*-heavy one-two-three. James Dean Bradfield's solo slot even included Wham!'s 'Last Christmas', but the mood was heavy. Again the final song was 'You Love Us'. Whatever had been boiling up through the show, through the tour, and through the year, finally burst out in an orgy of delight and destruction. Richey began smashing his head against his microphone; James Bradfield smashed his guitar and stormed off the stage; Nicky Wire demolished his bass and left. By now, Edwards' guitar and amp had been trashed. Finally, Richey, who had been hitting his head with a piece of broken guitar, used his body to crush Sean Moore's drum kit. It was his last public act as a Manic Street Preacher.

Afterwards, Nicky Wire said that those five minutes of release had been the best five minutes of his life. 'I was so nervous every night, that the end was just a relief,' he said. 'It was just brilliant. We were transported back to the days of "Motown Junk". Beautiful. It meant more than any of the songs. Until we saw the bill . . . ' The cost was estimated at various sums between £8,000 and £26,000.

Partly because of what would follow, these shows at the Astoria have become enshrined in poignancy. In 2007, the *Observer Music Monthly* listed the final night in its '25 Greatest Gigs Ever' feature. At the time, Caroline Sullivan (writing about the first night in the *Guardian* under the heading 'Bible of Hate') described Nicky Wire as Joey Ramone and James Dean Bradfield as Noddy Holder, ending with 'The sense was that it had been a ritual rather than a rock show, with the formerly central character of [Richey Edwards] now peripheral.'

The intensity of these shows – combined with the empathy felt towards the band in light of the year they'd just suffered – no doubt affected the group's placing in *Melody Maker*'s end-of-year poll. The Manics were voted the 'Best Band' ahead of Oasis, Blur, Suede, Nirvana, R.E.M. and Pulp. They also picked up the award for 'Best Live Band'. *The Holy Bible* came second in 'Album of the Year', behind *Parklife* but ahead of *Definitely Maybe*. Richey Edwards made the list of 'Sex Symbol of the Year' and came second place in 'Man of the Year', behind Kurt Cobain.

The day after the final Astoria show was Richey Edwards' twenty-seventh birthday. As a keen student of rock history, he – as much as anyone else – would have been only too aware that this was the age reached by numerous dead rock stars. Jimi Hendrix, Brian Jones, Janis Joplin and Jim Morrison all failed to reach their twenty-eighth birthdays, and of course Kurt Cobain had been twenty-seven when he shot himself earlier in the year. For Richey, there was no big birthday celebration this year – just a ride back home with Sean Moore and the prospect of a quiet Christmas with his parents in Blackwood.

**O**ne of Edwards' favourite rock books was Jerry Hopkins and Danny Sugerman's *No One Here Gets Out Alive* – a close study of The Doors. The book ended with a vague suggestion that Jim Morrison might have faked his own death and vanished due to some irregularities over the paperwork and quick burial of his coffin. Morrison died in Paris, where he'd moved to reinvent his life as a poet and not be a rock star any more. Richey Edwards knew this story well, and it was not until Stephen Davis' book on Morrison (*Life, Death, Legend*) was published in 2004 that any lingering conspiracy theorists were put right.

In Arthur Rimbaud's case, vanishing was definitely what he did well. Seen as a teenage genius, he decided to change his life at the tender age of nineteen. By then he'd turned against adult life, against the religion that had been forced upon him as a child and against the life as poet. Camus had called him 'the greatest', yet he destroyed his papers and vanished into the ether; many presumed him dead for years afterwards. In reality, Rimbaud had set out on foot and visited Germany, Holland and Denmark before settling in North Africa and running guns. His influence as poet, hellraiser and binge-drinker spread to the Beat Generation writers in the 1940s and 1950s, and to the punk bands of the 1970s.

# XIV

## A PRELUDE TO DESTINY

*January 1995*

Between Christmas and New Year's Eve 1994, the four members of Manic Street Preachers saw quite a lot of each other. Whether it was to swap presents or just hang out at their parents' or Nicky Wire's house, it was as though the troubles of the year had been put behind them. Richey was refraining from alcohol and eating well, relatively speaking. One evening they gathered together to watch a video of their show at the Clapham Grand from the previous March. Part way through the evening, Richey asked for a bowl and made a show of slowly unwrapping two chocolate bars and breaking them up into pieces in the bowl. On one hand, he was showing that he was eating; on the other hand, his meal consisted only of a couple of chocolate bars. 'Among us we'd take the piss out of it, and you'd laugh. It still had an edge to it amongst us, as four people,' said James Dean Bradfield. 'And he would take the piss out of himself as well. So it wasn't all po-faced.' But others remember it differently. 'It was macabre, shall we say. That's the word,' added Nicky Wire. 'He knew what he was doing to us and we knew what he was doing to himself. It was just a terrible situation.'

Edwards had been seen walking around Blackwood and seemed to be in a good mood; he even ventured back into the Red Lion alone. 'He just seemed really friendly,' said a local who was in there that day. 'He wasn't ever a star in here. Only with the youngsters. Most people couldn't give a fuck. But he wasn't trying to be a star either. I can definitely state that. He wasn't patronising. It was as if he wanted something from us, I think he was desperate to belong.'

Over the Christmas period Richey had been writing furiously and by the time the band met up in early January for five days of practice and rehearsals, he had accumulated a thick wedge of lyrics and prose – although he admitted that much of it wasn't exactly great. The band had booked the House in the Woods studio near Cobham in Surrey. There, Edwards presented Nicky Wire with a folder of around sixty song lyrics, which Wire photocopied and passed on to Moore and Bradfield. 'They were pretty heavy-going,' said Sean Moore. 'There wasn't a lot to pick out, to be honest. Most of it was pretty fragmented and rambling.'

'The lyrics in the last file he gave us were more poetry of a sort,' explained Nicky Wire. 'There was a lot of ranting.' There was certainly some useful material, however, which relieved James Dean Bradfield who had been worried that Edwards' writing would be unusable.

Among the new things Richey had prepared were lyrics for what would become 'Elvis Impersonator: Blackpool Pier', 'Kevin Carter', 'Small Black Flowers That Grow in the Sky', 'Removables' and 'The Girl Who Wanted to be God'. James Dean Bradfield worked up acoustic versions of Richey's lyrics for 'Elvis Impersonator: Blackpool Pier' and a 'bit more salsa, a bit more chintzy' (Bradfield) version of 'Kevin Carter'. When he heard a tape of the latter, Edwards said, 'I don't want my lyrics to sound like that.' Before leaving the sessions, Edwards passed a note to Bradfield suggesting that the next album sound like 'Pantera meets Nine Inch Nails meets *Screamadelica*'.

Richey seemed at ease during the week and was even described as being happy, something that he hadn't been for a long time. At the end of the stint he continued his end-of-sessions ritual with presents for the band, which included a copy of the *Daily Telegraph* and a Mars bar for Nicky Wire, and a CD for James Dean Bradfield.

The plan had been to tour America in the spring, with Richey and James going to North America ahead of the others to conduct interviews and drum up some advance publicity. Flights had been booked for 1 February, so they had a few weeks of down time.

Nicky Wire took the chance to take his wife for a short break in Barcelona. When he got back he received a phone call from James Dean Bradfield informing him that Richey had gone missing. While Wire had been away, Edwards' seventeen-year-old dog, Snoopy, had died on 14 January and Richey was naturally upset. He went with his sister to a local garden centre to buy a tree to mark the spot where the dog was buried. Rachel recalled that it was a really cold day and Richey gave his sister his bobble hat to keep warm. When he took off the hat he revealed a completely shaved head. Later, at his parents' house, Richey pulled out a little camera and took lots of photos of his parents. As he left that day he turned and took a long look at Rachel, eyeing her up and down to such an extent that she asked him if anything was wrong with her clothes. He left without replying.

Shortly afterwards, when Richey couldn't be contacted at his Cardiff flat, his parents assumed he was in London with the band. The band assumed he was in Blackwood with his parents. He'd actually gone to visit friends in Newport. While there, he called in at TJ's to see a gig by the 60ft Dolls. Dolls drummer Carl Bevan didn't recognise him. 'He had a loose expression,' he said. 'Like there was something loose in his head.' The day after Nicky Wire got home from Spain, Richey returned home and contacted the rest of the band. 'He did love his dog, that was a Manics thing,' explained Nicky Wire. 'We all had dogs. And they all died.'

'I wouldn't make too much significance out of it,' added James Dean Bradfield. 'He was always adept at too much symbolism. It wasn't a breaking point, to be honest. All of the bad things that happened to us in the past were almost like arbitrary disasters. That was a dog that had had a long life, a natural thing.'

'He was well on his way before then,' said Wire. 'It certainly didn't help, but something was gonna give. It gave in the summer, and it was just a question of whether he was gonna change it or not. He didn't seem to get enjoyment from many things by the end. He was upset, but I felt good, actually. When he cried naturally, it was nothing to do with the Priory, it was just his pet had died. It made him feel a real emotion, he was sad again. So he said.'

The band had earlier cancelled some upcoming shows in Japan but Richey still agreed to do an interview with Midori Tsukagoshi for the Japanese magazine *Music Life* on 23 January. Edwards collected the writer at the train station and Tsukagoshi was shocked at the sight of the man who greeted him. With the shaved head, Edwards was wearing striped pyjamas and the same Converse trainers that Kurt Cobain had been pictured wearing when he committed suicide. With his slight frame, he looked like he might have just stepped out of a concentration camp. He put Nirvana's *In Utero* in the tape deck and drove the writer back to his flat at Atlantic Wharf.

The interview that followed touched on many important subjects and is now known to be the last interview Edwards ever gave. As far as the general public is concerned, these were his last words. Tsukagoshi started with the obvious question about Edwards' appearance. The interviewer pointed out that the shaving of one's head could be taken as a very significant statement. 'I was bored with my old hairstyle, it was irritating me,' said Edwards. 'If I can't sleep I tend to have destructive ideas, and I have to do something to sort them out. I couldn't sleep and all I could think of doing was shaving my head. So I did. I'm very vain, and I was almost in love with my hairstyle. But in the end I just felt like abandoning things like that. I dumped a lot of notebooks, threw them in the river. They were full of notes, thoughts for lyrics, that kind of thing. Since Christmas I'd been writing a lot of stuff, but when I look at them again I realised eighty per cent of them just weren't good. Some people keep everything they write, but unless it's good, you shouldn't. I mean, you can see this flat isn't big enough to keep everything anyway. So I spent a whole night reading through it and then threw away what I didn't like.' Nicky Wire later disputed Edwards' statement about throwing things away, but with the waterfront right outside Richey's apartment he could probably have heaved them over his balcony and straight into the water. Wire couldn't possibly know what had been dumped and what hadn't. Later in the interview Edwards changed subjects abruptly and said, 'You know, I miss my dog, Snoopy. He died two weeks ago. That's why I shaved my head.'

Edwards was also questioned, and spoke candidly, about his decision not to get involved in any long-term relationships. 'I've never wanted to love somebody insincerely, and I don't mean only sexually but intellectually and mentally too,' he explained. 'For instance, you might be watching TV with someone you loved and see an attractive person on TV. It'd be insincere to me to have any feeling about the person on TV. Most people are more mature than me in that sense but I still can't deal with it. If my partner said, "That poster of River Phoenix looks gorgeous!" I'd have to say, "Bye". If I was in the street and my partner was thinking, "Wow! He's stunning!" I'd wonder why she was with me. Seriously, if I was in love with a woman, she'd have to be more attractive than Bette Davis, more than anyone else. I'd peel every picture off my walls.'

Late in the month, Richey was back to phoning Nicky Wire at night. He'd call on the premise of wanting to check the time or some detail about practice. He really just needed to talk and would spend two hours rambling about *Apocalypse Now* or the Mike Leigh film *Naked*. The conversation, or monologue, would ultimately end with Edwards being frustrated because he just couldn't get his point across.

During January, Tony van den Ende was working on a Manics video at an editing suite in London. Rob Stringer and Martin Hall were with him when Richey Edwards arrived, apparently having driven himself up from Cardiff. Van den Ende was shocked by Edwards' appearance – he hadn't yet seen him with a shaved head – plus he was wearing only pyjamas, with a ribbon tied around them, and slippers. Edwards hung around for about half an hour and then departed, apparently to drive back to Cardiff. It had been at least a five-hour round trip to spend thirty minutes in the editing suite.

On 29 January, the band reconvened at the House in the Woods for two more days of practice before the US dates, which would be their first for three years. Sony's Rob Stringer visited the band there and reported that Richey was in great spirits and was saying how much he was looking forward to America. As with Ian Curtis, it was trip he would never make.[34]

**I**f you closed your eyes and just listened you could hear nothing but a cacophonous din bouncing off the walls and the vaulted ceiling. With some concentration you'd realise that it was a hundred human voices meshed into one droning sound. Listen even harder and you'd recognise a multitude of languages and dialects all fighting to be heard above the others. Open your eyes and you'd find yourself not in the middle of a bustling marketplace or in the centre of a battle, but in line at a post office. The customers in this cavernous room were a mixture of East and West, turbans and long flowing gowns mixing easily with suits and ties – but then this city had always been the proverbial melting pot.

This was Istanbul. The year was 1933.

Third in line to be served was the Russian. Under the Russian's left arm was a thick, crumpled paper packet, tied up with a couple of rounds of string. In his right hand was a pungent cigarette, which was not being smoked; it just added to the smog, hanging idly to one side. The Russian watched as a hunched old woman purchased two stamps and shuffled away into the crowd. Then a well-tanned, healthy-looking Westerner handed over a white envelope and two coins before striding away. The Russian stepped up to the metal grille that separated the employees from the customers. In stuttering but proficient Turkish, the Russian asked for the parcel to be sent first-class to Paris. The fee was paid and he moved away from the counter, a wry smile forming on his face. The sending of this parcel would set in motion events that would gently echo through history. It would cause international outrage and form the basis of an enduring mystery.

Emerging from the post office, the Russian was met with a blast of searing heat that reflected from the whitewashed walls of the narrow street. Carefully negotiating a path in and around the stalls and shoppers, the Russian wandered along the packed thoroughfare before taking a right turn into a side alley, glad of the shade that greeted the exit from the main street and welcomed into the shadows that would cover him for the next seventy years.

*C isla*, or *Numbers*, was first published in Paris in 1930. Run by, and for, Russian émigrés in their mother tongue, the journal ruffled Western feathers with its views on culture and society. Articles and opinions were sent in from exiled Russians scattered around the world. In 1933, the editor received a mysterious parcel from Istanbul, more a manuscript than an article, with little more information on the author than the non-gender-specific name, M. Ageyev. The text was titled *Story with Cocaine* and outlined the decadent coming of age of a Russian teenager during the time of the revolution. The journal printed an abridged version of the story and the reception to it was so overwhelming that the publication of the full-length version, *Novel with Cocaine,* soon followed. The mysterious Ageyev was rumoured to be moving to Paris but he was never heard from again. Half a century later, the original Russian book was translated into French, and then English. The introduction to these later editions discussed how to carry out the perfect disappearance, such as that achieved by the author fifty years earlier. Numerous theories have since sprung up about the real identity of the author and what became of him or her. Reports of the writer being Vladimir Nabokov or the relatively obscure Marc Levi have hung around for decades, but the Russian seems to have slipped through the net.

# XV

## GONE

*31 January to 1 February 1995*

On Tuesday, 31 January 1995, an annoying single by Rednex, 'Cotton Eye Joe', was enjoying its fourth consecutive week at number one in the UK, while Celine Dion's even more annoying *The Colour of My Love* was in the midst of a six-week run as the number one album. It was on this gloomy Tuesday that James Dean Bradfield was a passenger in the silver Vauxhall Cavalier that Richey Edwards drove to the Embassy Hotel on London's Bayswater Road. Richey Edwards' own car was actually a white Ford Fiesta, the band owned the Cavalier, although only Edwards drove it. It wasn't a very rock 'n' roll vehicle to own, plus they'd bought it second hand. During the journey, Bradfield played Edwards a demo cassette of a new song called 'Small Black Flowers That Grow in the Sky' on the car stereo. Edwards said he thought the song sounded great and was happier than he had been when hearing the initial demo of his lyrics for 'Kevin Carter'. At around teatime, Edwards pulled into the underground car park at the hotel and they checked in. After taking the lift to the fifth floor, they settled into adjoining rooms overlooking Hyde Park. They agreed to freshen up and meet in half an hour.

When Bradfield returned to Edwards' room thirty minutes later he found Richey taking a bath. Bradfield asked if Edwards wanted to go and browse around the Queensway area, but Edwards said he'd prefer to go and see a film. Bradfield agreed that this was a good idea and said he'd return at eight thirty. When he returned, Edwards said he'd changed his mind and that he would have an early night so that he would be ready for the flight the next day. Bradfield said that he'd meet Richey first thing in the morning and went out to meet a friend for a drink. He was back at the hotel and in bed by eleven thirty p.m.

Richey spent the evening in his room. He telephoned his mother and told her that he wasn't really looking forward to the American trip, contradicting what he'd been saying to others. He slipped this into the conversation casually: it didn't seem like a big deal to Sherry. Apart from that, there was nothing unusual about the conversation. They said goodnight and have not spoken since.

Edwards seemed to know exactly what he was going to do and kept this information completely to himself. He sat on the bed and removed some books and videos (including *Equus* and *Naked*[35]) from his bag. He carefully placed them in a box and wrote a note that simply said, 'I love you'. Then he wrapped up the box like a birthday present. He decorated the outside of the box with collages and literary quotations, plus a picture of a Germanic-looking house and Bugs Bunny. The package was addressed to Jo, the mystery girl that he'd mentioned (in the interview with Midori Tsukagoshi), but someone who the band has since refused to comment on. Writing in the *Independent* on 20 January 1996, Emma Forrest wrote, 'The night before he disappeared, Richey gave a friend a book called *Novel with Cocaine*, and instructed her to read the introduction. All the introduction can reveal is that Ageyev spent time in a mental asylum before vanishing.' After initially agreeing to talk for this book, Ms Forrest later withdrew her help after saying that she'd got 'cold feet'. If that was indeed was Jo whom Richey met that night while James Dean Bradfield was out of the hotel he probably didn't confide his plans to her. What he did appear to do was give her a book that contained a clue about his possible plans. By the time she received the parcel from his room he would be well away. When Bradfield was later asked about Jo, he replied, 'He never talked about it so there's no point in us talking about it.' End of conversation.

After wrapping the parcel, Richey got some sleep but was up early. He dressed, collected his wallet, car keys, some Prozac and his passport, then quietly left room 516 and took the lift down to the lobby at around seven a.m. The desk staff noticed him step out of the lift, pass the front desk, trot down three steps and then exit through the automatic front door. He didn't check out or speak to them. He was carrying no luggage. He turned left and walked down to the car park. A minute or so later, he drove the Cavalier up the ramp onto St Petersburgh Place and then right onto Bayswater Road. He was soon on the motorway, heading west.

A couple of hours later James Dean Bradfield stood in the hotel lobby waiting for his bandmate. It wasn't like Richey to be late: he usually took great pride in being punctual for meetings, rehearsals and interviews. Bradfield soon decided to check Edwards' room but when he failed to get a reply he asked the duty manager to open it up. He was presented with a vacant room. The specially wrapped box was sitting on the bedside table, while the bed had clearly been slept in. Richey's toiletries and packed suitcase were still there, as was some of his Prozac. Bradfield contacted Martin Hall and it was decided that he would go ahead with the trip alone. Knowing that Richey had only recently gone missing for a couple of days, they assumed this would probably be something similar. Bradfield set off for the airport.

Exactly where Richey went during that morning may never be known, but he was doing *something* for eight hours before entering Wales. It seems likely that he drove to his Cardiff flat, arriving sometime around four p.m.

Every last detail about Richey Edwards' movements in January and February 1995 – and especially this last trip – would later be closely scrutinised. The trip should have taken three hours at most, which leaves several hours unaccounted for. Why would he have gone to his flat at all? Was it really Richey that made that trip? If it *was* Richey, did he go home for the purpose of collecting something? If so, what? These do not seem like the actions of someone who was about to commit suicide. What might he have been planning?

# BOOK 2

*'It's a rock and roll myth. I think what people miss is that he was in a Vauxhall Cavalier.'*

– Nicky Wire

*'We just wanted some conclusive evidence of what actually happened because we had nothing, even with private detectives and the police coming up with nothing. We had to come up with a decision or be in limbo for the rest of their lives.'*

– Sean Moore

*'We had nothing left to say about it.'*

– James Dean Bradfield

'Are disappearances classified and labelled, then?' I laughed.

Japp smiled also. Poirot frowned at both of us.

'But certainly they are! They fall into three categories: First, and most common, the voluntary disappearance. Second, the much abused "loss of memory" case – rare, but occasionally genuine. Third, murder, and a more or less successful disposal of the body.'

'You might lose your own memory, but someone would be sure to recognise you – especially in the case of a well-known man like Davenheim . . . In the same way, the absconding clerk, or the domestic defaulter, is bound to be run down in these days of wireless telegraphy. He can be headed off from foreign countries; ports and railway stations are watched; and as for concealment in this country, his features and appearance will be known to everyone who reads a daily newspaper. He's up against civilization.'

'Mon ami,' said Poirot, 'you make one error. You do not allow for the fact that a man who had decided to make away with another man – or with himself in a figurative sense – might be that rare machine, a man of method. He might bring intelligence, talent, a careful calculation of detail to the task; and then I do not see why he should not be successful in baffling the police force.'

– from *Poirot Investigates* – 'The Disappearance of Mr Davenheim' [1924]

# MISSING

You'd think it would be very difficult to go missing in this day and age. If you live in the UK you are more likely to be filmed by CCTV than if you live anywhere else in the world. In the last decade and a half, more than £200 million has been spent by governments on CCTV installation. If you're in London, you could conceivably be filmed every second you spend outside your own home. There are more than 100 cameras at Heathrow, 260 at the Houses of Parliament and thirty-five on Oxford Street (not to mention the in-store ones). Over two thousand cameras cover the nation's railway stations and if you drive along a major road you'll be picked up by camera after camera, allowing your journey to be accurately mapped. Since the events of 11 September 2001, the number of CCTV cameras has grown larger still. They can be found in bridges, tunnels, alleyways, shop fronts, schoolyards and car parks.

What if you wanted to drive from, say, London to Cardiff? And let's just say that you also wanted, for whatever reason, to then slip away from any prying eyes? On the drive from London to Cardiff, your car would be filmed almost constantly and an accurate path of your journey could be plotted using software that can read car number plates and place them at a particular location at a particular time. In the cities of Cardiff and London, you'd be filmed almost constantly while on the roads, so for anyone wishing to trace your movements it should be relatively easy. That wasn't quite the case back in 1995, however, when the number of CCTV cameras was far smaller.

Today, away from the glare of the omnipresent video eyes, you would also be leaving a trail of physical evidence that could be scrutinised by DNA-identification techniques. Even if you did manage to evade detection and slip away, this would only be the first step.

Once you had vanished, you would have to try and *stay* vanished. This would present a crucial choice: either retain your original identity or adopt a new one. The former option would only really be possible if you wanted to fend for yourself in a remote location, living where the world doesn't usually look (in a monastery, for example, or perhaps a private religious retreat). The latter option is also possible, but you'd have a lot of paperwork to extricate yourself from. Your life is carefully documented from the outset: birth certificate, baptism, first communion, school records, passport, dental records, exam certificates, driving licence, medical records, wage slips, tax records, National Insurance number, census returns, banking records, credit ratings, mortgages, utility bills, electoral registers, mobile phone records, and so on. Only when the paperwork trail comes to a stop has a person really gone missing.

More than 200,000 people go missing in the UK each year. The vast majority of these cases are cleared up quickly, and usually involve children. I was invited to Cardiff Central Police Station to discuss Richey Edwards and missing persons cases in general. In short sleeves on a lovely summer's day I was welcomed by Detective Chief Inspector Andrew Davies, and he showed me the Missing Persons set-up in Cardiff. We discussed the differences in approach and technology today in contrast to the way things were done back in 1995.

'There is a desire by the police to sight a missing person,' he explained. 'Otherwise it just sits on our records. Our records go back twenty and thirty years with people still listed as missing, and they're still a problem to me because every now and then I have to pay them some attention; it's a drain on resources.' At the time of my visit, Cardiff Central had nine 'long term' missing persons cases on its books (the oldest dating back to 1988), but they had recently been able to close a case that had been seventeen years old. My visit, which had started so promisingly, soon left me deflated when I was told that none of Richey Edwards' records were held in Cardiff. All of the paperwork had long since been transferred to London under the jurisdiction of the Metropolitan Police, who had primacy in the case because they had taken the initial missing person report. I would have to start again.

The earlier statement that over 200,000 people annually go missing in the UK, while not meant to be deliberately misleading, is nonetheless probably inaccurate. There are many problems with correctly determining the total number of missing persons, despite the perceived benefits of advanced computer technology. The main reason for these difficulties is the lack of a central organisation to collate all of the data. The police collect reports of missing persons in a standardised way, but some forces only add the names to the national database after they have been missing for a certain length of time. If one person goes missing three times in a year, this is counted as three different people going missing. The Missing People Helpline charity also collects data, but often finds itself dealing with a case that was never reported to the police: this further complicates any official statistics. On top of this, many missing persons simply aren't reported at all. The reasons for this are complex and varied. In extreme cases, a person may go missing without anyone even noticing, or it could be that questions are only asked after someone has not been seen for a long period of time. Disappearances can be a slow 'drifting away' or a sudden vanishing. It's when the questions are asked that the pain for friends and family really begins. Not knowing what has happened to someone may be even harder to take in than the truth about what actually occurred, but it should be noted that the number of missing persons who are eventually found dead is small (less than 10 per cent), but the longer they are missing, the more likely this outcome is. According to figures issued in 2003, less than 0.02 per cent of missing persons were found to have been murdered.

Typically, there are more than 1,100 long-term missing persons in the UK at any one time – that is, people who have been missing for twelve months or more. Those people who *are* found often wish to remain 'missing' – after all, these are usually people who deliberately disappeared in the first place. Any adult in the UK has the right to go missing – be it for personal, financial or professional reasons. Some missing persons are people with mental health problems who might not even realise what has happened to them. In 2003 the Missing Persons Helpline database revealed that of all the missing persons that were located, only 20 per cent of them decided to return home. A further 39 per cent made contact with those looking for them but did not return home. The remaining 41 per cent decided not to make contact with their friends and family. No one has the right to insist that a missing person make contact; by law, the family can only be informed that the missing person is alive.

•

Once someone has decided to go missing – assuming it isn't an off-the-cuff resolution – how would they go about pulling it off? I found only two books which covered the issue and neither was especially helpful. *How to Disappear Completely and Never be Found* was written in 1986 and so has limited relevance in terms of avoiding modern surveillance techniques and data trails, although it does contain some amusing anecdotes (wives disbelieving that their husbands could walk out on *them*, husbands upset that their model train sets were destroyed, and so on). *Cover Your Tracks Without Changing Your Identity* sounded a little more intriguing but petered out in about seventy pages and was more concerned with helping people into the wilderness of North America. A few websites offer more up-to-date advice regarding ways to disappear, along with warnings that they don't condone any criminal or terrorist activities. I wondered later whether my IP address might now be stored on some government database, indicating me as a potential terrorist because I'd visited these pages.

What did these websites actually tell me? A lot of the guidance was common sense: don't use your own car, pay for everything with cash, wear a baseball cap when you have to go into shops or areas with CCTV, change your clothes, haircut and hair colour, and do things that you wouldn't usually do (start or stop smoking, for example). Readers were also encouraged to write in with tips and suggestions. The overwhelming message was that running away is the easy part: hiding is harder and staying hidden is by far the hardest part. Saving up money, in cash, before you vanish was also, not surprisingly, recommended, as was using your own car as a decoy. The simplest decoy may be driving a car in one direction before abandoning it and doubling back. Doubling back and then taking a tangential route is confusing to any trackers, as is leaving a car just over a border (international or otherwise) to increase the number of agencies involved in the pursuit and to add the complication of their need to share information.

One other decoy method that crossed my mind was to get someone else to dump your car for you. By then, you could be anywhere else in the world and if you were to leave it near to a possible suicide spot the implications could confuse your pursuers even more. This would form what is known as either a 'Reggie Perrin' or a 'pseudocide', depending on where you come from. The former refers to the 1970s BBC comedy *The Fall and Rise of Reginald Perrin*, in which Leonard Rossiter (in the lead role) despairs of the daily monotony of life and fakes his own suicide by leaving his clothes on a beach. While a 'Reggie Perrin' has an air of comedy and sympathy to it, the use of 'pseudocide' is not only more clinical but often reserved for cases in which the perpetrator is staging his or her own disappearance for more sinister reasons. High-profile cases in recent years include Keith Hackett, Graham Cardwell, Andrew Hoy and John Darwin (the 'canoe man'). Each case highlights a slightly different take on the process.

Hackett was eventually given a five-month suspended jail sentence for wasting police time after he tried to fake his own death in connection with the Paddington rail disaster in which thirty-one people died. He had a police record as a sex offender, dating back to 1987, and in 1999 he used the rail crash to kill off his original persona and re-emerge as Lee Simm. This was a case in which the subject saw the news and reacted quickly to take advantage of the situation. Hackett called the police and, using the name Simm, pretended to be Hackett's landlord. He reported that he thought

Hackett might have been on the ill-fated train. He then called again – claiming to be a brother of Hackett – and said that he thought his brother had been in carriage H, which had been burnt out in the tragedy. Hackett's father and sister attended the memorial service for the victims while unaware that Hackett/Simm was alive and well. Police later became suspicious of Simm, and when they took Hackett's cousin to visit Simm they were able to confirm that Hackett and Simm were one and the same person.

Another, more Perrin-esque, pseudocide was 46-year-old Graham Cardwell, who left personal items on a beach near Grimsby and gave the impression that he'd been swept out to sea. He left behind a wife and three children. Eight months later, the police were tipped off and Cardwell was found living two hundred miles away in the West Midlands with a new name, a new job and a new home.

Essex salesman Andrew Hoy, a 31-year-old father of two, is suspected of faking his own murder to escape paying back the £20,000 he owed a local gang. Hoy had received death threats and moved his family to another town before we went missing. Two days later, his car was found with his bloodstained clothes in the boot. Forensic tests proved that he hadn't died in the clothes, and the police suspected that he had tried to make it look like murder. But murderers would have been unlikely to leave clothes and other potentially incriminating forensic evidence for the police to easily find.

The most famous British episode is the case of Lord Lucan, who vanished in 1974 on the night that nanny Sandra Rivett was killed in his family home. Some people believe he might have drowned in the English Channel while trying to escape, while others have suggested he could have slipped away to start a new life, assisted by wealthy friends and associates.

Another attempted pseudocide became embroiled in the Lucan story when former Labour MP John Stonehouse left his clothes on a beach and relocated to Australia under a new name, John Markham, with his secretary. Australian police suspected that he might be Lord Lucan and – after taking him into custody – discovered his real identity. Stonehouse was deported to the UK. Despite this failure, the number of people around the world who have successfully started a new life under a new name runs into the thousands.

Another method might be that of withdrawing to a spiritual retreat: whether you did this under your own name or an assumed one, it's likely that few questions would be asked. Unless you had committed a serious crime, the police would probably go no further than making the briefest of enquiries. If you went missing of your own free will, they would probably not bother to waste time contacting such institutions, and even if they did, they might be denied private details of the inhabitants. Even a famous person might not be recognised in a monastery or retreat, where media figures and notions of celebrity are of little consequence.

There are numerous establishments in the UK − including traditional Benedictine monasteries, Cistercian gatherings and Buddhist assemblies, plus several less formal spiritual centres and congregations − where it might be possible to exist in relative anonymity. If you were to travel overseas, the choices would increase further. There are approximately thirty to forty Benedictine monasteries in the UK alone, and these are home to around one thousand monks and nuns at any one time. There are fundamental criteria that must be satisfied in order to join a monastery: the candidate should be unmarried, free of responsibilities and not in debt. Being a Catholic is not essential before applying, although conversion to Catholicism often occurs in due course. Almost anyone with a strong religious calling could enter a monastery and − if they so wished − never directly encounter the outside world again.

**I** **met my agent**, Tim, at Marble Arch and we began to walk along the Bayswater Road. We were looking for the Embassy Hotel, which didn't seem to exist any more. Had it vanished into the ether like Richey Edwards? All we had to go on was a grainy black-and-white picture, which I'd printed out in low quality from my computer. Google hadn't helped and now we were looking at the print-out and wondering what angle it was taken from and whether we would still recognise the building if it had been renovated during the past thirteen years. As the walk went on and on, my agent seemed convinced that we wouldn't find it; in fact, he seemed more interested in stopping by the Café Diana at the end of the road. It's his favourite retro cafe, with each wall covered in pictures and memorabilia of the princess. I was starting to resign myself to his pessimism and turn my thoughts to a nice grilled sandwich when I spotted it. Just as we were reaching Notting Hill Gate, it was over the road from Hyde Park, and was now called the Ramada Jarvis Hotel. The photo we'd been following showed a view from a side street by the car park entrance, and we could easily have missed the building and walked on by.

As we approached the main doors we realised that we hadn't actually decided what we were going to do once we found it. I was doing my duty as a diligent researcher, while Tim was just along for the ride (he worked not far from here and liked a good detective romp).

We ambled down the car ramp but soon decided there was nothing much to see there and turned back just as a couple of hotel porters on a cigarette break turned to watch us – not that either of us looked much like a car thief. As we walked back out I wondered what was on Richey's mind as he drove up the ramp that February morning? Was his plan set in stone? Was it a loose idea that might change as he went? Did he just want to get away from the hotel as quickly as possible without being spotted? Was he alone?

We walked around to the entrance and into the lobby. We knew we wanted to look at the fifth floor, and headed confidently past the front desk to the lifts. Feeling like a couple of naughty schoolboys we pressed 'Five' and started our ascent. What would we do if someone challenged us or asked what we were doing? Just our luck, the cleaners were working along the fifth floor – a narrow, dark corridor. We looked at the numbers. Where was room 516, the room Edwards had departed from? It didn't exist. The numbers jumped past where it should have been. He would have had a view of Hyde Park if the room was where it was supposed to be. And if he had just wanted to end it all, he could easily have jumped from his room. He would have made quite a scene by doing that. No, he wasn't going to just kill himself – of that I felt sure.

After a swift exit we stopped to eat at Café Diana. Richey would have hated the place, but when he vanished he wouldn't have known about her suicidal tendencies, her eating disorders and her self-harming. Would he have felt a sense of connection to her then? With my stomach filled I said goodbye to Tim and set off on my drive, trying to recreate Richey's last movements, based on what is known about them. It wasn't totally 'authentic'; we hadn't been that keen for me to set off at seven a.m., and it wasn't quite 1 February, but I was off. Past the flyovers, the pharmaceutical towers and concrete. Past the turn-off for Heathrow, where he should have been going that morning en route to America. My car was being filmed by numerous cameras, charting my journey along a stretch of road on which, back in 1995, cameras had been few and far between.

I hit 'Play' on the car's CD player and *In Utero* burst into life. Richey was most likely listening to this as he drove. Nirvana's vast, majestic music gives extra air to the lungs as you speed away, leaving ten million people behind you, but the schizophrenic nature of the album moves, song-by-song, through pain and anguish. Kurt Cobain's opening words – 'Teenage angst has paid off well / Now I'm bored and old' – mirrored sentiments expressed by Richey in various interviews. It was the perfect soundtrack to his journey.

# XVI

## THE SIGHTINGS, THE SEARCH, THE BRIDGE
*February 1995*

*'There wasn't any huge panic at the point. It seemed weird, but everybody thought maybe he didn't want to go* [to America] *or he'd just gone out, or something.'*

– band spokesperson's comment to the *NME*, 25 February 1995

When it became clear that Richey had been missing for twenty-four hours, Martin Hall visited the Metropolitan Police at Harrow Road in West London to lodge a formal missing persons report at ten a.m. on Thursday, 2 February:

> Form 584(C): (abbreviated)
> Height: 5' 8"
> Eyes: Brown
> Circumstances: Subject is a member of a band . . . Subject has made a previous suicide attempt and is taking anti-depressants.

•

At this stage Richey's disappearance wasn't thought of as really serious. Everyone knew he'd had problems, and maybe this was just his way of dealing with not wanting to go to America – at least that's what people started to surmise after his mother spoke of her conversation with Richey from Tuesday night.

'Mam just said the words, "Richard's gone missing", recalled Rachel Edwards to the *Sun*. 'I stood there rooted to the spot. I was stunned, but at that point I believed he would come back. I think everyone thought Richard would return any second with a grin on his face. But as the hours went by it became more and more ominous. No matter where he was he had always phoned home and spoke to Mam, even if it was just to say, "Hello". Then the police became involved and the whole investigation started to retrace his movements. It was only when we went round to Richard's flat in Cardiff that we realised he had been back there. He left a trail of clues but we have never been able to work out what they meant.'

With the police now involved, the band and Richey's family were doing what they could to find out quickly where he might have gone. Graham Edwards, Nicky Wire and the Cardiff police visited Richey's Anson Court apartment and what they found only caused more worry and confusion over what Edwards might be up to. Richey, or someone, had obviously been home. Under the clipped magazine-page gaze of Marilyn Monroe and Liz Taylor, James Dean and Kate Moss, Keith Richards, Ian Curtis and the other portraits on the wall, was Richey's passport. It had been left on a desk in full view for anyone who walked in. Also found in the apartment was some Prozac, Richey's bank cards, and a £2.70 toll ticket from the Severn Bridge with 30p change. The ticket indicated that the crossing occurred at three p.m. While it's very likely that Edwards had returned to his flat and deposited these items himself, no one saw him return there, so the possibility of someone else doing it on his behalf cannot be completely discounted.

It could be that these items had been deliberately left in a place where they could quickly be found. If Edwards had wanted to dispose of them he could have thrown them into the river or taken them somewhere else where they would never be recovered. But why might he have wanted these things to be spotted? Could the ticket have been a clue as to where Richey was going to end up? And, if this was the case, why would he want to leave clues anyway? The leaving of the passport could perhaps be taken at face value as Richey saying, 'Look, I'm not leaving the country', or it could be viewed, as many chose to see it, as a decoy to stop people looking further afield. As would become apparent, it was relatively easy to acquire a short-term passport in 1995 and at least one sighting placed Richey at a passport office. Edwards leaving behind his medication, or at least some of it, was more worrying. The implications of what his unhinged mental state might lead him to do worried everyone.

Soon afterwards the police checked Richey's bank account and found that he'd been withdrawing his maximum £200 per day from cash machines for the two weeks leading up to his disappearance, giving him a total of at least £2,800 in cash. It was becoming ever more obvious that he'd been planning whatever he was doing for some time. From the day he vanished he never used his cash card again. Some speculated that he needed the money for the American trip, but he was on band business and wouldn't have needed such a large amount of cash. It was also mentioned that he'd ordered a new desk for his flat from a Cardiff store, but there was no record of that ever being paid for and, besides, that would only have accounted for half of the money he'd withdrawn. This money was required for something else – perhaps to cover other transport arrangements and alternative ID.

After Edwards had been missing for two days, Nicky Wire began phoning around hotels asking whether Richey had checked in during the previous twenty-four hours. The closest he got was a Swansea businessman called Richard Edwards. But if Richey had checked in to a hotel, he would have been unlikely to do so under his own name. The family placed a notice in the local paper's 3, 4 and 5 February editions that said, simply, 'Richard, please make contact, love Mum, Dad and Rachel.' Hall Or Nothing, meanwhile, called in a private investigator to check other possibilities – ports, airports and hospitals – but there were no signs at all.

James Dean Bradfield was in America alone, saddled with the task of handling the pre-tour press interviews. At each stage he had to explain that Richey hadn't made the trip because he had an ear infection. The wider world was unaware of Richey's disappearance, so no one outside the Manics' inner circle was looking for him. If he had been spotted by a member of the general public, they would have been unaware of the importance of the sighting.

Missing for four days. On Sunday, 5 February, David Cross – a nineteen-year-old Manics fan from Aberdare, Mid-Glamorgan – took a bus to the Newport bus station and got off to buy the Sunday newspapers from a nearby shop. He was a penpal of US-based Manics fan Lori Fidler. David Cross knew that Fidler was friendly with the band and with Richey in particular. As Cross went about his business on that Sunday morning, he was unaware that Richey was considered 'missing'. What happened next was recorded in his official statement to the police, taken on 21 February: 'As I approached the newsagent's I saw Richey James Edwards. He was stood alone near to a silver grey coloured car. I approached him as I was going to the shop. Although I do not know him, I said to him, "Hello, Richey, I'm a friend of Lori's." And he said, "How is she? How is she doing?" I said, "She's fine." He looked at me and said, "I'll see you later." He was wearing a dark, blue-coloured jacket. I noticed he looked withdrawn and pale. I am positive it was Richey Edwards.' It's known that Richey had friends in Newport but later enquiries revealed that none of them had heard from or seen Richey around this time. So, assuming this sighting was authentic, where had Richey been sleeping for the past few nights?

Lori Fidler is a name that kept cropping up in reports.[36] She was supposed to have told *The Sunday Times* that on 2 February she'd received a call that may have been from Edwards. 'I was out at the time,' she said, 'and my girlfriend took the call, the day after he went missing. There was that beep-beep on the line showing it was from overseas. The man on the other end just said, "Hi Lori," and then hung up. I think it was him.'

Missing for six days. One of the most intriguing stories from the first week of Richey's disappearance came from Anthony Hatherall, a forty-something taxi driver from Newport. His account seems to have some credibility because he was not a Manics fan and appeared to have nothing to gain from his story. It began at seven a.m. on Tuesday, 7 February at the King's Hotel. Here, Hatherall picked up someone he later described to police as 'a tall, slim man with a gaunt face'. Hatherall also commented that the passenger spoke with a cockney accent, but the taxi driver thought it was a fake one from the off and so asked for £40 of the fare to be paid upfront. The passenger then began directing Hatherall around various South Wales locations. First, he asked to be taken to Uplands, then to Risca and up the valley to Blackwood. His Cockney 'accent' occasionally slipped into a Welsh one and the passenger said he was looking for his boss who had broken down but that he didn't know where he was. Despite the fact that he was supposedly looking for someone, the passenger asked if he could lie down on the back seat and said that Hatherall should avoid using the motorway because he 'was always using the motorway'. Eventually they reached Blackwood and went to the bus station, but after simply saying 'This is not the place', the passenger asked to be taken to Pontypool railway station. Upon arrival at the station, the passenger said he had to get out and make a call. He returned a few minutes later and the journey continued. It was later ascertained that Pontypool train station did not have a public telephone. The final leg of the trip saw the passenger ask to be dropped off at Aust services over the Severn Bridge. The passenger paid the remainder of the £68 fare, then Hatherall drove off without a second glance. A service station was a strange place for someone to alight unless they had a way of getting away from there – a previously parked car or a friend to collect them. And if this person had left the car there in the first place, how had he got from there to Newport? If this had been Richey, then it's possible that no one was looking out for him at the time (the date of the private investigator being hired is unknown). With his shaved head making him less recognisable to fans and members of the public, it's conceivable that Edwards could have been coming and going as he pleased, all the time unnoticed.

Richey's family and friends naturally became more concerned after he had remained missing for several days. They had hoped that he would return or have been found soon enough that they would not need to go public, but – as a week passed without so much as a hint as to where he was – it soon reached the point where a public appeal would have to be made.

Two weeks missing. On Wednesday, 15 February, the South Wales police issued the first public statement about Richey's disappearance. It read:

Police are anxious to trace Richard James Edwards, aged 28 years [sic], a member of the pop group Manic Street Preachers, who has been missing from the London area since Wednesday 1st February 1995 when he was seen leaving the London Embassy Hotel at 7 a.m. It is known that on the same day, he visited his home in the Cardiff area, and he is still believed to be in possession of his silver Vauxhall Cavalier motor car, Registration No L519 HKX.

Richard's family, band members and friends are concerned for his safety and welfare and stress that no pressure would be put on him to return if he does not wish to do so. They stress that his privacy will be respected at all times.

Police are asking anyone who has seen Richard, knows of his whereabouts, or has seen his car, to contact them at Cardiff Central Police Station on 0222 222111, and ask for the Crime desk or CID office.

Should Richard himself hear or see this appeal, his family and friends are anxious for him to contact one of them or the police to let them know he is safe and well. They again wish to stress that Richard will not be urged to return or reveal his whereabouts if he does not wish to do so.

A brief band statement issued via Hall Or Nothing on the same day stated that they had nothing to add and asked for 'sensitivity regarding this matter'. Graham Edwards then made an appeal on Cardiff's Red Dragon Radio with DJ Adrian Masters. 'All we know is that he left the Embassy Hotel in London on the first of the month and he left without giving any reason, and just sort of disappeared into thin air,' said Graham Edwards. 'Obviously everyone in the family is concerned, and we just want to get in touch with him to know that he is OK. We've phoned all his friends and all the acquaintances that we can think of; nobody seems to be in touch with him at all. All I'd like say is, Richey, if he's listening, please get in touch, just a phone call just to let us know you're all right. If he needs time to be on his own, then that's OK with everybody, but if he does have a problem that we can help with, he'll have strong support from his family and also from his band, Nick, James and Sean.'

This sudden burst of press interest generated many more enquiries and led the South Wales police to issue a further statement on 16 February. This announced that 'Although there is still no news on Richey, there is no evidence that he has come to harm.'

Unbeknown to all involved, and while these appeals and statements had been filtering through the media, a massive piece of the puzzle was about to come to light. Two days earlier, on 14 February, Richey's silver Vauxhall Cavalier had been given a parking ticket at the Aust services. The next day, it was still sitting there – apparently untouched – so the services manager alerted the police. Twenty-four hours later, on Thursday, 16 February, Avon and Somerset police identified the car as Richey's and informed his family. There were now four police forces involved in the case: the Metropolitan Police (investigating the scene of his reported disappearance), the South Wales police (at the address of his permanent residence), Gwent police (conducting interviews with friends and family) and now the Avon and Somerset police (looking into the discovery of his car). In this pre-internet age, information was sometimes slow to circulate.

What tests had the car been subjected to? My attempts to gather any information from the Metropolitan Police had been ongoing for well over a year, and eventually I gave up after the vast majority of my questions went unanswered. One of my last communications with the Met Press Office told me that the car 'was searched by police and nothing of any evidential value was recovered'. This told me nothing. 'In your email you said that this information in your opinion would not cause any distress to the family,' they continued. 'The family in communication with us on this matter at the end of 2008 disagree.' My questions about the car remain unanswered, as do those about Richey's hotel room and his Cardiff flat. In 1996, *Select* magazine was given access to Richey's police file and even reproduced the missing person report in the pages of their magazine. By 2008, all such access was locked behind a closed door.

How long the car had been left at the services is unknown. No one had spotted Richey there, he hadn't checked into the motel on the site, and no one had seen him leave. Again, the question has to be asked: was Richey ever there, or did someone dump the car on his behalf? Assuming that he did leave it there himself – in the midst of the constant stream of businessmen, long-distance lorry drivers, families on days out and other assorted flotsam – Edwards could have been invisible in his own personal pain, while life passed by and through him. Services manager Tom Cassidy told the *NME*, 'I reported it to the police, the car could have been a stolen vehicle for all we knew, and on the Thursday they traced it. The car was locked and there were no clues from that as to what may have happened. There was nothing suspicious about it at all, no suitcase or note or anything that we could see. We know as little about this as anyone else. We wish we could be more helpful but all we know is the car was here and that's it. Nobody saw him here, but then a lot of people pass through every day.'

Even if Richey had been the passenger in Anthony Hatherall's taxi on 7 February, this still leaves seven days on which he is completely unaccounted for. Closer inspection of the car revealed that it seemed to have been 'lived in'. Empty cigarette packets were scattered about inside and the battery was flat, which some people saw as evidence he'd been sleeping inside the car, using its heater and playing tapes. A carrier bag was found inside, containing the photos of his parents he'd taken on his last trip to see them. In the cassette deck was Nirvana's *In Utero*.

Two arguments question the length of time that the car had been left there. On the one hand, if it had been there for many days it would probably have been given a parking ticket before 14 February. On the other hand, the battery would have been unlikely to be flat if he'd only just arrived. One possible explanation is that he arrived on the thirteenth, then slept there overnight and ran the battery flat while sleeping in the car. He could then have left it there on the fourteenth once he realised it could take him no further. The next problem is where he went next. If he was going to throw himself off the bridge, why hadn't he done so two weeks earlier? If he had planned his disappearance (as suggested by his taking out the money), what had he been doing for two weeks and where had he gone to now? He could have been preparing any number of possible escape routes and places to stay. If he was still in South Wales after two weeks, this suggests that he wasn't planning to go far – unless that was yet another decoy. Had he been sleeping in his car for two weeks? Had he been using his cash to stay in B&Bs under an assumed name? Had he been staying somewhere in preparation for a permanent move?

DI Frank Stockholm was running the Cardiff Central branch of the investigation in 1995. 'Until we have positive sightings there is not much more we can do,' he said. 'All the inquiries that can be made have been. We are now relying on information from other people. If Richard Edwards wanted to disappear then he is quite entitled to. Our only concern is for his safety. If he is prepared to contact us in the strictest confidence then we wouldn't pass the details on, we wouldn't tell anybody except for his parents if that is what he wanted. If he is unwell and needs medical treatment then we can arrange that, he can be seen by a police doctor and then he can leave. We just want him to get in touch so we know he is alright. He could have hitched a lift on the M4 or M5 and gone somewhere else. He could have left the country. We are keeping a very open mind. He could be anywhere.'

In the week after the news of the car find had filtered out, the public began getting in touch with the police – but this was a trickle rather than a flood. If news of the disappearance had been spread earlier, would someone somewhere have a positive idea about where he was? Would someone have spotted him at Aust? David Cross and Anthony Hatherall contacted the police, as did Lori Fidler about her phone call. A woman from Guildford reported seeing a hitchhiker with a guitar case, but that was soon ruled out.

The Manics cancelled all upcoming engagements, including dates in the USA, Europe and Japan. The planned single release of 'Yes' was postponed indefinitely. Everyone was entering a state of limbo. Everyone could only run through the details, over and over, in their heads. Everyone could only sit and wait.

•

For those outside the inner circle of friends and family, it was easier to speculate about possible outcomes without the burden of intense personal grief. Many fans and the music press at large had watched as Richey unravelled in front of them. Few could look away – it was grimly fascinating: a sick sideshow in the world of pop. With Richey gone, an obvious place to look for clues was to investigate each key person's last encounter with him. Had they missed a subtle hint? Had he done or said anything that should have raised their suspicions? What more could they have done?

The night before Edwards vanished is ripe for further investigation. Why had he concealed his unhappiness about the American trip from his bandmates (if indeed he had), but quite openly told his mother his true feelings? Precisely when had he passed on *Novel with Cocaine*? What was in the box left in the room and what exactly was decorated on the outside?[37] Was it true that he'd left a bath full of water? Who really was Jo? The answers to at least some of these questions remain in the Met Police file, which I was told is one of the biggest missing persons files they've ever had.

'If you want to be that cryptic about it, you could spend half your life investigating everything,' said James Dean Bradfield.

'The front cover [of the box] is Bugs Bunny, so I thought perhaps he's in Disneyland,' added Nicky Wire. 'The only grey area is the service station. It's just like the lyrics he gave us beforehand. I went through a phase when I was just looking over and over because there was collages in there and stuff. Me and James saw this picture of a house and it was like, "Is that where he is? It looks like a mad house in Bavaria." We were going, "Perhaps he's there." You can go in his flat and you can look at every book, every thing. At the end of the day, you haven't got a clue.'

When Richey vanished, he left behind some of his Prozac. It's well known that Prozac lingers in the body even after someone stops taking their medication. So in Richey's case he may not have felt any of the effects for several days after disappearing, but when he did they were likely to be the textbook withdrawal symptoms that coming off certain drugs can engender: dizziness, nausea, fatigue, headache, abdominal cramps, chills and anxiety. Depending on the dose he'd been taking, if he stopped his medication on 31 January these effects might have begun kicking in any time after 5 or 6 February.

Although there were only two basic outcomes of Richey's disappearance – he's alive or he's dead – these can be split into sub-sections with various possibilities of what might have happened and when. The most depressing of these was that he killed himself. This could have been before 14 February 1995, when the car was spotted, on 14 February (perhaps as some kind of symbolic gesture), or at any time after 14 February – maybe even years later. Another strong argument was that he could have vanished for a new life in any number of ways, either at home or abroad. People usually assume that he was alone, but the fact that he might have had an accomplice cannot be discounted out of hand.

•

The British seem to love a good mystery story, and a good old vanishing act has always managed to hold the public's imagination. From Agatha Christie to Lord Lucan, it's a fascination that endures. So what leads us to think that he might have pulled off one of the great vanishing acts? The obvious fact is that a body has never been found. Also, he was interested in the possibility of being able to drop out of sight and be reborn in a new life. His well-documented unhappiness regarding adult life could have been strong enough for him to want to follow that route. If he committed suicide, he never left any note or explanation and this might be seen as surprising given his apparent interest in suicide notes. Then there are the facts that came to light after he'd vanished: the £2,800 withdrawn from his bank account (more than enough to buy a second-hand car in 1995) and his car having been on the move for almost two weeks after his disappearance. Was the fact of his leaving behind his passport, bank card and medication a deliberate symbolic gesture to indicate that he no longer needed any of those things, or was the passport a red herring? In 1995, the sum of £1,000 would have been enough money to get someone with a boat to drop you off on a

French beach in the middle of the night with no questions asked.

How easy would it have been for Richey to get another passport in 1995? Depending on how long he'd been making plans to disappear, he could have contacted the passport office, claimed that he had lost his original passport and been issued with a second one. He could then have left his original passport in his flat and used the new one to travel. There were no digital scans in use at this time. A second option would have been to walk into a post office and collect a British Visitor's Passport, which would have been difficult for police to trace and which required only a birth certificate for authentication. This security-downgraded option would have been sufficient for moving through most of Europe. He could also have obtained a passport on the black market – a difficult but not impossible feat.

As well as being well versed in famous suicide cases, Richey Edwards was also fascinated by celebrity suicide notes. He'd used van Gogh's in 'La Tristesse Durera', and he'd said that Tony Hancock's ('Things just went wrong too many times') was one of the most beautiful things he'd ever read. He'd also played around with the concept by wearing 'Kill Yourself' T-shirts for photo shoots. The Manics' first single had been 'Suicide Alley', and they'd covered 'Suicide is Painless'. It seems hard to believe that someone so literate and so aware of suicide notes could commit suicide and not leave a note, if only to spare his family the pain of not knowing what had happened to him.

The statistics of UK suicides make for especially startling reading: recent information released by the Priory Group stated that there is one suicide every eighty-four minutes in the UK and Ireland. Men are more likely than women to kill themselves and account for 75 per cent of all cases, with male suicides peaking during the ages of 25 to 34. 'People coming out of depression have a higher suicide rate than those who are severely depressed,' said Professor Chris Thompson, Director of Healthcare Services for the Priory Group. Richey seemed to be getting better shortly before he vanished. Most friends thought he seemed happier over Christmas 1994 than he had been in quite a while.

'I can honestly say that the five days at the House in the Woods was the only time when I thought he was back to being Iggy/Keith Richards, as opposed to Ian Curtis,' stated Nicky Wire. 'But that could have been because he [knew he] was going. It's so hard to speak about it, because for all we know, he could have gone insane. The morning he left, for all we know, he could have gone mad.'

•

Richey Edwards wasn't the only celebrity missing person in February 1995. Comedy actor Stephen Fry walked out of the West End production of *Cell Mates* on 22 February, just days after it had opened to poor reviews. He secretly travelled to France and Belgium while considering suicide. 'The reviews would not have affected me so badly if I'd not suspected they were true,' said Fry. 'I don't know what would have happened if I had carried on performing.' He was treated for a mild form of bipolar disorder, and later returned to work.

Missing for one month. The police were now receiving what seemed to be ever more elaborate theories about where Richey was and what he might be doing. Oxford University undergraduate Anna Bowles wrote to the *NME* and South Wales police that she thought Richey had gone to Germany to mark the fiftieth anniversary of the Holocaust, which he'd studied at Swansea. 'I believe Edwards has gone to Germany on a visitor's passport to visit locations which are significant to the Allied Forces' liberation of the concentration camps,' she wrote. The letter was forwarded to the Met but its suggestion wasn't explored further.

Sinead O'Connor became involved when she told police that Richey might be staying with a mutual acquaintance in Hereford. O'Connor had tried to kill herself in September 1993 (while on tour with Peter Gabriel) by overdosing on sleeping tablets and vodka. She and Edwards had been in touch before he disappeared, but when the police checked out her theory it proved to be another dead end. The police visited Henlow Grange health farm in Bedfordshire after reports of a 'quiet, withdrawn musician' being in residence, but again it came to nothing. As March approached, the whereabouts of Richey Edwards were still a complete mystery.

**O**n I drove under grey skies. I could have taken junction 11 for *The Oracle*, whatever that was. Maybe I should have taken the chance. Maybe it could have helped me. I could also have turned towards the Douai monastery near Reading or the Downside monastery near Bath. As I saw the first mention of South Wales, Kurt was singing 'Rape Me'. I was up to track eight, 'Milk It', by the time I saw a sign stating that Cardiff was still 188 miles away.

I stopped for petrol during 'All Apologies'. As I pulled out from my service stop the interior of the car was filled with the silence at the end of the song, giving me time to think. After a while I was lost in what might have been going through Richey Edwards' head, then I noticed that the CD clock was still ticking along until the track timer reached 23:59 and the album burst back into life.

My mood was becoming increasingly grim – a perfect match for the grey skies and misty weather. Mentions of the M48 services started to appear at the bottom of the signs, counting down the miles as if I was driving to the edge of the world – and in a way, I was. The edge of the world, the end of the world. The end of the story, or just its beginning? These trees by the road must be bigger now, I thought. How much had they grown in the years since Richey drove past them?

Over the brow of a hill I was suddenly driving down towards the flood plain and the bridge was visible before me; the new one could be seen away to the left. Would Richey have seen the new bridge being constructed as he drove down this road on 1 February 1995?

•

The service station seems to have changed its name back and forth over the years. I thought it was now 'Aust', but the sign says 'Severn View'. As I drove up the hillside from the roundabout I spotted the new, small services building – from here you can't even see the old services, never mind the 'Severn View' of its title. As I parked, I saw a small plaque at the edge of the car park, reading 'PC Steven Jones fell near here in 1999'. Around the back, past the petrol station, are the old services buildings – now the offices of a company called Motion Media. Beyond the 'No Unauthorised Entry' signs is a large grass bank at the side of the old services car park. As I sat there with the engine idling, gazing at the vast hill before me, I started to think I'd seen it before. I was pretty sure it hadn't been pictured in any of the newspapers or magazines I'd surveyed. Then it hit me. I had been here before. In a kind of special-effects moment I could now visualise the area covered in people wearing T-shirts and shorts, eating sandwiches and drinking from bottles and cans, the sun shining down. It was 1995, June or July – I forget which – and I was on the way to see R.E.M. at the Cardiff Arms Park with some friends. We'd stopped here on the way. It could only have been a matter of weeks after Richey Edwards' car had been removed from the very car park I'd parked in. I don't recall making the connection at the time, although of course I'd read in the *NME* about his disappearance. I guess that perhaps I hadn't taken it so seriously back then; after all, a lot of people thought he'd just turn up somewhere, somehow, during the months of that hot summer.

Now, I noticed a few things I hadn't back then. There were steep cliffs directly behind the old services buildings. Apparently, if you go past the 'No Entry' sign, there is a path that leads down towards the bridge – over the very tops of the toll plaza booths and onto the pavement which parallels the road over the bridge – making it the only stretch of UK motorway with a pedestrian path alongside it.

Parking is now free for the first two hours, then it costs up to £8 for a day. What did it cost in 1995? And how did Richey's car sit there for so long – if, in fact, it did – without being spotted sooner? As I readied to leave I checked my map and found that within minutes I could be on the M48, M4, M5, heading north or south or to Cardiff or London. That is, practically anywhere. Two hours back to London, four hours to the UK's largest Benedictine monastery at Ampleforth near York, eight hours to the relative wilderness of the Scottish Highlands.

So, on to Cardiff. The toll price is now £5.30. The Severn Bridge is massive. The pathway running alongside the road has only tiny railings. From the bridge it's a *long* way down to the water. On the Welsh side the motorway seems unkempt, two lanes, and it was quiet for much of my journey. I breezed into Cardiff, through the Cardiff Bay developments that looked like a big, unfinished theme park with empty new streets. My hotel was a converted mill overlooking the apartment block in which Richey used to live. After checking in and walking around the area for an hour or so I returned to my room and phoned for room service. While waiting, I switched on the TV and started channel-hopping. On BBC One it was *Crimewatch*.

# XVII

## LIMBO

*March to December 1995*

The Severn is Britain's longest river. It eventually flows into the Bristol Channel and then into the vastness of the Atlantic Ocean. At high water, the river is a mile wide at the Severn Bridge. Because the river is tidal at this point, its currents and sheer size make it a daunting proposition. The local coroner said that if a body entered the Severn it might never be recovered.

•

It didn't take long for hoax callers to start dogging the investigation. A series of people claimed to either be Richey or know where he was staying. The drain on police resources was considerable. The *Sun* had a call from 'Richey' saying he was OK and that he'd been in touch with his parents. His parents had a caller saying, 'Hello Mum, it's me' before the phone went dead. Despite these painful taunts, the family decided not to change their number in case Richey did try to call.

By early March it was clear to all that this wasn't just a brief get-away or a lost weekend. It took James Dean Bradfield a number of weeks to come to terms with the seriousness of the situation and then he was overcome by a numbness that he couldn't shake off. Nicky Wire kept in close contact with Richey's parents and sister, but everything seemed so futile and he could see first-hand the effect it was having on them. For several months, Wire couldn't help wondering if every phone call and every knock at the door might be Richey.

'Wherever Richey has been in the world he has always got in

touch,' Sherry Edwards told the *Daily Mail*. 'Whether it was a quick telephone call or a postcard we always knew how he was doing.' The family clearly realised that press coverage was vital at the time and continued speaking to journalists as much as they could, but this coverage wasn't exactly overwhelming. This wasn't like a possible child abduction – the sort of case that grips the headlines for weeks on end. This was an unstable rock star who had done this type of thing before.

Graham Edwards spoke to Welsh-language publication *Golwg* for their 23 March issue. 'It's true that he had a bit of a breakdown last year and that he spent some time in a private clinic in London,' he said. 'Maybe what's happened now is a repetition but it has taken a different form. He didn't say anything to us, we had no idea that he was going to do anything like this. Like the majority of parents, we think we are on a different level to our children in truth. So his music wasn't something we could enjoy together. But we get on well as a family, generally a very happy family, maybe a bit boring.'

'He just said nothing,' said Rachel Edwards when talking about Richey's last visit. 'But now I realise he knew it would be the last time he ever saw me, which makes me think he had everything planned out.'

By May the police had given up actively searching for Richey. This was standard procedure; there was no evidence of foul play or that he had come to any harm. They had to focus their resources elsewhere. Rachel Edwards, however, chose to continue with her own enquiries. Since there was no central database of unidentified bodies, she systematically contacted every coastguard and coroner in the area. She also made contact with monasteries and religious retreats, but most were duty-bound not to reveal the identities of their inhabitants. The family wondered whether Richey might have withdrawn to one of these retreats.

The procedure for joining a monastery varies slightly from one to the next, but in general they initially suggest that a prospective candidate should stay for a weekend or a few days to experience a monk's life: the multiple daily celebrations of mass, the discipline of living in a basic bedroom, working with the other monks, devoting life to prayer and living in near silence. These were all things that Richey might have thrived on. If this early stage goes well the candidate may stay for ever-lengthening periods before becoming a novitiate, essentially a trainee monk. Years later, the novitiate may progress to being a fully-fledged monk. Only at this point does the individual take his vows of obedience, stability and *conversatio morum*. The first of these is, as at least one monastery's website describes, 'about the self-abandonment of love', as the candidate gives his life to the love and will of another. 'Stability' is the 'virtue of being steadfast and trusting when we doubt our ability to continue', a point that Richey seems to have reached during the events of 1994. *Conversatio morum* approximately translates as 'changing the way you live' and includes chastity, which, given Edwards' indifferent attitude towards sex, would hardly have been difficult for him to come to terms with. Another monastery website talks about two vocations that have to be followed: one to monastic life and another to abandoning home and culture in a profound sense. If Richey wished to do so, he might have had time to visit a monastery before dumping his car.

•

In March 1995 Dave Grohl debuted his new, post-Nirvana, post-Kurt Cobain band, the Foo Fighters. Oasis and Blur were battling to be the kings of Britpop – both would have number one albums by the end of the year, as would Pulp and Elastica. Radiohead were also about to make a big breakthrough. 'I stopped reading the press when they printed I was going to top myself,' said Thom Yorke. 'My girlfriend rings me up, really really upset, saying, "What's all this, what have you been saying?" You know, that's when I stopped reading it. That was enough for me. I had people warning me a few months before Richey disappeared, before he went away the first time, warning me that he was in a bad way. I thought that basically it was the British press that did it to Richey. Full stop. Although I've got lots of friends who are journalists, the few who I think were basically responsible for him having a breakdown I will always hold responsible and I will always see what we do in that light.' This interview was a strange one. No one else had held the press responsible for Richey's troubles. Many people weren't even sure that being in a band had anything to do with it. Perhaps Yorke was too far away from what was really happening to know for sure.

With the music world moving along with barely a blip, the three remaining Manics eventually drifted back to doing what they did best. Nicky Wire had kept to himself and stayed at home, Sean Moore, likewise, remained based at his Bristol home, kitting out his loft, and James Dean Bradfield retreated to London. But in early May – at a meeting with the band, Martin Hall and Richey's parents – it was agreed that it was OK for the three musicians to start working again. Soon afterwards, they began rehearsing at Cardiff's Soundspace Studios.

By mid-July, a new series of stories were making the news. A sixteen-year-old girl from Skipton said that she'd seen Richey wandering the streets with a green rucksack and looking ill. No one gave much credence to that 'sighting' but within a week a more worrying development made headlines. On 21 July, the body of a tattooed man was found at Beachy Head in East Sussex. Local coroner Michael Davey contacted the Met at Harrow Road saying, 'This may be Richard Edwards. There has been very great press interest in this as he is a member of Manic Street Preachers popular music group [sic], known very well by you, I've no doubt. Please be aware before making public.' The body turned out to be some other unfortunate individual, but for a while all of the Manics' camp were again holding their breaths. The family of the deceased asked for his identity to be kept private.

A German fan, Monika Pommer, then claimed that she'd been sent a postcard by Richey with a London postmark of 3 February 1995. She refused to give the card, or even a copy of it, to the police. Instead, she wrote to the Met saying, 'I cannot and do not wish to surrender his last postcard. I do not think he would like me to do so, it is much too personal. I am always carrying it with me now that I think it was meant as some sort of goodbye. Personally, I do not know if he is alive, but I would like to know the truth. If Richey does not return until August 20, 1995, or no other messages or news are confirmed, I will go to Cardiff to say goodbye by throwing flowers into the sea. I do not care what others think about it, I will never forget him. I will always love him. Sincerely yours, Monika Pommer.' (Pommer did send an earlier card from Edwards, written in December 1994, but the contents of that card have never been publically divulged. It has been reported that the Metropolitan Police still have the card.)

By late summer, the Met changed tactics and decided it might be beneficial to give the press access to the inner workings of the investigation. They even allowed police documents to be photographed and reproduced in the media. This would not be permitted today. Detective Sergeant Stephen Morey spoke to several publications and caused a mini-stir with some of his own opinions. 'You can hop a yacht and be over [seas] without a passport, landing in a small port,' he explained. 'It takes a wee bit of planning and a little bit of negotiation with the yacht skipper, but I would have thought it can be done. I'd have thought that if something like that happened, with the publicity that has happened, we would have been notified. Personally, and this is my own personal view and not the view of the Metropolitan Police Service, I believe that Richard Edwards may no longer be with us.

'At every street corner there is potentially a Manics fan who would recognise him. He has so many out there. It is not as though he was just an ordinary unknown who has disappeared. Every fan is unwittingly looking for him. He has drawn no money since he left the hotel six months ago, nor asked his parents for any. In these circumstances I have to move towards the theory that Richey is no longer with us.'

Around the same time a feature appeared in the *Sunday Times* under the title, 'The Point of No Return?', and quoted Lori Fidler. Fidler later issued a statement disputing the article and her part in it. 'Without going into detail, I would like to say that ninety-five per cent of "the facts" printed were not true,' she said. 'I had no contact with the paper and still have no intention of it.'

There was no united front regarding what was best for the

246 · A VERSION OF REASON

investigation. Despite the openness of the police and continued appearances by the family, Gillian Porter at Hall Or Nothing was quoted as saying, 'We don't want to comment. We don't think any publicity is going to help now.' She did divulge that the note and parcel that Richey had left in the hotel room had been delivered to 'Just a friend of his, I am sure they were passed on.'

By now the Manics had been rehearsing for four months and had demos of around twenty new songs, some of which had been started before Richey disappeared. 'Loads of those lyrics had been around for a while,' explained James Dean Bradfield. 'No music has been written to any of his lyrics since he's gone missing.'

'We didn't feel comfortable with that,' added Nicky Wire. 'There's about fifty songs in there [the folder that Edwards left behind]. To be honest with you, they're no more horrific than *The Holy Bible*. You can't get any more low than that, can you really?'

In the first week of September, they travelled to France and set themselves up at the Chateau De La Rouge Motte studio. The first thing they recorded was a cover version of Burt Bacharach's 'Raindrops Keep Falling on My Head', and this was followed by a new composition titled 'A Design for Life'. Recording continued back in Bath and then with producer Mike Hedges[38] at London's Abbey Road Studios, where string sections were added. The aim was to return in 1996 with a new album.

•

Rachel Edwards' next public plea was via London Weekend Television's *Missing at Christmas* programme. Presented by John Suchet, the programme showed Rachel discussing Richey's physical traits. She talked about his shaved head and tattoos, and made a direct appeal to her brother. Although the latest 'sightings' included reports of Richey in Brighton, Cambridge, Liverpool, Whitby and reading books in a shop on Charing Cross Road in London, the show prompted only eight phone calls offering possible new information.

Richey Edwards was neither the first nor the last musician to vanish, but he might just have been the most calculated. The reasons for other's flights are varied. In the case of Syd Barrett's transformation into a recluse and Jeremy Spencer (of Fleetwood Mac) being admitted to the Children of God religious cult, both were put down as 1960s casualties, while Joe Strummer escaped to Paris because he 'wanted a break'. Marvin Gaye ran away to Belgium when faced with a $2 million tax bill and the breakdown of his marriage, while Killing Joke's Jaz Coleman chose Iceland as his sanctuary because he feared the world was about to end. All were located eventually. The 1983 film *Eddie and the Cruisers* explored the myth of the vanishing rock star with the fictional story of Eddie Wilson faking his own death and taking off with the master tapes of his band's unreleased second album.

Many of these escapes were, if not spur of the moment, then not completely thought out. Richey's case might have been very different. 'Richey is a very ritualistic person,' said Sony's Rob Stringer. 'He doesn't act arbitrarily, and the scary thing is, he's the most well-read person I've ever known, he would be able to tell you the last words of all the world's most famous suicides. He would know the contents of Kurt Cobain's suicide note off by heart, and he would know twenty different ways to disappear completely. He will have planned it. He may be in Tibet for all I know.' One report claimed that Stringer had loaned Edwards a book about staging a disappearance – something Stringer later denied. Whether or not Stringer did this, Rachel Edwards commented that Richey was well aware of such books. Edwards was certainly aware of celebrity drop-outs. 'One of the best things I've ever read is J. D. Salinger,' Richey told *EP* magazine. 'After his big success, *Catcher in the Rye*, he locked himself away in a basement for twenty years. But he was still writing. He'd got stacks of manuscripts on his shelves, but no one's ever seen them.' Asked if he himself could do that, Edwards replied, 'I'd like to think so.'

Perhaps the most intriguing link between Edwards and a famous vanishing is that of Arthur Rimbaud. The Frenchman's dissatisfaction with 'modern life' was mirrored by Edwards' and his destruction of all his writings draws comparisons with Edwards throwing his into the river and/or passing them onto Nicky Wire for the rest of the band. Edwards also paraded around a photo-shoot with Rimbaud's words written across his back. Rimbaud was presumed dead for many years after he vanished.

Edwards was also aware of writer Harold Brodkey, whose epic novel *The Runaway Soul* mined the author's childhood memories. It took him twenty-seven years to write. Brodkey later documented his own death from AIDS, writing into his final days in January 1996. Edwards could quote in interviews that 33 per cent of jump suicides had torn shoulder muscles from a reflexive instinct to grab onto the bridge and to live.

While many people have looked to Richey Edwards' intelligence to highlight their hopes that he vanished rather than died, one of many unanswered questions is whether he had the presence of mind to carry out any plans that he might have formulated. Assuming that he was still around when his car arrived at Aust on 14 February, he could have gone fourteen days without taking his medication. No one can know what mental and emotional state he would have been in at that point and what the avenues of escape might have looked like to a possibly confused mind. With statistics backing up the theory that 'recovering' depressives are often more likely to commit suicide, Richey fitted that profile. He was also clearly feeling the stress of the upcoming US trip and the band's forthcoming tour. He'd already broached the idea of being a 'stay at home' member of the band, but he couldn't face that option. His choices were becoming limited.

Why did he return to Wales? 'Basically, whatever he was doing, he was looking to escape,' said Andrew Evans, an arts and media psychologist, to *Melody Maker*. 'People often get that with fame. If you're too long in a situation that's stressful, the desire for escape becomes paramount. Then again, it's entirely possible he was disoriented, and trying to sort out his head by returning to his roots, memories and home surroundings, trying to piece together a puzzle. But he was certainly clever enough to escape. He could have done it with someone, in Wales, maybe. Someone who he could trust implicitly, perhaps an old friend, dating back to school days. Was there another person involved?'

Those closest to Richey were sceptical that the breakdown was explicably linked to his fame as a rock star. James Dean Bradfield speculated that the outcome might well have been the same had Edwards followed the path to becoming a teacher or lecturer. Richey's actions might have been in his psychological make-up all along, just waiting to surface.

The Vauxhall Cavalier was taken back to Blackwood and parked outside the Edwards' house. But after souvenir hunters repeatedly stole parts of the vehicle, it was sold and given a new set of number plates. The Manics were busy preparing to play a comeback gig of sorts as support to the re-formed Stone Roses at Wembley Arena on 29 December, with Richey nowhere in sight.

Years before, Edwards had been asked what he would most like to be. His answer? 'Any animal that hibernates.'

# XVIII

## EVERYTHING MUST GO

*1996 to 1998*

The first Manic Street Preachers album to be released after the disappearance of Richey Edwards was called *Everything Must Go*. It was a title that resonated on several levels, with Richey's jettisoning of his place in society and the band's need to cast off their own collective past and move ahead among them. I'd been watching an old compilation video that gathered together the Manics' TV appearances and promotional videos from 1994 and 1996. Placed side by side and back to back, the changes from the *Holy Bible* era to *Everything Must Go* were stunning. Not counting the absence of Edwards, if you didn't know better you'd have sworn that it was a different band. Not only had the musical style and lyrical content changed almost beyond recognition, but the way the band dressed was about as different as it could be. The Manics hadn't embraced Britpop's retro tracksuit tops or the football-hooligan urban street-cred of Oasis, but they seemed to have stepped into (or out from) the pages of the Next directory. I struggled to think of any other band that had been so visually on the edge becoming so 'safe' in the space of one album. The aggressive war-ready uniforms had served a purpose, but with a change of musical tack – and the obvious loss of a driving force in the band – they had also decided that the songs had to say what was needed. They now dressed to let the music talk and their look be as bland as possible.

When they appeared with a four-piece string section on *Top of the Pops* to promote 'A Design for Life', I immediately thought back to 'Faster', with all the bowls of fire and camouflage netting. The trio now dressed in untucked shirts – fresh out of the packet – and slacks and cargo pants. This was a middle-aged catalogue shoot, and not one of James Dean Bradfield's slicked-back hairs was out of place. All three band members were relatively subdued in their movements and expressions. This was certainly a measured departure. If they looked like a walking advert, it was almost the case that they were exactly this: years later, *Q* magazine carried notes in its margins about the band's designer shirts and where they could be bought, along with phone numbers for those interested in making further enquiries.

The album-interview-tour treadmill was cranking up again but this time they had to steel themselves for the expected avalanche of questions about their missing bandmate. Right away, they were asked what Richey's family made of the band continuing. It emerged that Graham and Sherry Edwards had encouraged them to continue as soon as possible; they thought that the Manics' return to the spotlight might even flush out Richey from wherever he was hiding. All sides had also carefully set up the legal paperwork to differentiate the Manics' earnings pre- and post-Richey. As the band was using songs that Edwards had worked on, he was due to receive a portion of the writing credits for *Everything Must Go*. Edwards was given three full lyrical writing credits and two co-writing credits on the album, which – as it turned out – would be the biggest selling of their career to date. 'We've set up a trust fund so that all Richey's royalties go into this account under his name,' explained Wire. 'If he ever turns up, he's got his share. It was really depressing, doing all that legal shit. You've gotta wait seven years until he's declared dead. We were signing all these forms. We wanted everything to be proper, but doing that, it just makes him seem like a number. It was really sad.'

The interviews also revealed some of the pain and hurt that the band had been keeping from the public eye during the previous year. Nicky Wire talked about having to visit his local GP and being told that he should consider bereavement counselling, but it was more complicated than that. 'How can you go to bereavement counselling when you don't even know if someone's dead?' said Wire.

The band, and Nicky Wire in particular, had been keeping in close contact with Richey's family. As well as dealing with his own emotions, Wire was also seeing first-hand what effect the disappearance was continuing to have. The sense of not knowing was suffocating. The band – having perhaps been as close to Richey as his family during the previous few years – would not have been surprised to hear that he'd restarted his life somewhere in the UK. 'He could be in a sewage works in Barry, for all we know,' said Wire. 'Done a Reggie Perrin.'

'That's more plausible to me,' agreed James Dean Bradfield. 'Something that's very mundane. Rather than some kind of pilgrimage. To do something in isolation.'

Like any gripping mystery, the Richey Edwards disappearance brought out a number of conspiracy theories and now that the Manics were back in the spotlight, they had to field some awkward questions. Martin Hall had been approached by writers convinced that the band secretly knew where Edwards was, while a growing number of voices were muttering that the band had since made contact with Edwards and were keeping quiet about his whereabouts. After being asked these sorts of questions one time too many, James Dean Bradfield exploded, 'Once and for all, all of the stories that are going around, we haven't got a fucking clue! We swear on our lives. We've had journalists going up to Martin saying, "We know where he is", and it really upset him. And there's still the same level of scepticism. I've tried to blank it out, to a certain degree. I won't give anybody the illusion that I'm sitting here waiting, because we've all nearly fucked ourselves up over it and I've developed some kind of immunity towards it. I'd rather be shocked than wait on something now. Because I can't wait round any more.' For people who had never had to experience the disappearance of a loved one, some of the band's comments seemed harsh. The group admitted that they had put up barriers between themselves and Edwards and that the longer it went on the harder it would be for him to make contact again. Wire said that if Edwards returned he'd be constantly worrying about him, looking for signs, physical and otherwise, of any recurring disintegration. James Dean Bradfield got straight to the point. 'I couldn't be friends with him again, just for the sake of us three,' he said. 'If it went off again, just imagine how much it could fuck you up. It's my biggest nightmare. What would I do if Richey turned up and wanted to know me again?'

These had been the demons they wrestled with when sessions started for the next Manics album, an album that Terri Hall for one thought would never happen. She'd felt sure that Nicky Wire wouldn't have wanted to continue the band without Edwards. But while the search was on, Wire had sat at home with his thoughts and started sketching out ideas. One of many contradictions around the enigma of Nicky Wire is the anti-rock-star lifestyle that he withdraws to when the band isn't working. Gardening and watching TV take up much of his time; he's an avid sports fan but he doesn't travel much and rarely goes out unless he has to. The first new piece that Wire composed in 1995 was a long two-page poem tentatively titled 'A Design for Life'. He passed it on to James Dean Bradfield, who soon called him back saying he thought they'd got a great song.

Wire, by default, had been burdened with the sole responsibility of writing lyrics for the next album. After writing only about a quarter of the last album, this was a giant step, but the band had the fall-back position of a handful of songs they'd started working on with Richey before he vanished. Many of these used Edwards' words or were co-compositions between Edwards and Wire. When it came to actually recording, it was much the same as ever: Edwards was hardly a factor in that side of the Manics' work anyway.

The first day back at Soundspace was awkward but by the end of it they had played 'A Design for Life' and began feeling more optimistic about their future. 'We weren't going to try to write any music to the lyrics that [Richey] left,' said James Dean Bradfield. 'We would do songs that were already written, and they were Manic Street Preachers songs. Richey had heard them all in some form or another. We created ourselves a safety net, and once we'd got in there it was pretty easy, to be honest. From then on, it was just like normal itinerary really, thinking of a producer and writing songs, just getting on.' One positive thing, if that's possible, that arose from Richey's absence was that the remaining three band members had the weight of Edwards' musical expectations taken from their shoulders. The anticipated tensions about the band's future direction were no longer there; in some ways, the musicians now had more freedom to work and experiment on brand new material, even if Edwards was never far from their thoughts. Bradfield was also looking forward to singing a whole line, as he put it, rather than a sometimes-confusing collection of words. Ironically, perhaps, it was partly Richey's absence from the Manics that led to the band releasing more accessible material that gained them larger audiences than ever before.

The new album's title, *Everything Must Go*, was taken from a play that Nicky's brother Patrick had been writing and the song of the same name became an anthem of both the Manics' rebirth and their rejection of their past. Wire's words ask for forgiveness – of the fans who might have criticised them for continuing and of Richey for moving on without him. The talk of asking for explanations and escaping their own history seemed self-explanatory.

The songs featuring Edwards' words proved a little more troublesome. Richey had left the lyrics for 'Kevin Carter', which was based on the life of the eponymous Pulitzer Prize-winning photographer. It was a semi-controversial choice to include the song on the album because Carter had festered with self-disgust after one of his photos of a dying child in Africa afforded him an unwanted celebrity status. He failed to cope with this situation and eventually killed himself. The story might have had parallels with Edwards' own. Either way, the band decided to use it and James Dean Bradfield spent many late nights wrestling with the music to fit the words, constantly asking himself if he thought Richey would approve of the music that he was adding to Edwards' lyrics. The result was one of the harder-rocking tracks on the album and wouldn't have been too far out of place on *The Holy Bible*. 'Removables' had been around for a few years, and was typical of the abstract lyrical approach that Edwards was fond of. The other Richey lyrics were either tracks he'd heard the band play before he vanished or co-compositions with Wire.

In the summer of 1996, the fanzine culture that had served the Manics well in their earlier years was reaching its zenith. By the mid-1990s, the music press classifieds overflowed with fanzine adverts and some papers even ran reviews of them. This was the precipice of the internet age, and soon much of this sub-culture would be swept away as band discussion turned digital. The country was in high spirits with the Blur-versus-Oasis Britpop chart battle harking back to the heyday of the Beatles-versus-Stones rivalry of the 1960s. The Tory government had been in power for so long that people of a certain age couldn't ever remember Labour being in power, but that change was fast approaching. Meanwhile, the new Sky-led football revolution was peaking as England readied itself to host Euro 96 – a further boost to the booming 'lad' culture.

Over the summer, the Manic Street Preachers were offered lucrative support slots with Oasis. To warm up for the first of these dates, the Manics played a cosy gig at Manchester's Hacienda club. This was perhaps the only time that Richey's loss really spilled over onto the stage. Nicky Wire cracked under the emotion and burst into tears, but once that was out of his system the rest of the shows went smoothly. A splattering of festival dates followed as sales of the album continued to soar. Riding the coat-tails of Britpop no doubt helped: even though they weren't really part of that 'movement', the Oasis support slots linked them to it by association. More than ever before, the music was being left to do the talking. 'We had to become more anonymous and live behind the music for the first time ever,' said Wire. 'And I just really missed being couched in that visual air that we used to have.' Despite only some of their songs featuring Richey's lyrics and the absence of Richey himself, the year was seen as the Manics' career summit. Of course no one will ever know how different they would have been if Edwards had remained a part of the band, not touring but working in the background on their lyrics.

In February 1997, the Manic Street Preachers – self-styled outsiders of 1990s British rock – reached their zenith in terms of public acceptance when they won Brit Awards for 'Best Album' and 'Best Band'. This broke the Britpop-only stranglehold that had seen Blur win four awards at the ceremony in 1995 and Oasis take home three awards a year later. Vinnie Jones and Colin Jackson were on hand to present the 'Best Band' statuette, which James Dean Bradfield dedicated to 'the wisdom of Mr Philip Hall and the coolness and intelligence of Mr Richard Edwards'.

'This is also for every comprehensive school in Britain which the government is trying to eradicate,' added Nicky Wire from the stage, addressing the final days of the Tory government. 'They produce the best bands, the best art and the best everything. The best boxers, too.' Noel Gallagher was filmed smiling from the crowd and seemed genuinely pleased. Then they played 'A Design for Life', and this was seen as their crowning glory.

•

Missing for two years. Things seemed to have moved no further forward than they had on the day Richey vanished, and a certain amount of frustration was creeping in. Rachel Edwards spoke to BBC Radio Wales for their *Eye on Wales* documentary, broadcast in mid-March. She revealed that the police effort had not been co-ordinated and that there were holes in the investigation that might have helped had they been identified earlier. The most shocking revelation was that footage from the 24-hour surveillance cameras perched atop the 450-foot bridge towers had not been analysed until two years after Richey's disappearance. 'I have been told by a police officer from the Met that the tapes had been destroyed and now, two years down the line, I find out that they are there,' said Rachel Edwards. 'It would have made a big difference to know that those tapes had been viewed and to know that Richard wasn't on them.' Problems were highlighted in the communications between the Avon and Somerset police and the Metropolitan Police, along with the lack of any national policy to control information about missing persons.

A Met spokesperson went on record to talk about the CCTV footage. The cameras had been recording as usual during February 1995. My understanding is that they were viewed among a bank of monitors running in real-time while officers manned the CCTV centre. There was nothing untoward noticed at the time, but of course they weren't specifically looking for Richey Edwards at this point. It was unlikely that anyone would have been intently looking at the screens of the relevant cameras all of the time. 'The pictures from the camera were being watched by the police at the time of Richey's disappearance and nothing suspicious has been spotted,' said the spokesperson. 'If there were any figures on the bridge they would be so far away as to be unidentifiable. I doubt if we would able to tell if a figure was a man or a woman.' The footage did not show anyone jumping from the bridge.

•

The next big Richey story was delayed. The incident had happened back in November 1996, but it didn't make the news until March 1997. This very delay caused some doubt as to its authenticity from the beginning. Vyvyan Morris, a 48-year-old college lecturer from Swansea, claimed to have spotted Edwards at a hippy market in Goa, India. Morris was known locally as a singer and wrote a pop music column for the *Swansea Evening Post*. When he returned to Wales he said that he'd told the editor and various reporters at the *Post* about the possible sighting, and that – surprisingly – no one was interested. 'I was quite pleased,' said Morris. 'I just thought, "Good, leave the poor bugger alone." But my main concern of course was for his parents and family. So I just kept it low-key after that, and then I mentioned it last weekend in that interview about Badfinger, and it's all gone hysterical. I didn't want it to come out like that.' Many of Morris' comments seemed ambiguous: if he was glad that his editor wasn't going to act on the story, why did he tell him in the first place? And if his thoughts were only for Richey's parents and family, why didn't he inform just them, discreetly, as soon as he got home?

Morris had been travelling with his girlfriend and had found himself at an outdoor market in Anjuna when he spotted someone he thought he recognised sitting at a cafe. Initially, he couldn't place the face. By the time he realised who he thought it was, the man had left to get on a bus. Morris later told the police that he hadn't been able to place the man at first because the man was heavier than he remembered Richey having been and because he had long, matted hair and a suntan. After the man had left, Morris claims to have asked a local resident, Jim Reid (originally from Bath), about him. Morris was told that the man's name was Rick and that he'd been in Goa for about eighteen months. 'I can't be one hundred per cent certain, but I'm sure it was him,' Morris informed the *NME*. 'I still believe he's out in India and he wants to be left alone.' That was the quote that made all the headlines.

Once this story was in the press, a stream of 'official' statements was unleashed. For the band, Terri Hall revealed that: 'In the past few months, Richey has supposedly been seen in seven different countries, like Berlin [sic], Poland and the US.' Rachel Edwards told reporters that she was aware of previous 'sightings' in Goa. The Metropolitan Police gave the standard issue, 'We were made aware on February 28 of a reported sighting of Mr Edwards in Goa in November 1996. If necessary, we will be making further enquiries through Interpol.' Within two weeks, however, the story had been dropped. Police sources explained that they would not be taking things any further because this would be difficult if he had travelled under a false identity, because he seemed to be 'missing' by his own free will, and because no crime had been committed. 'If it was a murder inquiry or something major, then yes [an officer might travel overseas],' said a spokesman. 'But if it's just a missing person, it can't be done. I think the Goa angle will now be moved to the back burner.'

In May 1997, the *NME* received another letter about Richey Edwards. The writer was a young whippersnapper named Doherty – Peter Doherty. The future Libertine wrote a mini-rant against the Manics' supposed highbrow aspirations. 'With Richey went all feeble hopes of purity and guitars and profound graffiti,' he wrote. 'PS. That's the final word on the Manics. Forever. So all fanzines must stop. Let it be known.' Little did anyone know that a decade after Edwards vanished, the young correspondent would have his own cult following, be admitted to addiction clinics and be the subject of letters to the same publication.

•

As the third anniversary of the disappearance came and went without incident or any real news, the only Richey-related stories seemed to be concerned with misguided young souls involved in apparently trying to emulate Edwards. Every case was a potential tragedy but it was surprising that more of these cases didn't come to light bearing in mind the number of followers he had. An inquest into the tragic death of Christopher Goodall, a sixteen-year-old Manics fan from Glossop, was told that he'd wanted to end his life after breaking up with his girlfriend and that he was only too aware of Richey's story. Goodall had drowned in the Severn after a pilgrimage to the Severn Bridge the previous autumn. The Gloucester coroner recorded an open verdict and stated, 'Clearly Christopher was influenced by this media pop idol and undoubtedly he was in a very disturbed state when he decided to go to the Cardiff–Newport area, probably following what he had read about his idol.' Soon after the inquest, another sixteen-year-old, Sally Allen, vanished from her North Yorkshire home and for three weeks travelled to Bristol, Cardiff and London on a Richey-related pilgrimage of her own. Eventually, she grew homesick and went home before any real harm was done.

The post-Richey Manics bandwagon rolled on with the 1998 album *This is My Truth Tell Me Yours*, which gave the band its first UK number one album. Boosted by the number one single 'If You Tolerate This Your Children Will Be Next' and 'You Stole the Sun From My Heart', the album cemented the band's place as the country's favourite alt-trio.

·

On the 'Robinson Crusoe' island of Fuerteventura in the Canary Islands, British-born barmaid Tracy Jones arrived for work at the Underground Bar in Corralejo. She was faced with the usual trickle of customers and it seemed to be a day like any other until one of her customers started calling over to a thin man sitting alone at the bar. 'You're Richey from the Manic Street Preachers!' He called. The thin man was visibly shaken and jumped up from his seat and ran to the door; in seconds, he was gone. Speaking to Tenerife's *Island Sun* newspaper, Jones said, 'We were sure it was just like Richey.' An off-duty British police officer witnessing this added credence to the story; after all, why would someone just up and run away? There were numerous ferries from Fuerteventura to other islands in the chain, and moving between them was easy and could ensure anonymity. The news was soon all over the UK press. The Metropolitan Police were alerted and Richey's family took it seriously enough that they booked flights to visit the area themselves. Nothing like this had come to light for years – just a succession of unbelievable 'reports' with nothing to back them up, such as the recent claim that Richey was incarcerated in a South Wales mental hospital. Could there have been something substantial behind the Canary Islands sighting? For the first time, it seemed that Graham and Sherry Edwards might have had cause for optimism.

# XIX

---

## FOREVER DELAYED

*1999 to present*

At the beginning of 1998, PC Michael Cole had taken control of the Missing Persons desk at Paddington and so inherited the Richey Edwards case. Twelve months later he was able to look back on a year that had seen the largest number of police hours spent on the case since 1995, despite the generally held opinion that it had been scaled down. Many of those hours had been spent chasing leads relating to the report from the Canary Islands in the autumn of 1998, which everyone agreed had seemed the strongest lead to date. As more enquiries were made, however – and with Graham and Sherry Edwards ready to fly out – the story started to break down. 'We were going because we needed to know the truth about this report,' said Sherry, 'but now it seems there is nothing in it.' The holidaying policeman had simply vanished into thin air. It seemed likely that he would have said something upon his return to the UK, but no one knew who he was or where he'd gone. Under closer questioning, the barmaid admitted that she hadn't noticed any tattoos or scars on the person's arms – this was surely something that, surgery permitting, would have stood out to any casual observer. After discussing the matter with the UK police, Richey's family decided not to proceed and cancelled their trip.

PC Cole had thrown himself into this high-profile case. He told *Melody Maker*, 'The search for Richey has been stepped up substantially. I have been in touch with Interpol. I have contacted every coroner's office in Britain, every sanctuary and every religious body. I have a file here that is six inches deep, full of inquiries from the last year. I've got to keep an open mind. There is no evidence to suggest that he is not living. I do not see any reason why the search for Richey Edwards should stop.' And it didn't.

Rachel Edwards, now employed as a care worker, spent most anniversaries of Richey's disappearance working with the press to ensure that there was sufficient media coverage each February. In 1999, it was no different and she spoke extensively to the *Sun*. She explained that time hadn't helped to heal any of the hurt that the disappearance had caused and that the family were still 'tormented'. 'I cannot rest until I find out what has happened,' she said. 'He is not a rock star in a famous band to us, he is our flesh and blood and it hurts every day he is not here with us. It is that pain that drives me on to try to find him because I have to know the truth. I put everything off in my life in the hope that if I wait long enough he will return to share it all with me.'

•

The Manics had loomed large in the latest *Melody Maker* Readers' Poll, winning 'Best Band' and 'Best Live Act' with Nicky Wire topping 'Man of the Year' and Richey Edwards topping 'Most Sadly Missed' ahead of Green On Red, with Kurt Cobain in a surprising third place. As a side note, Nicky Wire was also voted 'Unsexiest Man' but also the second 'Sexiest Man' and one of the 'Fools of the Year'. The band had enjoyed four years of previously unattained fame and adulation, and were privately saddened that Edwards had missed out on the vindication. The *Melody Maker* poll results were issued just before the fifth anniversary of Richey's vanishing and Rachel made another emotional appeal to him while Sherry Edwards took the unusual step of writing an open letter to her son via the pages of the *Sunday Mirror*. The moving letter ended with her writing, 'I can never give up hope that you will return one day and, wherever you are, I hope the pain you carried inside has gone away. You are my precious son and I will never give up looking for you.'

•

The build-up started in early 2002. Soon Richey would have been missing for seven years – the milestone at which point a missing person could be declared legally dead, the relative could inherit any trust funds and the case could be closed. It was hoped that people could then achieve a form of closure and try to move on. So would the Edwards family take this route? In reality, the seven-years rule – widely quoted in the media – was misleading. The rule was generally only applied if a case was challenged during a High Court hearing. With the support of senior police officers, a family could usually make such an application at any time even if a body had not been recovered. But these facts didn't stop the family being hounded about the seventh anniversary.

'We want our son back, not the money,' said Graham Edwards. 'We will never declare him dead. As far as we are concerned he is still alive and we have always felt the same. We're not going to get a death certificate, not now and not in the future. The Trust Fund will be staying exactly as it is.' Rachel Edwards, meanwhile, told the *Observer*: 'Each one of those sightings has only made it worse for us. The thing is, when we said we weren't going to have him declared dead people suddenly said, "Then you must think he's alive", but the only reason we didn't do it is because we don't know he's dead. I also can't say he's alive because I have no evidence.' She also revealed that she'd now been in touch with twenty-seven coroners around the River Severn and had been informed of eight different unidentified bodies. None of them were her brother, but they were eight people who had slipped through society's net. Was anyone even looking for these people?

•

In March, two fishermen found a size-eight training shoe near Chepstow – two miles downstream from the spot where Richey's car had been found. Before the family could be alerted, the *Daily Star* printed a report saying that the remains of Richey Edwards might have been found. Soon afterwards Gwent police found the other shoe nearby. Each shoe was caked in mud and contained a decomposing foot. Families of possible relatives were informed as the police searched for further remains. They concluded that the body couldn't have entered the water too far away as the feet were found quite close together, and that they had been in the water for some time. After the evidence was sent for forensic analysis, the police began checking out the actual shoes. They contacted the manufacturers and found that the particular design and model had only been sold during 2001. This pretty much discounted Edwards, although it was possible that he might have entered the river long after 1995. DNA tests later proved the remains to be of a 25-year-old man who had been missing since the summer of 2001.

In July 2003, another scare surfaced when a full skeleton was found near an oil refinery in the Bristol Channel. An anxious few weeks followed until tests proved that this was again someone else. Since then, the number of sightings and unidentified bodies has slowed to almost nothing. For several years the only news involving Richey came about in relation to recordings issued by the Manic Street Preachers.

The month that the Bristol Channel skeleton was found also saw the release of a double compilation CD, *Lipstick Traces*, which gathered together Manics B-sides, out-takes and live tracks. This was notable for the previously unreleased 'Judge Yr'self', credited as an equal composition between all four band members and the last song Richey worked on before disappearing. It had been written for use on the *Judge Dredd* film soundtrack but it was shelved when Richey vanished. A year later the Manics' next album, *Lifeblood*, included the track 'Cardiff Afterlife', which Nicky Wire explained was about – and dedicated to – Edwards.

The Canary Islands again became the centre of Richey Edwards news when, in October 2004, the *Lanzarote Gazette* ran the story of another 'sighting', this time on Famara beach. Lee Wilde claimed he'd met Richey on the deserted beach and exchanged a few words. 'I know people will find this difficult to believe and that they'll think I'm some sort of crackpot, but I am convinced that is who I saw,' said Wilde. 'I know what I saw and I'm totally certain of it. He was talking about the view. There was something quite different about him. He was incredibly thin, a drawn complexion and greying hair. [His arms were] wrapped in leather bracelets and fabric that looked like rags, but in a fashionably untidy way, I don't think they were bandages but on the areas of his arms that weren't covered you could make out scars which looked worse than they really were because of his tanned skin.' Unfortunately, this report became just another in the series of dead ends and false alarms.

•

Released in 2007, the eighth Manic Street Preachers album – *Send Away the Tigers* – brought a return to both commercial success and critical acclaim. It did well enough to wipe away the lingering discontent of the mediocre solo projects and lacklustre albums of the early twenty-first century. The tour that followed gained positive reviews and by the start of 2008 the band were on their way to being seen as some kind of alternative national treasure, the elder statesmen who just about proved they could still rock. This rebirth of sorts paved the way for the *NME* to honour them in early 2008 with their annual 'Godlike Genius Award'. In terms of news the rest of the year seemed pretty quiet (although the band played festivals across Europe), until early November when fans were hit with a lightning strike.

Missing for thirteen years. After so long it was widely believed that the final batch of lyrics that Richey left with the band before disappearing would never be seen or heard in public. Talk about a possible book of his writings had long since faded away. So when Nicky Wire posted on the Manics website that the band was going to record a new album and only use Richey Edwards' lyrics the shock waves were palpable. Twelve years previously, James Dean Bradfield had said, '[There are] between thirty and forty poems, all in a book, we just don't feel as if we can have any kind of accountability towards them. Some of those lyrics, as soon as you put Manics' music to them, they just become symbolically more emotionally charged anyway, and we don't really want to burden ourselves with that responsibility to certain members of our audience. We feel as if we'll release those in book form some day, because he obviously left them to be used in some sense, they're bound together as a piece of work.'

Time had obviously changed the band's feelings about these lyrics. 'Finally it feels like the right time to use them (especially after the last eighteen months being so amazing with *Send Away the*

Tigers,' wrote Wire. 'Musically, in many ways it feels like a follow up to *The Holy Bible* but there is also an acoustic side – tender, romantic, nihilism. It's a record that celebrates the genius of his words, full of love, anger, intelligence and respect. We have to make this great. Wish us luck.' What the success of the previous eighteen months had anything to do with the decision is unknown. But the band went into the studio with Steve Albini, the man who had produced Nirvana's *In Utero*, and started working. Tentative album titles were *Journal for Plague Lovers* and *I Know I Believe in Nothing But It is My Nothing*. Rumoured song titles included 'Jackie Collins Existential Question Time', 'Doors Closing Slowly' and 'Me and Stephen Hawking'.

In the autumn the Edwards family finally started proceedings to 'get the estate in order' and in October they were granted a probate to register Richey as presumed dead. It was the *Mail on Sunday* that broke the story on 23 November. Terri Hall explained that 'The band has been aware this was coming. It is hugely emotional for all of us. This is the parents' choice and the band is happy to go with what the parents decide is best. We all dream Richey will come back one day. You hope he is still around somewhere. But it is no longer a realistic hope and if this offers some kind of closure then the band will be content with that.' The family's lawyer, David Ellis, added that it was 'an acceptance that his affairs have got to be sorted, that's not the same as an acceptance that he is dead'. Discussion had most likely been going on between band and family for some time. It might not be a coincidence that the sorting out of Richey's trust fund was undertaken at around the time of the announcement of a new album that would generate songwriting royalties for Edwards' account. This also meant that – even if they believed he might still be alive – the family had control over Richey's estate and could offer legal input into what would be done with the left-behind lyrics and their use on the new album.

The legal documents stated that Edwards had died 'on or since' 1 February 1995. With no will, no spouse and no children, his estate of £455,990 was inherited by his parents. After death duties, this sum was released as £377,548. The following day's newspapers carried a small mention of these developments, presumably kept minimal because the story had broken so late on the Sunday that only token coverage could be given. Alongside a picture of a gaunt-looking Richey, the *Sun* buried the story in a tiny capsule on page fourteen with the heading, 'RICHEY "DEAD"'.

Later, the obituaries began to appear. The *Daily Telegraph* started the ball rolling on Tuesday, 25 November, but their tribute was filled with errors, claiming that Edwards had been self-destructive since his teenage years, that he vanished on 2 February 1995 and that his hotel room door had been broken down to reveal lyric sheets in the bedroom. The *Guardian* gave two-thirds of a page to Richey on Wednesday 26th, calling him a 'Thomas Chatterton or Pete Doherty'. On Friday 28th, the *Independent* filled a whole page with their tribute. Among other errors, this also claimed that Edwards had been self-harming since childhood. These pieces had likely been on file for several years and their sloppiness was disappointing. But like the discrepancies in the stories of Richey's birth date, his life seems to have ended amid the same confusion.

XX

# FOREVER AND EVER

Where is Richey Edwards today? I don't mean physically, I mean where is he in the country's collective consciousness? Where is he in our thoughts? Where is he in our hearts? Without wanting to sound like Tony Blair, what is his legacy? In the early twenty-first century, outside of the close-knit Manics 'community', he was in danger of drifting away from any kind of relevance to the next generation of music fans. If you wanted angst, Kurt Cobain was the 'lost 1990s rock star' of choice. If you wanted to watch an emotional car crash before your very eyes, then Pete Doherty was your man. But in recent years Edwards' star has begun to rise again.

Richey began to cast a shadow over British pop culture as soon as he walked out of his hotel in 1995. He made a transition into literature and several titles have been based on or around him, or are blatantly influenced by his legacy.

Dave Franklin's novel *Manic Streets of Perth* concerned a girl who becomes fixated on the missing guitarist after her own boyfriend vanishes. P. P. Hartnett ('Possibly the most uncompromising, provocative and downright shocking author presently writing in Britain') wrote *Rock 'n' Roll Suicide* – a book that was clearly a bastardised version of Richey's and the Manics' story. Not only are the band's lyrics paraphrased all over the book, but the lead character says that he wanted to be so skinny that he rotted from view, he crumbles two bars of light milk chocolate into a small bowl, his family dog dies and he finally plays a comeback gig in Cuba.

Storm Constantine's *Thin Air* (from 1999) opens with the protagonist,

Dex, standing in a car park looking down at a beach, deciding whether or not it would be necessary to carry out his 'plans'. He had been drinking heavily and was found banging his head against a wall. His car was eventually found at the seaside but he had vanished into the thin air of the title. Edwards also lingers around the edges of books such as Emma Forrest's *Namedropper* and Iain Sinclair's *Landor's Tower*.

Edwards was also a big fan of comic books and especially of *2000AD* and Judge Dredd. He'd spend hours browsing the Forbidden Planet shop in Cardiff or Negative Zone in Newport during breaks from his record-buying trips. He used a line from *2000AD* ('Be pure. Be vigilant. Behave.') in the song 'P.C.P.' He was jealous when that very same comic based the character Domino on Nicky Wire in an August 1992 issue. He then made his own transition into ink in June 1993 when the character 'Clarence' from the 'Crazy Sked Moaners' burned '4 Rael' [sic] into his forehead with a laser beam during the story *Muzak Killer: Live! Part 3*.

In 2007, Edwards made an appearance as himself in the graphic novel *Rue Britannia* – a classy comic book that presented a twisted story about Britpop's legacy. The main character, David Kohl, comes across the ghost of his ex-girlfriend Beth – a glammed-up, feather-boa-wearing Manics fan who can't get over Richey's disappearance and is stuck in 1995. When he meets the current, real, version of Beth, she's a civil servant and hasn't listened to the Manics in years. Later, he's sent to visit a mystical figure called Indie Dave, who is in fact a thinly disguised representation of Richey Edwards as the authors imagine him twelve years after he vanished. Still skeletally thin – and going thin on top, too – he lives in seclusion on the edge of a small northern village where he spends his time in the dark listening to Joy Division and The Clash. Back with the ghost of Beth, Kohl ends up talking to her on the Severn Bridge. 'Waiting for a man whose main characteristic is his absence is a stupid waste of time,' he tells her. 'And Manics fans are anything but stupid.'

•

While I was writing this book, a news story came along that just seemed to run and run. For a while it seemed that every day something was revealed which was more incredible than the previous day's snippet. This was the saga of the 'Canoe Man', John Darwin. Darwin was presumed drowned in the North Sea near Hartlepool in March 2002. His body was never found, even though the sea was calm that day, but his damaged canoe was washed up. His wife Anne was left with ownership of two adjoining houses, and five years after her husband's disappearance she sold them for a combined £455,000. She was planning on moving to Panama, leaving her two grown-up sons elsewhere in England. Then, at the end of 2007, John Darwin walked into a London police station and said, 'I think I'm a missing person.' He pretended to have lost his memory, but the police weren't fooled. As the investigation took shape it emerged that Darwin had in fact been living back with his wife, in the adjoining house, for several years without anyone suspecting. The couple were later found guilty of fraud and money-laundering, and were sentenced to six years each in prison. I mention this story not only because it's a case of pseudocide gone wrong, but also because it highlights what would seem to be a highly unlikely scenario had it been in a Hollywood movie. Life truly is stranger than fiction. I also mention it because a number of conspiracy theorists cling to their claims that the Manics and Richey's family know where he is. Some people refuse to rule out the possibility that they could have been in touch with Edwards. If someone can live in the very house he's supposed to have vanished from, then perhaps anything is possible.

●

Richey lived much of his life in emulation of his heroes and heroines. Their influence on him was so strong that it was sometimes hard to tell where Richey ended and his heroes began. When he wanted to cut his fingers off, was it because of Steve Clark's stagefright or did it echo Sylvia Plath's *Cut*; when he decided to make his break, it had to be done in a newsworthy fashion – like Yukio Mishima; when he was about to go, he cut off his hair just before an American tour – just like Ian Curtis; when he vanished, it seemed just like Arthur Rimbaud, or was it more like the mysterious M. Ageyev? When delving into Edwards' story one has to ask what went on inside his mind when the vicarious nature of his life began to run dry. When he'd copied everyone he thought was worth copying, what was left inside? Did he realise that he was becoming an empty shell? Did he see the end of that particular road and decide to head off down a new one, alone, to get away before the baggage of being a Manic Street Preacher, a Generation Terrorist and an unofficial spokesman for the 'outsiders' among his fan base became too much?

It would be good to think that Richey Edwards is still alive, perhaps living peacefully in a monastery or some other religious retreat. However unlikely this may seem, it's not impossible. Getting to one wouldn't have been that difficult, and he would probably have had enough money to use as a deposit (although many such institutions eventually allow free room and board to someone willing to work for and join the organisation). If he had entered a monastery under an assumed name, any police enquiries would have come up empty. Away from the public glare he would have fewer responsibilities and could practise discipline without it being a danger to him. Certain unresolved factors in Edwards' case have led some people to hope that he did indeed find a way to survive in seclusion: it's likely that he possessed a sum of money when he vanished, he was apparently still alive two weeks after disappearing and no suicide note or body was ever located. But it's unlikely that anyone will ever really know for sure.

•

'Richey was a smart kid and great icon. His sensitivity was too rare in rock 'n' roll and his intelligence was always intriguing. He always seemed very aware of the mythology of rock 'n' roll and maybe he got lost in that Rimbaud myth. Hopefully he's still out there somewhere; he was smart enough to just disappear.'

– John Robb

'There was nothing poetic about what Richey did. It was mental illness.'

– Rob Stringer

'[Suicide is] a strong thing to do. It's only the thought of hurting the people who are left that stops you from doing it.'

– Richey Edwards

'I lose track of how many years he's been missing. It really is a long time. It does make you feel . . . it's hard to explain. It's not like someone who's passed away and who you can think of in a different context. Being selfish about it, at least if you knew it was final perhaps all the grief would come out, because I'm not sure it has really, which is a bit frightening.'

– Nicky Wire

# NOTES

1. The Manic Street Preachers' song '1404', which was an extra track issued on the 2007 single 'Autumnsong', was based on the Owain Glyndwr revolt and the melancholy of what might have been had he succeeded. Nicky Wire was also reported to have considered writing a screenplay based on Glyndwr's story.

2. Richey Edwards has passed the chasm into literature several times with *Landor's Tower*, *Rue Britannia*, *2000AD*, *Rock 'n' Roll Suicide* and *Thin Air* being just some of the examples where his myth burrowed him further into popular culture.

3. Surprisingly, Cardiff had only been Wales twenty-fifth biggest town in 1801. Half a century later it was the fourth, after Methyr, Swansea and Newport. By 1881, it was the biggest.

4. The Durutti Column actually did use a sandpaper sleeve for their 1979 album *The Return of the Durutti Column* on Factory Records. Members of Joy Division apparently helped in assembling these awkward sleeves. It's unknown whether Edwards heard about the Debord idea first or came to it after reading about The Durutti Column.

5. Other pre-Richey gigs by the Manic Street Preachers in 1986 included shows on 6 June (Six Bells Workingman's Club), 27 September (The Level, Ebbw Vale) and 4 October (The Little Theatre, Blackwood), all as support for Funeral In Berlin.

6. *DOA* was a film about the Sex Pistols' tour of the USA with other bands, such as the Dead Boys and Sham 69.

7. A listings and entertainment magazine covering the South Wales region, published in Swansea.

8. The Sex Pistols famously held a photo-shoot at the gates of Buckingham Palace in a fake contract-signing stunt.

9. The Membranes put out eight post-punk-inspired albums between 1977 and 1990, with an ever-changing line-up.

10. 'I was freelancing for *Sounds* at the time and writing about loads of new bands,' says Robb. 'I did the first interviews with the Stone Roses and Nirvana

278 • A VERSION OF REASON

and accidentally came up with the phrase 'Britpop', which was in use even back then in the early eighties!'

11. Paul Cannell started out doing the artwork for Flowered Up and designed the logo for Heavenly Records before working with Primal Scream. He committed suicide in 2005.

12. The footage had been filmed on 6 December 1990 at London's Town & Country 2 venue.

13. Gilbert's Syndrome is a failure of the liver to detox certain substances.

14. Having previously decorated the tour van with collages, Edwards would continue to do the same in hotel rooms and recording studios.

15. The live review was a full page under the headline 'Blood on the Tracks', but little of the text concerned the actual show.

16. The band were also in debt to Philip Hall who had loaned the band £45,000 of his own money, such was his belief in them.

17. Rodin's *I Am Beautiful* sculpture showed a man lifting a bundled woman into the air. Serrano's photograph *Piss Christ* featured a plastic crucifix submerged in a glass of urine. Dali's 1951 painting *Christ of Saint John of the Cross* shows Christ on the cross from above but the figure is hanging without any blood, nails or crown of thorns in the picture.

18. Arthur Rimbaud, mentioned here by Edwards for the first time, would become central to the Richey Myth.

19. Traci Lords shot to fame when it was revealed that many of the pornographic films she starred in had been made while she was underage.

20. The Wildhearts went through many personnel changes before splitting up in 1997. They re-formed in 2001.

21. This, in turn, had been a cover of the 1965 version by The Four Seasons.

22. A burning book section of the video seems to show (or show a book that mentions) *Emile*, Jean-Jacques Rousseau's 1762 musings on the philosophical nature of man.

23. Nicky Wire to *Melody Maker*: 'In a bar in Portugal he started doing the moonwalk in front of all these people, and I remember thinking, "He's not tortured tonight, he's pissed!"'

24. James Dean Bradfield was keen to let each band member concentrate on their individual strengths. 'People should do what they're best at,' he said. 'I'm not going to let Richey try a solo just because I think it'll do his self-esteem a load of good, because he can't do it.'

25. *Times Square* – now a cult-classic, but once a box-office bomb – was oft-referenced in the Manics' career, although most of the seminal soundtrack (The Ramones, The Cure, Lou Reed, XTC, Talking Heads and Roxy Music, among others) didn't filter into the Manics' music. The exception was the unexceptional 'Damn Dog', which they'd covered on *Generation Terrorists*. 'Roses in the Hospital' was taken from a scene in the film in which one of the characters actually eats roses in a hospital.

26. Primo Levi survived the Holocaust but chose to take his own life in 1987.

27. The case eventually went to court but no one was convicted.

28. The last two songs that Philip Hall heard were called 'Mausoleum' and 'Die in the Summertime'. 'Oh, thanks for that,' he said after listening to the early demos, demonstrating a sense of humour even though he was seriously ill by then.

29. The twelve steps can be summarised as follows. The patient:

[1] has to admit they are powerless compared to their addiction and their life has become unmanageable.

[2] should submit to the fact that a power greater than themselves could restore their life.

[3] has to decide to turn over their will and life to the care of God as they understand Him.

[4] should make a 'searching and fearless' moral inventory of themselves.

[5] must admit to God, themselves and another human being the nature of their problems.

[6] should be ready to let God remove the defects of character.

[7] must humbly ask God to remove their shortcomings.

[8] must make a complete list of all the people who they have hurt and be ready to make amends with each one.

[9] must make amends to these people except if this would injure them or others.

[10] should continue taking personal inventory and admit when they are wrong.

[11] should seek improved contact with God, as He is understood, through prayer and meditation, while asking for knowledge of His will.

[12] must try and pass this message to other addicts and practise these principles in all areas of their life.

30. The blurb for Earnie Larson's book reads (in part): 'Meditation for every day of the year, complete with an inspirational quote and a thought-for-the-day. It addresses such subjects as: Why self-esteem seems so fragile; how to define ourselves in terms of our own standards and values; why attitude is so important when we make mistakes; the difference between conceit and self-approval; how self-doubt triggers unattractive behaviours; and how self-esteem blooms when we have a sense of purpose in life.'

31. In the 1780s, Jeremy Bentham designed a prison, or Panopticon – a circular design with all cells open to the centre of the building where guards could be housed to watch all of the prisoners easily.

32. Finding your own self-worth and admiring yourself for it, whatever that involves. Kate (Moss), Kristin (McMenamy), Emma (Balfour), Karen (Sky Agony Aunt) were the women listed in the lyric.

33. Richey Edwards also found basic day-to-day skills hard to master – taking laundry back for his mother to wash even though he owned a washing machine in his own flat, for example.

34. Ian Curtis' widow Debbie has commented on the repeated haircutting that he

underwent before his suicide.

35. *Equus* starred Richard Burton as a psychiatrist investigating a seventeen-year-old youth responsible for the blinding of horses with a metal spike. The young man has serious issues with religion (he was forced to read the Bible as a child), his own sexuality and horses, who he sees as the eyes of God. In *Naked*, Mike Leigh presents viewers with the grim tale of Johnny (played by David Thewlis), who runs away from Manchester after raping a woman in an alleyway. He ends up in London and comes across a parade of unusual and sometimes seedy characters before heading out into the world again. While not explained explicitly, Johnny seems likely to be suffering from manic depression or a similar mental illness.

36. Lori Fidler was also mentioned in a telephone call to the police in early March 1995. A Philip Keen, of Irvine, Scotland, told them that he thought Edwards was staying at Fidler's apartment on East 21st Street in New York. He also sent a fax to the *NME* with the same suggestion but he didn't seem to have any proof to back up his claims.

37. Requests to the Metropolitan Police as to details about this box were, perhaps unsurprisingly, rebuked. The reason given was that it could infringe Richey Edwards' human rights, even though this was after he had been declared legally dead.

38. Mike Hedges' work with The Cure and Siouxsie and The Banshees brought him to the Manics' attention.

# THANKS AND ACKNOWLEDGEMENTS

More than usual, this book has proved to be a long and sometimes difficult haul to the finish line; thanks and love to Carolyn and Milan for putting up with the more difficult bits!

Richey Edwards is a subject that some potential interviewees naturally shied away from, so heartfelt thanks to the friends and colleagues who agreed to talk on the record (and to those who wished to remain anonymous): Stephen Gatehouse, Dr Eleanor Breuning, Tony van den Ende, Becky Rigby, John Robb, Paul Lester, Kevin Cummins, DCI Andrew Davies, Ria Gibbs and Sally Killian.

Sara Hawys Roberts always provided helpful advice, and throughout my research many others oiled wheels and provided contacts, including Rowland Williams, Jill Lewis, Jackie Evans, Ross Miller at the Missing People charity, Bernadette Ford, Ed Stearns, Graham Palmer, Mark Hunter and Stuart Wilks. Thanks also to Liz Gould, Martin Hall and Terri Hall at Hall Or Nothing for relaying messages back and forth.

At Orion Books I would like to thank Ian Preece, Jane Sturrock, Angela McMahon, Lucie Stericker, Rabab Adams, Stephen Fall and everyone else involved in getting this book into your hands.

Finally, I never realised what use having an agent would be until I actually got one. Many thanks to Tim Bates and all at Pollinger for their help and guidance on this project.

# BIBLIOGRAPHY

Books read for background information and used in the preparation of this manuscript:

Martin Clarke, *Manic Street Preachers: Sweet Venom* (Plexus, London, 1997)

John Davies, *A History of Wales* (Penguin, London, 2007)

Wallace Fowlie, *Rimbaud and Jim Morrison* (Souvenir Press, London, 1995)

Ian Hamilton, *In Search of J. D. Salinger* (Random House, New York, 1988)

Ronald Hayman, *The Death and Life of Sylvia Plath* (William Heinemann Ltd, London, 1991)

Michael Heatley, *Manic Street Preachers: In Their Own Words* (Omnibus Press, London, 1998)

Steve Lamacq, *Going Deaf for a Living* (BBC, London, 2000)

Duncan MacLaughlin with William Hall, *Dead Lucky – Lord Lucan: The Final Truth* (John Blake, London, 2003)

Aubrey Malone, *Literary Trivia* (Prion, London, 1999)

Mick Middles, *Manic Street Preachers* (Omnibus Press, London, 1999)

Andrew O'Hagan, *The Missing* (Picador, London, 1995)

Sylvia Plath, *The Bell Jar* (Faber, London, 2003)

Simon Price, *Everything (A Book About Manic Street Preachers)* (Virgin, London, 1999)

James Reidel, *Vanished Act: The Life and Art of Weldon Kees* (Bison Books, Lincoln, Nebraska, 2003)

Graham Robb, *Rimbaud: A Biography* (Picador, London, 2000)

Christopher Ross, *Mishima's Sword: Travels in Search of a Samurai Legend* (Fourth Estate, London, 2006)

Ewart Smith, *Blackwood Yesterday* (Old Bakehouse Publications, Abertillery, 1991)

Jennifer Watkins-Isnardi, *In the Beginning* (Blake, London, 2000)

David Williams, *The Rebecca Riots* (Arrowsmith, Bristol, 1986)

## Books on the Richey Edwards reading list:

*(listed with the date and publisher of the version I held a copy of)*

James Baldwin, *Another Country* (Penguin, London, 2001)

James Baldwin, *Go Tell It on the Mountain* (Penguin, London, 2001)

J. G. Ballard, *Crash* (Vintage, London, 1995)

Brendan Behan, *Borstal Boy* (Corgi, London, 1975)

William Burroughs, *Junky* (Penguin, London, 1977)

Joseph Conrad, *Heart of Darkness* (Penguin, London, 1989)

Fyodor Dostoevsky, *Notes from Underground* (Vintage, London, 1993)

Bret Easton Ellis, *Less Than Zero* (Picador, London, 1986)

Ralph Ellison, *Invisible Man* (Penguin, London, 1965)

Jean Genet, *Miracle of the Rose* (Castle Books, New Jersey, 1965)

Joseph Heller, *Catch-22* (Vintage, London, 2005)

Masuji Ibuse, *Black Rain* (Kodansha, Tokyo, 1979)

Franz Kafka, *Metamorphosis and Other Stories* (Vintage, London, 2005)

Franz Kafka, *The Trial* (Vintage, London, 2005)

Yukio Mishima, *The Temple of the Golden Pavilion* (Vintage, London, 2001)

Hubert Selby Jr., *Last Exit to Brooklyn* (Flamingo, London, 1993)

William Wharton, *Birdy* (The Leisure Circle, London, 1978)

# SOURCES

## I: A PROLOGUE TO HISTORY

John Robb, 'Teenage Rampage', *Sounds*, 26 January 1991
James Brown, 'Indecent Exposure', *NME*, 11 May 1991
Bob Stanley, *Melody Maker*, 1991

## II: THE GREEN, GREEN GRASS OF HOME

James McMahon, 'The Lost Godlike Genius', *NME*, 8 February 2008
Dorian Lynskey, *Q*, March 2001
Phil Sutcliffe, 'Fun Boy Three', *Q*, November 1996
Simon Price, 'Archives of Pain', *Melody Maker*, 3 December 1994
*Q Cash for Questions*, *Q*, November 2007

## III: SCULPTURE OF A MAN

Simon Price, 'Archives of Pain', *Melody Maker*, 3 December 1994
Taylor Parkes, 'Manic Depression', *Melody Maker*, 20 August 1994
Simon Price, 'Singalongamanics', *Melody Maker*, 29 August 1992
Phil Sutcliffe, 'Fun Boy Three', *Q*, November 1996
Richard Lowe, 'Blackwood Calling?', *Select*, October 1991
Dorian Lynskey, *Q*, March 2001
Darren Waters, 'The Manic Truth Comes Out', *Western Mail*,
    22 August 1998

## IV: VAGUE LITTLE CUTS

Darren Waters, 'The Manic Truth Comes Out', *Western Mail*,
    22 August 1998

James McMahon, 'The Lost Godlike Genius', *NME*, 8 February 2008

Richard Lowe, 'Blackwood Calling?', *Select*, October 1991

Amy Raphael, 'Love Will Tear Us Apart', *Esquire*, November 1998

Stuart Bailie, 'Manic's Depressive', *NME*, 1 October 1994


## V: STRAIGHT OUTTA BLACKWOOD

Claire Rees, *Wales on Sunday*, 1 June 2008

Keith Cameron, 'Out Demons Out!', *Mojo*, February 2005

*Record Collector*, May 1997

Gina Morris, 'The Full Story', *Select*, May 1995

Mandi James, 'P.C.P.', *Volume*, Autumn 1994

Stuart Clark, '4 real 4 ever', *Hot Press*, 26 November 2002

Johnny Dee, 'Urgh!', *Smash Hits*, 20 August 1991


## VI: DESTROY THE HIERARCHY

Amy Raphael, 'Love Will Tear Us Apart', *Esquire*, November 1998

James McMahon, 'The Lost Godlike Genius', *NME*, 8 February 2008

Jason Arnopp, 'Five Years Gone', *Kerrang!*, 29 January 2000

Gina Morris, 'The Full Story', *Select*, May 1995

William Shaw, *Q The 90s*

Stuart Clark, 'Hey Preachers!', *Hot Press*, 7 September 1994

Steve Lamacq, 'Blood on the Tracks', *NME*, 25 May 1991

Andrew Perry, 'Rebels Without a Clue', *Select*, April 1991


## VII: NOTHING TO CLING TO

Paul Elliott, 'Life Becoming a Landslide', *Kerrang!*, 1996

'Seven Days in the Life of Richey Edwards', *Select*, December 1992

Johnny Dee, 'Urgh!', *Smash Hits*, 20 August 1991

Simon Reynolds, 'Rock 'n' Roll Suicide', *Melody Maker*, 30 July 1991

Sally Margaret Joy, 'Dai Hard', *Melody Maker*, 1993

Stuart Bailie, 'Non-stop Neurotic Cabaret', *NME*, 30 May 1992

Keith Cameron, 'Out Demons Out!', *Mojo*, February 2005

Jason Arnopp, 'Five Years Gone', *Kerrang!*, 29 January 2000

Caitlin Moran, 'Gorgeous in Spite of Himself', *The Times*, 7 October 1994

Tom Hibbert, 'Pathetic', *Q*, May 1992

Andrew Collins, 'The Newport Dolls', *NME*, 1991

David Quantick, 'It Takes an Advance of Millions . . . ', *NME*,
  15 February 1992

Simon Price, 'Singalongamanics', *Melody Maker*, 29 August 1992

Mark Day, 'The Politics of Glamour', *Rock Power*, January 1992

'Seven Days in the Life of Richey Edwards', *Select*, December 1992

Richard Lowe, 'Blackwood Calling?', *Select*, October 1991


**VIII: THIS SECTION IS NOT CALLED FROM DESPAIR TO WHERE**

Stuart Clark, 'Oh Lord . . . ', *Hot Press*, 28 July 1993

Val Savage, *Insane Fanzine*, October 1993

Sally Margaret Joy, 'Dai Hard', *Melody Maker*, 1993

Everett True, 'Manic Depression', *Melody Maker*, 29 May 1993

John Harris, 'From Sneer to Maturity', *NME*, 19 June 1993

Stephen Dalton, 'Dead End Street', *Select*, December 1993


**IX: BANGKOK**

Simon Price, 'Archives of Pain', *Melody Maker*, 3 December 1994

'Noisy Mothers', *Raw Power*, 2 February 1994

Jason Arnopp, 'Five Years Gone', *Kerrang!*, 29 January 2000

Mandi James, 'P.C.P.', *Volume*, Autumn 1994

Keith Cameron, 'Cool LA Shakers', *NME*, 12 October 1996

Stuart Clark, 'Hey Preachers!', *Hot Press*, 7 September 1994

Keith Cameron, 'Out Demons Out!', *Mojo*, February 2005

Barbara Ellen, 'Siamese Animal Men', *NME*, 28 May 1995

'I Don't Care', *Metal Hammer*, Summer 1994

'Blood, Sweat and Tears', *The Face*, June 1994

Stuart Bailie, 'Manic's Depressive', *NME*, 1 October 1994

David Bennun, 'All That Glitters', *Melody Maker*, 29 January 1994


**X: HELL IS IN HELLO**

Stuart Bailie, 'Manic's Depressive', *NME*, 1 October 1994

Taylor Parkes, 'Manic Depression', *Melody Maker*, 20 August 1994

Andrew Collins, 'One Foot in the Past', *Word*, January 2005

## XI: THE BIBLE

Simon Price, 'Archives of Pain', *Melody Maker*, 3 December 1994

Stuart Clark, 'Hey Preachers!', *Hot Press*, 7 September 1994

## XII: A MAN WHO WOULD MUTILATE HIMSELF

Simon Price, 'Archives of Pain', *Melody Maker*, 3 December 1994

Stuart Bailie, 'Manic's Depressive', *NME*, 1 October 1994

Caitlin Moran, 'Gorgeous in Spite of Himself', *The Times*, 7 October 1994

Stuart Maconie, 'Smile, It Might Never Happen', *Q*, December 1994

Keith Cameron, 'Out Demons Out!', *Mojo*, February 2005

Stuart Bailie, 'Everything Must Go On', *NME*, 11 May 1996

Simon Price, 'Archives of Pain', *Melody Maker*, 3 December 1994

Jason Arnopp, 'Five Years Gone', *Kerrang!*, 29 January 2000

Paul Stokes, 'We Felt it was Time . . . ', *NME*, 8 November 2008

Midori Tsukagoshi, 'Manic Street', *Music Life*, March 1995

James McMahon, 'The Lost Godlike Genius', *NME*, 8 February 2008

## XIII: FEVER AND EXHAUSTION

Stuart Maconie, 'Smile, It Might Never Happen', *Q*, December 1994

## XIV: A PRELUDE TO DESTINY

Phil Sutcliffe, 'Fun Boy Three', *Q*, November 1996

## XV: GONE

Andrew Collins, 'One Foot in the Past', *Word*, January 2005

Keith Cameron, 'Out Demons Out!', *Mojo*, February 2005

## XVI: THE SIGHTINGS, THE SEARCH, THE BRIDGE

Rosie Dunn, 'I Can Never Rest', *Sun*, 23 February 1999

'From Despair to Where?', *Melody Maker*, 25 February 1995

'Motorcar Emptiness', *New Musical Express*, 4 March 1995

Caroline Sullivan and Alex Bellos, 'Sweet Exile', *Guardian*, 22 February
1995

## XVII: LIMBO

Edward Verity, 'Parents Pray for the Lost Preacher', *Daily Mail*, 2 March 1995

'Richey Where Are You?', *Golwg*, 23 March 1995

Sue Reid, 'The Point of No Return?', *Sunday Times*, 6 August 1995

Andy Richardson, 'Boom Shake the Gloom!', *NME*, 9 December 1995

Dave Simpson, 'Vanishing Point', *Melody Maker*, 31 January 1998

Andrew Mueller, 'Manic Depression', *Melody Maker*, 1 April 1995

John Harris, 'From Despair to Where?', *NME*, 25 February 1995

## XVIII: EVERYTHING MUST GO

Cliff Jones, 'More!', *Mojo*, December 1996

'Richey's Out in India . . . ', *NME*, 15 March 1997

'Richey Sister Hits Out at Police', *NME*, 29 March 1997

'Son Copied The Possible Fate . . . ', *South Wales Argus*, 27 April 1998

Stuart Maconie, 'Everything Must Grow Up', Q, October 1998

## XIX: FOREVER DELAYED

Rosie Dunn, 'I Can Never Rest . . . ', *Sun*, 23 February 1999

'Richey: The Search Goes On', *Melody Maker*, 8 May 1999

'I Won't Give Up Hope . . . ', *Sunday Mirror*, 13 February 2000

Jay Rayner, 'Why Did They Have to Go?', *Observer*, 10 March 2002

Dorian Lynskey, 'Not So Manic Now', *Guardian*, 1 October 2004

Andrew Young and Nick Constable, 'After 13 years . . . ', *Mail on Sunday*, 23 November 2008

## XX: FOREVER AND EVER

Stephen Phelan, 'Living With Ghosts', *Sunday Herald*, 30 January 2005

Dorian Lynskey, Q, March 2001

# DISCOGRAPHY

Richey Edwards' major releases before he disappeared

## SINGLES

'New Art Riot' / 'Strip it Down' / 'Last Exit on Yesterday' /
'Teenage 20/20'
> Damaged Goods [YUBB 4], 12", 1,000 copies, black & white label,
> June 1990
> Damaged Goods [YUBB 4], 12", 1,000 copies, coloured labels, 1990
> Damaged Goods [YUBB 004P], 12", 3,000 copies, pink vinyl,
> November 1991
> Damaged Goods [YUBB 4CD], CD, 3,000 copies, January 1992

'Motown Junk' / 'Sorrow 16' / 'We Her Majesty's Prisoners'
> Heavenly [HVN8 12], 12", January 1991
> Heavenly [HVN8 CD], CD, January 1991

'You Love Us' / 'Spectators of Suicide'
> Heavenly [HVN10], 7", May 1991

'You Love Us' / 'Spectators of Suicide' / 'Starlover' / 'Strip it Down' (live)
> Heavenly [HVN10 12], 12", May 1991
> Heavenly [HVN10 CD], CD, May 1991

'Stay Beautiful' / 'R. P. McMurphy'
> Columbia [657337 7], 7", July 1991

*'Stay Beautiful' / 'R. P. McMurphy' / 'Soul Contamination'*

    Columbia [657337 6], 12", July 1991
    Columbia [657337 8], 12" poster sleeve, August 1991
    Columbia [657337 2], CD, July 1991

*'Love's Sweet Exile' / 'Repeat'*

    Columbia [657582 7], 7", November 1991

*'Repeat (U.K.)' / 'Love's Sweet Exile' / 'Democracy Coma'*

    Columbia [657582 6], 12", November 1991

*'Repeat' / 'Democracy Coma' / 'Love's Sweet Exile' / 'Stay Beautiful' (live)*

    Columbia [657582 8], 12", limited edition, November 1991

*'Love's Sweet Exile' / 'Repeat (U.K.)' / 'Democracy Coma'*

    Columbia [657582 2], CD, November 1991

*'You Love Us' / 'A Vision of Dead Desire'*

    Columbia [657724 7], 7", January 1992

*'You Love Us' / 'A Vision of Dead Desire' / 'It's So Easy' (live)*

    Columbia [657724 6], 12", limited edition, January 1992

*'You Love Us' / 'A Vision of Dead Desire' / 'We Her Majesty's Prisoners' / 'It's So Easy' (live)*

    Columbia [657724 2], CD, January 1992

*'Slash 'n' Burn' / 'Motown Junk'*

    Columbia [657873 7], 7", March 1992
    Columbia [657873 4], cassette, March 1992

*'Slash 'n' Burn' / 'Motown Junk' / 'Ain't Going Down'*

    Columbia [657873 6], 12" with free print, March 1992

*'Slash 'n' Burn' / 'Motown Junk' / 'Sorrow 16' / 'Ain't Going Down'*

    Columbia [657873 0], CD, March 1992

*'Motorcycle Emptiness' / 'Bored Out of My Mind'*

    Columbia [658083 7], 7", June 1992
    Columbia [658083 4], cassette, June 1992

*'Motorcycle Emptiness' / 'Bored Out of My Mind' /*
*'Under My Wheels' (live)*

> Columbia [658083 8], 12" picture disc, June 1992

*'Motorcycle Emptiness' / 'Bored Out of My Mind' / 'Crucifix Kiss' (live) /*
*'Under My Wheels' (live)*

> Columbia [658083 9], CD, June 1992

*'Theme from M\*A\*S\*H (Suicide is Painless)' / 'Everything I Do (I Do it*
*for You)'\**

> Columbia [658382 7], 7", September 1992
> Columbia [658382 4], cassette, September 1992
> \* by Fatima Mansions

*'Theme from M\*A\*S\*H (Suicide is Painless)' / 'Everything I Do (I Do it*
*for You)'\* / 'Sleeping with the NME'*

> Columbia [658382 6], 12", September 1992
> Columbia [658382 2], CD, September 1992
> \* by Fatima Mansions

*'Little Baby Nothing' (7" version) / 'Never Want Again' / 'Suicide Alley'*

> Columbia [658796 7], 7", January 1993
> Columbia [658796], cassette, January 1993

*'Little Baby Nothing' (7" version) / 'Never Want Again' /*
*'Dead Yankee Drawl' / 'Suicide Alley'*

> Columbia [658796 2], CD, January 1993

*'Little Baby Nothing' (7" version) / 'R. P. McMurphy' (live) /*
*'Tennessee' (live) / 'You Love Us' (live)*

> Columbia [658796 5], CD, January 1993

*'From Despair to Where' / 'Hibernation'*

> Columbia [659337 4], cassette, June 1993

*'From Despair to Where' / 'Hibernation' / 'Spectators of Suicide'*
*(Heavenly version)*

> Columbia [659337 6], 12", June 1993

*'From Despair to Where' / 'Hibernation' / 'Spectators of Suicide'*
*(Heavenly version) / 'Starlover' (Heavenly version)*

    Columbia [659337 2], CD, June 1993

*'La Tristesse Durera (Scream to a Sigh)' / 'Patrick Bateman'*

    Columbia [659477 4], cassette, July 1993

*'La Tristesse Durera (Scream to a Sigh)' / 'Patrick Bateman' /*
*'Repeat' (live) / 'Tennessee'*

    Columbia [659477 6], 12", July 1993

*'La Tristesse Durera (Scream to a Sigh)' / 'Patrick Bateman' /*
*'What's My Name?' (live) / 'Slash 'n' Burn' (live)*

    Columbia [659477 2], CD, July 1993

*'Roses in the Hospital' / 'Us Against You' / 'Donkeys'*

    Columbia [659727 7], 7", October 1993
    Columbia [659727 8], cassette, October 1993

*'Roses in the Hospital' / 'Us Against You' / 'Donkeys' / 'Wrote for Luck'*

    Columbia [659727 2], CD, October 1993

*'Life Becoming a Landslide' / 'Comfort Comes'*

    Columbia [660070 4], cassette, January 1994

*'Life Becoming a Landslide' / 'Comfort Comes' / 'Are Mothers Saints?'*

    Columbia [660070 6], 12", January 1994

*'Life Becoming a Landslide' / 'Comfort Comes' / 'Are Mothers Saints?' /*
*'Charles Windsor'*

    Columbia [660070 2], CD, January 1994

*'Faster' / 'P.C.P.'*

    Columbia [660447 4], cassette, May 1994

*'Faster' / 'P.C.P.' / 'Sculpture of a Man'*

    Columbia [660447 0], 10", May 1994

*'Faster' / 'P.C.P.' / 'Sculpture of a Man' / 'New Art Riot (In E Minor)'*
    Columbia [660447 2], CD, May 1994

*'Revol' / 'Too Cold Here'*
    Columbia [660686 4], cassette, August 1994

*'Revol' / 'Too Cold Here' / 'You Love Us' (live) /*
*'Life Becoming a Landslide' (live)*
    Columbia [660686 0], 10", August 1994

*'Revol' / 'Too Cold Here' / 'You Love Us' (live) / 'Love's Sweet Exile' (live)*
    Columbia [660686 2], CD, August 1994

*'Revol' / 'Drug Drug Druggy' (live) / 'Roses in the Hospital' (live) /*
*'You Love Us' (live)*
    Columbia [660686 5], CD, August 1994

*'She is Suffering' / 'Love Torn Us Under'*
    Columbia [660895 4], cassette, September 1994

*'She is Suffering' / 'The Drowners' (live) / 'Stay With Me' (live)*
    Columbia [660895 0], 10", September 1994

*'She is Suffering' (radio edit) / 'She is Suffering' (acoustic)*
    Columbia [660972 1], CD, September 1994

*'She is Suffering' / 'Love Torn Us Under' / 'The Drowners' (live) /*
*'Stay With Me' (live)*
    Columbia [660895 2], CD, September 1994

*'She is Suffering' (radio edit) / 'La Tristesse Durera (Scream to a Sigh)'*
*(vocal mix) / 'La Tristessa Durera (Scream to a Sigh)' (dub mix) /*
*'Faster' (dub mix)*
    Columbia [660895 5], CD, September 1994

## ALBUMS

### GENERATION TERRORISTS

'Slash 'n' Burn' / 'NatWest-Barclays-Midlands-Lloyds' / 'Born to End' / 'Motorcycle Emptiness' / 'You Love Us' / 'Love's Sweet Exile' / 'Little Baby Nothing' / 'Repeat (Stars and Stripes)' / 'Tennessee' / 'Another Invented Disease' / 'Stay Beautiful' / 'So Dead' / 'Repeat (UK)' / 'Spectators of Suicide' / 'Damn Dog' / 'Crucifix Kiss' / 'Methadone Pretty' / 'Condemned to Rock 'n' Roll'

> Columbia [471060 1], 2LP, February 1992
> Columbia [471060 1], cassette, February 1992
> Columbia [471060 2], CD, February 1992
> Columbia [471060 9], 2LP*, June 1992
> * 2 picture discs

### GOLD AGAINST THE SOUL

'Sleepflower' / 'From Despair to Where' / 'La Tristesse Durera (Scream to a Sigh)' / 'Yourself' / 'Life Becoming a Landslide' / 'Drug Drug Druggy' / 'Roses in the Hospital' / 'Nostalgic Pushead' / 'Symphony of Tourette' / 'Gold Against the Soul'

> Columbia [4740649], LP, June 1993
> Columbia [4740649 1], LP*, June 1993
> Columbia [4740649], cassette, June 1993
> Columbia [4740649 2], CD, June 1993
> * picture disc

### THE HOLY BIBLE

'Yes' / 'Ifwhiteamericatoldthetruthforonedayit'sworldwouldfallapart' / 'Of Walking Abortion' / 'She is Suffering' / 'Archives of Pain' / 'Revol' / '4st 7lb' / 'Mausoleum' / 'Faster' / 'This is Yesterday' / 'Die in the Summertime' / 'The Intense Humming of Evil' / 'P.C.P.'

> Epic [477421 1], LP, August 1994
> Epic [477421 9], LP*, August 1994
> Epic [477421 1], cassette, August 1994
> Epic [477421 2], CD, August 1994
> * picture disc

## Major releases after Richey Edwards disappeared but which include his lyrics

### EVERYTHING MUST GO

Includes: 'Elvis Impersonator: Blackpool Pier' / 'Kevin Carter' / 'Small Black Flowers That Grow in the Sky' / 'The Girl Who Wanted to Be God' / 'Removables'

### LIPSTICK TRACES

Includes: 'Judge Yr'self'

### JOURNAL FOR PLAGUE LOVERS

The band have suggested that this entire album, due for release in 2009, will consist of lyrics written by Richey Edwards.

Includes: 'Peeled Apples / 'Jackie Collins Existential Question Time' / 'Me and Stephen Hawking' / 'This Joke Sport Severed' / 'Journal for Plague Lovers' / 'She Bathed Herself in a Bath of Bleach' / 'Facing Page: Top Left' / 'Marlon J. D.' / 'Doors Closing Slowly' / 'All is Vanity' / 'Pretension/Repulsion' / 'Virginia State Epileptic Colony' / 'William's Last Words'